McGraw-Hill Dictionary of Information Technology and Computer Acronyms, Initials, and Abbreviations

Other McGraw-Hill Books by Jerry M. Rosenberg

McGraw-Hill Dictionary of Business Acronyms, Initials, and Abbreviations

McGraw-Hill Dictionary of Wall Street Acronyms, Initials, and Abbreviations

McGraw-Hill Dictionary of Information Technology and Computer Acronyms, Initials, and Abbreviations

Jerry M. Rosenberg, Ph.D.
Professor
Graduate School of Management
Department of Business Administration
Faculty of Arts and Sciences
Rutgers University

McGraw-Hill, Inc.
New York St. Louis San Francisco Auckland Bogotá
Caracas Lisbon London Madrid Mexico Milan
Montreal New Delhi Paris San Juan São Paulo
Singapore Sydney Tokyo Toronto

Library of Congress Cataloging-in-Publication Data

Rosenberg, Jerry Martin.
  McGraw-Hill dictionary of information technology and computer acronyms, initials, and abbreviations / Jerry M. Rosenberg.
      p.   cm.
    ISBN 0-07-053936-7 :   —ISBN 0-07-053735-6 (pbk.) :
    1. Electronic data processing—Acronyms—Dictionaries.
    2. Electronic data processing—Abbreviations—Dictionaries.
    3. Information technology—Acronyms—Dictionaries. 4. Information technology—Abbreviations—Dictionaries. 5. English language—Acronyms—Dictionaries. 6. Abbreviations, English—Dictionaries.
    I. Title. II. Title: Dictionary of information technology and computer acronyms, initials, and abbreviations.
    QA76.15.R68 1992   91-24861
    004'.03—dc20   CIP

Copyright © 1992 by McGraw-Hill, Inc. All rights reserved. Printed in the United States of America. Except as permitted under the United States Copyright Act of 1976, no part of this publication may be reproduced or distributed in any form or by any means, or stored in a data base or retrieval system, without the prior written permission of the publisher.

1 2 3 4 5 6 7 8 9 0   DOC/DOC   9 7 6 5 4 3 2 1

ISBN 0-07-053936-7 {HC}
ISBN 0-07-053735-6 {PBK}

The sponsoring editor for this book was Betsy Brown, the editing supervisor was Alfred Bernardi, and the production supervisor was Suzanne W. Babeuf. It was set in Century Schoolbook by McGraw-Hill's Professional Book Group composition unit.

Printed and bound by R. R. Donnelley & Sons Company.

*For my ever-expanding family—
With continuing love.*

Preface

Fifteen years after I had published the first in a series of five business-oriented dictionaries, I began to see the need for yet another type of dictionary. This time, the proposed book would be a lexicon containing business acronyms, initials, and abbreviations. What had I noticed in my day-to-day life as a business consultant and educator to convince me of the compelling need for such a book?

First of all, everyone knows that in today's business world we are all confronted daily with a variety of common (and not so common) abbreviated terms. Whether these terms are communicated in written or verbal form, confusion can arise, since most of them frequently convey several different meanings. For example, IBM is a three-letter word that is quickly identified throughout the world as initials for International Business Machines. However, these same three letters also stand for the Institute for Burn Medicine, Industrias Biologicas Mexicana (Mexican Biological Industries), intercontinental ballistic missile, and the International Brotherhood of Magicians. And the two-letter words, IB or IM, have a list of several dozen possible spelled-out forms.

An anecdote taken from my own professional life might serve to further highlight the potential trouble that can come about when one of these terms is misinterpreted. As a young college professor, I once had occasion to take a plane trip to Boston in order to attend a professional conference. Seated next to me on the plane was a relentless name-dropper who, during the course of his career as a reporter, claimed to have interviewed JFK (President John F. Kennedy), LBJ (President Lyndon B. Johnson), and so on and so forth! After he had exhausted this line of conversation, the reporter turned to me and asked if I did consulting work. Seeing that my opportunity to speak (and to shine) had at last arrived, I answered by saying that yes, indeed, I did consulting in Boston for ADL. The reporter was quite impressed to hear that I worked for Arthur D. Little, a first-rate consulting firm. His enthusiasm waned, however, when I corrected his error and informed him that I was a consultant to the Anti-Defamation League!

The story is amusing, but it nicely summarizes the reason I have written this book. Clarity and precision are necessary components of business communications. They will be improved only when we are aware of the many different meanings that have been applied to each acronym, initial, abbreviation, or symbol by the general business community at large. Thus, I have tried to include in this volume as many of the commonly used designations from the world of computers and information technology as is possible. When this book is used in conjunction with a computer dictionary, the user should be amply equipped to comprehend clearly and communicate effectively.

Lastly, there are a few decisions made in the preparation of this book that the reader should be aware of as he or she begins to use it:

1. Conventional symbols have been used without specific identification, for instance: - (hyphen); / (diagonal); & (ampersand); = (equal sign); * (asterisk).
2. The use of capital, lowercase, or a combination of both capital and lowercase letters for the spelled-out versions of abbreviations or acronyms has never been universally agreed upon. In most cases in this book, I have used the preferred or most commonly used form. When an abbreviation involves the use of proper names, then capital letters are the correct choice. Otherwise, the form of capitalization that is adopted is more a matter of style than of correctness.

Acknowledgments

My library contains hundreds of sources of information that were used to prepare my five earlier dictionaries. These volumes have also been put to use in creating this book. In addition, both American and foreign agencies have been helpful in providing relevant information. I also received a good deal of assistance from trade associations (who, along with government departments, appear to be in the habit of creating new terms on a daily basis).

To the best of my knowledge, I have not quoted from any other copyrighted source. However, I have acquired much indirect assistance from the authors of numerous books, journal articles, and reference materials. Any attempt to list them here would be impossible.

Betsy Brown and Bill Sabin, my editors at McGraw-Hill, have been enlightened professional supporters of this dictionary. My wife, Ellen, my daughters, Elizabeth and Lauren, and my son-in-law, Robert, continue to be my inspiration. Time away from them, whether it is spent researching an article or struggling with a complex set of acronyms, initials, and abbreviations, is more than compensated for by their affection.

Finally, I acknowledge my reader—the ultimate judge. I continue to seek your critical comments and urge you to bring any errors or suggestions to my attention.

Jerry M. Rosenberg

About the Author

JERRY M. ROSENBERG, Ph.D., is professor at the Graduate School of Management and Department of Business Administration at Rutgers University. He is the author of the *McGraw-Hill Dictionary of Business Acronyms, Initials, and Abbreviations* and the *McGraw-Hill Dictionary of Wall Street Acronyms, Initials, and Abbreviations*—both just published by McGraw-Hill. Dr. Rosenberg's previous reference works include the *Dictionary of Business and Management*, the *Dictionary of Banking and Financial Services*, the *Dictionary of Computers and Information Processing*, and the *Dictionary of Artificial Intelligence and Robotics*. In addition, Dr. Rosenberg serves as a consultant to the *Oxford English Dictionary* and the *Random House Dictionary*. He is acclaimed "America's foremost business and technical lexicographer."

McGraw-Hill Dictionary of Information Technology and Computer Acronyms, Initials, and Abbreviations

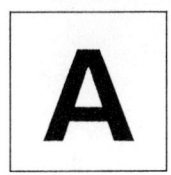

a: absolute
accumulator
adder
address
alphabetic
ampere
amplitude
analog
angstrom
area
asynchronous
attribute
automatic
AA: Arithmetic Average
AAAS: American Association for the Advancement of Science
AAC: Automatic Aperture Control
AACS: Advanced Automatic Compilation System
AADC: All-Application Digital Computer
AADS: Automatic Applications Development System
AAE: American Association of Engineers
AAEE: American Association of Electrical Engineers
AAGR: Average Annual Growth Rate
AAIMS: An Analytical Information Management System
AAL: Absolute Assembly Language
AAME: American Association of Microprocessor Engineers
AAO: Authorized Acquisition Objective
AAP: Analyst Assistance Program
Associative Array Processor
Attached Applications Processor
AARS: Automatic Address Recognition Subsystem
AAS: Advanced Administrative System
Automatic Addressing System
AAU: Address Arithmetic Unit
AAVD: Automatic Alternate Voice Data
AB: Address Bus
ABAC: Association of Business and Administrative Computing
ABACUS: Agents and Brokers Automated Computer Users System
ABB: Array of Building Blocks
ABC: Approach By Concept
ABCS: Automatic Base Communication Systems
ABDL: Automatic Binary Data Link
ABE: Arithmetic Building Element
ABEL: Acid/Base Electrolyte Disorders
ABEND: Abnormal End of Task
ABFD: Affordable Basic Floppy Disk
ABL: Accepted Batch Listing
Architectural Blockdiagram Language
Automatic Bootstrap Loader
ABLP: Air Bearing Lift Pad
ABM: Asynchronous Balanced Mode
Automated Batch Mixing
ABMPS: Automated Business Mail Processing System

ABMS: Automated Batch Manufacturing System
ABOL: Adviser Business-Oriented Language
ABPS: Automated Bill Payment System
abs: absolute
ABSLDR: Absolute Loader
ABW: Advise By Wire
ac: accumulator
AC: Acoustic Coupler
   Actual Count
   Adaptive Control
   Address Counter
   Alternating Current
   Automatic Configuration
   Automatic Control
ACA: Asynchronous Communications Adapter
ACAM: Augmented Content-Addressed Memory
ACAMPS: Automated Communications And Message Processing System
ACAP: Advanced Computer for Array Processing
ACAPS: Automated Cost And Planning System
ACAS: American Computer Appraisal Service
ACB: Adapter Control Block
   Asynchronous Communications Base
ACBGEN: Application Control Block Generation
ACBR: Accumulator Buffer Register
acc: accept
   accumulate
   accumulator
ACC: Asynchronous Communications Control
ACCA: Asynchronous Communications Control Attachment
ACCAP: Autocoder to COBOL Conversion-Aid Program
ACCAT: Advanced Command and Control Architectural Testbed
acce: acceptance
ACCEL: Automated Circuit Card Etching Layout
ACCESS: Access Characteristics Estimation System
   Argonne Code Center Exchange and Storage System
   Automatic Computer-Controlled Electronic Scanning System
ACCLAIM: Automated Circuit Card Layout and Implementation
ACCT: Ad Hoc Committee for Competitive Telecommunications
accum: accumulator
ACD: Automatic Call Distribution
   Automatic Call Distributor
   Destination Accumulator
AC-DC: Alternating Current to Direct Current
AC/DC: Alternating Current to Direct Current
ACDMS: Automated Control of a Document Management System
ACE: Adaptive Computer Experiment
   Asynchronous Communication Element
   Automated Computing Engine
   Automatic Checkout Equipment
ACEA: Association of Computing in Engineering and Architecture
ACEC: American Consulting Engineers Council
ACES: Automated Code Evaluation System

ACF: Access Control Field
Advanced Communication Function
ACG: Automatic Code Generator
ACH: Attempts per Circuit per Hour
ACI: Adjacent Channel Interference
Alternating Current Inputs
ACIA: Asynchronous Communications Interface Adapter
ACID: Acceleration, Cruising, Idling, Deceleration
Automatic Cross-Referencing and Indexing Document Generator
ack: acknowledge
acknowledgment
ACKI: Acknowledge Input
ACKO: Acknowledge Output
acko: acknowledgment (ready to receive)
ACK1: Acknowledgment (message received ok – send next message)
ackt: acknowledgment
ACL: Application Control Language
Audit Command Language
ACLR: Access Control-Logging and Reporting
ACLS: Automatic Carrier Landing System
ACM: Advanced Composite Materials
Alterable Control Memory
Association for Computing Machinery
Associative Communications Multiplexer
Asynchronous Communication Control Module
Authorized Controlled Material
ACMS: Advance Configuration Management System
Application Control and Management System

ACNS: Advanced Communications Network Service
ACO: Alternating Current Outputs
Automatic Call Origination
ACOL: Application Control Language
ACORN: Associative Content Retrieval Network
Automatic Conversion and Test Score Analysis Package
ACOS: Application Control Operating System
ACOUSTINT: Acoustical Intelligence
ACP: Accomplishment/Cost Procedure
Advanced Computational Processor
Ancillary Control Processor
Arithmetic and Control Processor
ACPA: Association of Computer Programmers and Analysts
acpt: accept
acceptance
ACQM: Automatic Circuit Quality Monitoring
ACQS: Association of Consultant Quantity Surveyors
ACR: Access Control Register
Address Control Register
Alternate Recovery
ACRE: Automatic Call Recording Equipment
ACRODABA: Acronym Data Base
ACS: Advanced Communications Service
Associated Computer System
Australian Computer Society
Automatic Checkout System
Automatic Control System
Auxiliary Core Storage
ACSAP: Automated Cross-Section Analysis Program

ACSES: Automated Computer Science Education System
ACSL: Advanced Continuous Simulation Language
ACSM: Assemblies, Components, Spare Parts and Materials
ACSTI: Advisory Committee for Scientific and Technical Information
ACSYS: Accounting Computer System
ACT: Active Control Technology
Actuarial Programming Language
Analogical Circuit Technique
Automated Contingency Translator
ACTA: Automatic Computerized Transverse Axial
ACTD: Automatic Telephone Call Distribution
ACTEL: Alternating Current Thin-Film Electroluminescence
ACTRAN: Audocoder-to-COBOL Translation
ACTS: Advanced Communications Technology Satellite
Application Control and Teleprocessing System
ACTSU: Association of Computer Time-Sharing Users
ACU: Address Control Unit
Arithmetic Control Unit
Association of Computer Users
Automatic Calling Unit
ACUA: Automatic Calling Unit Adapter
ACUG: Association of Computer User Groups
ACUTE: Accountants Computer Users Technical Exchange
ACV: Analysis of Covariance
ACVS: Automatic Computer Voltage Stabilizer
ACW: Access Control Word
ad: address

A/D: Analog/Digital
A-D: Analog-to-Digital
ADA: Ada (Augustra Byron) (computer language)
Automatic Data Acquisition
ADABAS: Adaptable Data Base System
ADAC: Analog to Digital/Digital to Analog Converter
Automatic Direct Analog Computer
ADACS: Automated Data Acquisition and Control System
ADAEX: Automatic Data Acquisition and Computer Complex
ADAL: Action Data Automation Language
ADAM: Adaptive Dynamic Analysis and Maintenance
Advanced Data Access Method
Advanced Data Management
Automatic Direct Access Management
ADAPS: Automated Design and Packaging Service
ADAPSO: Association of Data-Processing Service Organizations
ADAPT: Automatic Density Analysis Profile Technique
ADAPTICOM: Adaptive Communication
ADAPTS: Analog/Digital/Analog Process and Test System
ADAS: Automatic Disk Allocation System
ADAT: Automatic Data Accumulation and Transfer
ADATE: Automatic Digital Assembly Test Equipment
ADAU: Auxiliary Data Acquisition Unit

ADB: Adjusted Debit Balance
ADBS: Advanced Data Base System
ADBT: Access Decision Binding Time
ADC: Analog-to-Digital Converter
Area Distribution Center
A/DC: Analog to Digital Converter
ADCAD: Airways Data Collection and Distribution
ADCC: Asynchronous Data Communications Channel
ADCCP: Advanced Data Communications Control Procedures
ADCIS: Association for the Development of Computer-based Instruction Systems
ADCOM: Association of Data Center Owners and Managers
ADCON: Analog-to-Digital Converter
ADCP: Advanced Data Communication Protocol
ADCU: Association of Data Communications
add: addition
ADD: Automatic Document Distribution
ADDAM: Adaptive Dynamic Decision Aiding Methodology
ADDAR: Automatic Digital Data Acquisition and Recording
ADDAS: Automatic Digital Data Assembly System
ADDDS: Automatic Direct Distance Dialing System
ADDF: Address Field
addit: additional
ADDM: Automated Drafting and Digitizing Machine
addr: adder
address
addressing

ADDR: Address Register
ADDS: Advanced Data Display System
ADDSB: Address Disable
ADDSRTS: Automated Digitized Document Storage, Retrieval and Transmission System
ADE: Advanced Data Entry
Automated Design Equipment
Automatic Data Entry
ADEM: Automatic Data Equalized Modem
ADEPT: Advanced Development Prototype
ADES: Automated Data Entry System
ADEX: Advanced Data Entry Executive
ADI: Alternating Direction Implicit
Alternating Direction Iterative
Automatic Direction Indicator
ADIO: Analog-Digital Input-Output
ADIOS: Analog Digital Input-Output System
Automatic Diagnosis Input-Output System
ADIP: Automated Data Interchange Systems Panel
ADIS: Automatic Data Interchange System
ADIT: Automatic Detection and Integrated Tracking
adj: adjustment
ADL: Automatic Data Link
Automatic Data Logger
ADLC: Advanced Data Link Controller
ADLIPS: Automatic Data Link Plotting System
ADLM: Account Data List Management
ADM: Activity Data Method
Adaptive Data Base Manager
Adaptive Delta Modulation

Advanced Development Models
admin: administration
administrative
administrator
ADMINID: Administrative Identification
ADMIS: Automated Data Management Information System
admn: administration
admr: administrator
ADMS: Advanced Data Management System
Automated Document Management System
Automatic Digital Message Switching
ADMSC: Automatic Digital Message Switching Centers
ADONIS: Automatic Digital On-Line Instrumentation System
ADOPT: Approach to Distributed Processing Transaction
ADOS: Advanced Diskette Operating System
ADP: Acoustic Data Processor
Association of Database Producers (UK)
Automatic Data Processing
ADPACS: Automated Data Processing and Communications Service
ADPC: Automatic Data Processing Center
ADPCM: Adaptive Differential Pulse Code Modulation
ADPE: Automatic Data Processing Equipment
ADPE/S: Automatic Data Interchange System
Automatic Data Processing Equipment and Software
ADPREP: Automatic Data Processing Resource Estimating Procedures

ADPS: Automatic Data Processing System
ADP/TM: Office of Automatic Data Processing and Telecommunications Management
adr: address
addressing
ADR: Alternate Data Retry
Analog-Digital Recorder
Automatical Digital Relay
ADRA: Automatic Dynamic Response Analyzer
ADRAC: Automatic Digital Recording And Control
ADREN: Address Enable
ADROIT: Automated Data Retrieval and Operations Involving Timeseries
ADRS: Adaptive Data Reporting System
Analog-to-Digital Data Recording System
ADRT: Analog Data Recording Transcriber
ADS: Accurately Defined Systems
Activity Data Sheet
Advanced Debugging System
Analog Digital Subsystem
Autographed Document Signed
Automated Design System
ADSE: Alternative Delivery Schedule Evaluator
ADSEL: Address Selective
ADSG: Alternative Delivery Schedule Generator
ADSOL: Analysis of Dynamical Systems On-Line
ADSP: Advanced Digital Signal Processor
ADSS: Advanced Software System
ADSTAR: Automatic Document Storage And Retrieval
ADT: Active Disk Table
Asynchronous Data Transceiver

Attribute Distributed Tree
Automatic Detection and Tracking
Autonomous Data Transfer
ADTD: Association of Data Terminal Distributors
ADTS: Automated Data and Telecommunications Service
Automatic Data Test System
ADU: Automatic Data Unit
Automatic Dialing Unit
adv: advice
advise
ADVAST: Advanced Station
ADX: Asymmetric Data Exchange
Automatic Data Exchange
Automatic Digital Exchange
AE: Arithmetic Element
AEC: Automatic Energy Control
AECT: Association for Educational Communications and Technology
AED: ALGOL Extended for Design
Association of Equipment Distributors
Automated Engineering Design
ADECAP: Automated Engineering Design Circuit Analysis Program
ADEPS: Automated Engineering Documentation Preparation System
AED: Automated Engineering Design
AEDS: Advanced Electric Distribution System
Association for Educational Data Systems
AEIMS: Administrative Engineering Information Management System
AEL: Audit Entry Language
AEMS: American Engineering Model Society
AERIS: Automatic Electronic Ranging Information System

AES: Automatic Extraction System
AESC: Automatic Electronic Switching Center
AESOP: Automated Engineering and Scientific Optimization Programming
AESS: Aerospace and Electronics Systems Society
AET: Acoustic Emission Testing
Automatic Exchange Tester
AEVS: Automatic Electronic Voice Switch
AEWM: Acoustic Emission Weld Monitor (monitoring)
AEWS: Advanced Early Warning System
AF: Arithmetic Flag
Aspect Factor
Audio Frequency
AFAM: Automatic Frequency Assignment Model
AFC: Automatic Field Control
Automatic Frequency Control
AFCAD: Automatic File Control And Documentation
AFCS: Attitude Flight Control System
AFES: Automatic Feature Extraction System
affil: affiliated
AFI: Automatic Fault Isolation
AFIPS: American Federation of Information Processing Societies
afirm: affirmative
AFIS: Automated Financial Information System
AFL: Abstract Family of Languages
AFM: Application Functions Module
AFO: Advanced File Organization
AFOS: Advanced Field Operating System
Automation of Field Operations and Services
AFPA: Automatic Flow Process Analysis

AFP/SME: Association for Finishing Processes of the Society of Manufacturing Engineers
AFR: Advanced Fault Resolution
Automatic Field/Format Recognition
AFRC: Automatic Frequency Ratio Controller
AFSK: Audio Frequency Shift Keying
AFSM: Association of Field Service Managers
AFT: Analog Facility Terminal
Automated Funds Transfer
Automatic Fund Transfers
AFTS: Automated Funds Transfer System
AFU: Autonomous Functional Unit
AG: Address Generator
Association Graph
Attribute Grammer
AGC: Automatic Gain Control
Automatic Generation Control
AGT: Arithmetic Greater Than
AGU: Address Generation Unit
AH: Acceptor Handshake
AHCS: Advanced Hybrid Computing System
A&I: Abstracting and Indexing
AI: Artificial Intelligence
AIA: Accident/Incident Analysis
Automation One Association
AIC: Automatic Intercept Center
AICS: Association of Independent Computer Specialists
Automated Industrial Control System
AID: Algebraic Interpretive Dialogue
Analog Interface Device
Automated Industrial Drilling
Automatic Information Distribution
Automatic Interaction Detection
AIDAPS: Automatic Inspection, Diagnostic And Prognostic Systems
AIDAS: Advanced Instrumentation and Data Analysis System
AIDE: Accountability In Data Entry
Automated Integrated Design and Engineering
AIDES: Automated Image Data Extraction System
AIDE/TPS: Advanced Interactive Data Entry/Transaction Processing System
AIDS: Acoustic Intelligence Data System
Advanced Impact Drilling System
Advanced Interactive Debugging System
Advanced Interactive Display System
Advanced Interconnection Development System
American Institute for Decision Science
Automatic Illustrated Documentation System
Automatic Interactive Debugging System
Automatic Inventory Dispatching System
AIET: Average Instruction Execution Time
AIFU: Automated Instruction Fetch Unit
AIG: Address Indicating Group
AIIE: American Institute of Industrial Engineers
AIL: Arithmetic Input Left
Array Interconnection Logic

AIM: Abridged Index Medicus
Access Isolation Mechanism
Advanced Informatics and Medicine
Advanced Information in Medicine
Associative Index Method
Asynchronous Interface Module
Automated Inventory Management

AIM/ARM: Abstracts of Instructional Material/Abstract of Research Material

AIMIS: Advanced Integrated Modular Instrumentation System

AIMS: Annual Improvement Maintenance and Support
Automated Industrial Management System

AIOD: Automatic Identification of Outward Dialing

AIOP: Analog Input/Output Package

AIP: Alphanumeric Impact Printer
Automated Imagery Processing

AIPU: Associative Information Processing Unit

AIR: Acoustic Intercept Receiver
Arithmetic Input Right
Automatic Interrogation Routine

AIRES: Automated Information Resource System

AIRS: Alliance of Information and Referral Services
Automatic Image Retrieval System

AIS: Advanced Information Systems
Analog Input System
Automated Information System
Automatic Intercept System

AISB: Society for the Study of Artificial Intelligence and the Simulation of the Brain

AISC: Association of Independent Software Companies

AIST: Agency of Industrial Science and Technology (Japan)

AIT: Advanced Information Technology

AIU: Abstract Information Unit

AJG: Automatic Job Stream Generator

ak: acknowledge

AKM: Automatic Key Management

AKO: A Kind Of

AKR: Address Key Register

al: alphabet
alphabetic

AL: Assembler Language
Assembly Language

ALABOL: Algorithmic And Business-Oriented Language

ALADIN: Algebraic Automated Digital Iterative Network

ALAP: Associative Linear Array Processor

ALB: Arithmetic and Logic Box
Assembly Line Balancing

ALBO: Automatic Line Build-Out

ALC: Adaptive Logic Circuit
Assembly Language Coding

ALCAPP: Automative List Classification And Profile Production

ALCU: Arithmetic Logic and Control Unit
Asynchronous Line Control Unit

ALD: Advanced Logic Design
Asynchronous Limited Distance
Automated Logic Diagram

ALDEP: Automated Layout Design Program

ALDP: Automatic Language-Data Processing
ALDS: Analysis of Large Data Sets
ALE: Address Latch Enable
Automatic Line Equalization
ALEC: Analysis of Linear Electronic Circuits
ALEM: Association of Loading Equipment Manufacturers
ALF: Application Library File
Automatic Line Feed
ALFA: Automatic Line Fault Analysis
ALFC: Automatic Load-Frequency Control
ALG: Asynchronous Line Interface
ALGEC: Algorithmic Language for Economic Problems
ALGOL: Algorithmic Language
ALICE: Application Language Interface Conversion and Extension
ALIS: Advanced Life Information System
ALIT: Automatic Line Insulation Test
alloc: allocation
ALM: Alarm Master
Asynchronous Line Module
ALMS: Automated Logic Mapping System
ALMSA: Automated Logistics Management Systems Activity
ALN: Attribute Level Number
ALP: Arithmetic and Logic Processor
Assembly Language Program
Automated Learning Process
alph: alphabet
alphabetic
alphanum: alphanumeric
ALPROS: ALGOL Process Control System
ALPS: Advanced Linear Programming System
Assembly Line Planning System
ALRS: Arithmetic Logic Register Stack
ALS: Advanced Logistics System
Arithmetic Logic Section
ALSC: Automatic Level and Slope Control
ALSPEC: Automated Laser Seeker Performance Evaluation System
alt: alternate
ALT: Average Logistic Time
ALTAPE: Automatic Line Tracing And Processing Equipment
ALTINSAR: Alternate Instruction Address Register
ALTRAN: Algebra Translator
ALU: Advanced Logical Unit
Arithmetic and Logic Unit
Asynchronous Line Unit
ALV: Arithmetic Logic Unit
A/M: Amperes per Meter
AM: Access Manager
Address Marker
Address Mode
Address Modifier
Addressing Mode
Amplitude Modulation
Associative Memory
Asynchronous Modem
AMA: Associative Memory Address
Associative Memory Array
Asynchronus Multiplexer Adapter
AMA/MTR: Automatic Message Accounting – Magnetic Tape Recording
AMAPS: Advanced Manufacturing, Accounting, and Production System
AMARC: Automatic Message Accounting Recording Center

AMAVU: Advanced Modular Audio Visual Unit
AMC: Autonomous Multiplexer Channel
AMCAP: Advanced Microwave Circuit Analysis Program
AMCAT: Addressograph Multigraph Computer Access Terminal
AMD: Associative Memory Data
AMDF: Absolute Magnitude Difference Function
AMDS: Advanced Microcomputer Development System
AME: Angle Measuring Equipment
Automatic Microfiche Editor
Automatic Monitoring Equipment
Average Magnitude of Error
AMEDA: Automatic Microscope Electronic Data Accumulator
AMEDS: Automated Measurement Evaluator and Director System
AMEME: Association of Mining, Electrical and Mechanical Engineers
AMES: Automatic Message Entry System
AMFIS: Automatic Microfilm Information System
AMH: Automated Materials Handling
AMHS: American Material Handling Society
AMI: Association of Multi-Image
Average Mutual Information
AMIS: Acquistion Management Information System
Automated Management Information System
AML: Advanced Math Library
A Manufacturing Language
Amplitude Modulated Link
Application Module Library

AMLC: Asynchronous Multiline Controller
AMM: Additional Memory Module
Advanced Manufacturing Methods
Alternative Method of Management
Analog Monitor Module
AMMA: Automated Media Management System
AMME: Automated Multi-Media Exchange
AMMINET: Automated Mortgage Management Information Network
AMMS: Automated Multi-Media Switch
AMMSS: Automatic Message and Mail Sorting Systems
AMNIP: Adaptive Man-Machine Non-Arithmetical Information Processing
AMO: Area Maintenance Office
AMOS: Adjustable Multi-Class Organizing System
AMOSS: Adaptive Mission-Oriented Software System
amp: ampere
amplifier
AMPCR: Alternate Microprogram Count Register
AMPP: Advanced Microprogrammable Processor
AMPS: Advanced Mobile Phone Service
Assembly Manufacturing Payroll System
Assignment Management Planning System
Automatic Message Processing System
AMR: Arithmetic Mask Register
Automatic Message Routing
AMRF: Automated Manufacturing Research Facility
AMRPD: Applied Manufacturing

Research and Process Development
AMS: Administrative Management Society
Application Management System
Asymmetric Multiprocessing System
Automated Maintenance System
AMSCO: Access Method Services Cryptographic Option
AMSDL: Acquisition Management System and Data Requirements Control List
AMSEC: Analytical Method for System Evaluation and Control
AMSO: Automated Microform Storage and Retrieval
AMSP: Array Machine Simulation Program
AMST: Automated Maintenance Support Tool
AMT: Advanced Manufacturing Technique
Advanced Manufacturing Technology
Automated Microfiche Terminal
AMTD: Automatic Magnetic Tape Dissemination
AMTRAN: Automatic Mathematical Translator
AMU: Association of Minicomputer Users
a/n: alphanumeric
an: alphanumeric
ANA: Automatic Number Analysis
ANACOM: Analog Computer
ANACONDA: Analytical Control and Data
anal: analysis
analyst
ANALIT: Analysis of Automatic Line Insulation Tests
ANAPAC: Analysis Package
ANATRAN: Analog Translator
ANC: All-Numbers Calling
ANCHOR: Alpha-Numeric Character Generator
ANCOVA: Analysis of Covariance
ANCS: American Numerical Control Society
AND: Alpha-Numeric Display
ANDMS: Advanced Network Design and Management System
ANDVT: Advanced Narrow-band Digital Voice Terminal
ANI: Automatic Number Identification
ANIRC: Annual National Information Retrieval Colloquium
ANL: Automatic New Line
ANLP: Alpha-Numeric Logic Package
anlyst: analyst
ANOM: Analysis Of Means
ANOVA: Analysis Of Variance
ANRF: Area Normalization with Response Factors
ANS: American National Standard
ANSA: Advanced Network System Architecture
ANSC: American National Standards Committee
ANSC X3: American National Standards Committee for Computers and Information Processing
ANSC X4: American National Standards Committee for Office Machines and Supplies
ANSI: American National Standards Institute
ANSIM: Analog Simulator
ANSR: Add-On Non-Stop Reliability
ANSWER: Algorithm for Non-Syn-

chronized Waveform Error Reduction
ANSYS: Analysis System
AOCR: Advanced Optical Character Reader
Advanced Optical Character Recognition
AOCU: Arithmetic Output Control Unit
Associative Output Control Unit
AOD: Arithmetic Output Data
AOE: Auditing Order Error
AOF: Advanced Operating Facilities
AOG: AND/OR Graph
AOH: Add-On-Header
AOI: Acousto-Optical Imaging
ADD-OR-Inverter
AOIPS: Atmospheric and Oceanographic Information Processing System
AOL: Application Oriented Language
AOM: Acoustic-Optic Modulator
AON: All Or None order
AOQ: Average Outgoing Quality
AOQL: Average Outgoing Quality Limit
AORS: Abnormal Occurrence Reporting System
AOS: Advanced Operating System
AOSP: Automatic Operating and Scheduling Program
AOU: Arithmetic Output Unit
Associative Output Unit
AOV: Analysis Of Variance
Attribute (Object) = Value
AP: Application Program
Argument Pointer
Arithmetic Processor
Array Processor
Associative Processor
Attached Processor
Audio Processing
APACHE: Analog Programming And Checking

APAL: Array Processor Assembly Language
APAR: Authorized Program Analysis Report
Automatic Programming and Recording
APAS: Adaptable-Programmable Assembly System
APB: Application Program Block
APC: Area Positive Control
Associative Processor Control
Automatic Peripheral Control
Automatic Phase Control
Automatic Potential Control
APCC: Association of Professional Computer Consultants
APCHE: Automatic Programmed Checkout Equipment
APCM: Adaptive Pulse Code Modulator
Authorized Protective Connecting Module
APCS: Associative Processor Computer System
Attitude and Pointing Control System
APD: Approach Progress Display
Automated Payment and Deposit
APDL: Algorithmic Processor Description Language
APDM: Associative Push Down Memory
APE: Application Program Evaluation
APET: Application Program Evaluator Tool
APEX: Assembler and Process Executive
Automated Planning and Execution Control System
APF: Authorized Program Facility
APG: Application Program Generator
API: Automatic Priority Interrupt

APICS: American Production and Inventory Control Society
APIS: Array Processing Instruction Set
APL: Algorithmic Programming Language
A Programming Language
Automatic Program Load
Automatic Program Loading
APLL: Analog Phased-Locked Loop
Automatic Phased-Locked Loop
APM: Automatic Predictive Maintenance
APMS: Automatic Performance Management System.
APO: Automatic Power Off
APOLLO: Article Procurement with On-Line Local Ordering
APP: Advance Procurement Plan
Associative Parallel Processor
APPI: Advanced Planning Procurement Information
APPLE: Analog Phased Processing Loop Equipment
Associative Processing Programming Language
appr: approximate
approximately
approximation
approx: approximate
approximately
APPU: Application Program Preparation Utility
APR: Active Page Register
Automatic Programming and Recording
APRICOT: Automatic Printed Circuit Board Routing with Intermediate Control of the Tracking
APRIL: Accounts Payable, Receivable, Inventory Library Automatically Programmed Remote Indication Logging
APROC: Adaptive Statistical Processor
APRS: Automatic Position Reference System
APRST: Averaged Probability Ratio Sequential Test
APS: Assembly Programming System
Auxiliary Power System
APSL: Access Path Specification Language
APSM: Auxiliary Power Supply Module
APSS: Automated Program Support System
APT: Automatic Program Control
Automatically Programmed Tool
APTE: Automatic Production Test Equipment
APTF: Automated Program Testing Facility
APTI: Automatic Print Transfer Instrument
APTIF: Average Process Time Inverted File
APTP: Arithmetic Proficiency Training Program
APTR: Association Printer
APU: Analog Processing Unit
Arithmetic Processing Unit
Assessment of Performance Unit
Asynchronous Processing Unit
Auxiliary Power Unit
AQD: Analysis of Quantitative Data
AQL: Acceptable Quality Level
A&R: Analysts and Researchers
AR: Accumulator Register
Address Register
Arithmetic Register
Aspect Ratio

Associative Register
Automated Register
Automatic Restart
ARA: Attitude Reference Assembly
Automatic Route Advance
ARAC: Array Reduction Analysis Circuit
ARAL: Automatic Record Analysis Language
ARAMIS: Automation Robotics and Machine Intelligence System
ARASEM: Artificially Random Self-Motivated
ARAT: Automatic Random Access Transport
arb: arbitrary
arbitration
ARC: Attached Resource Computer
Automatic Revenue Collection
ARCADE: Automatic Radar Control And Data Equipment
ARCAIC: Archives and Record Catologing And Indexing by Computer
ARCS: Advanced Reconfigurable Computer System
Automated Reproduction and Collating System
Automated Revenue Collection System
Automated Ring Code System
ARD: Answering, Recording and Dialing
Automatic Release Date
ARDA: Analog Recording Dynamic Analyzers
ARDI: Analysis, Requirements Determination, Design and Development, and Implementation and Evaluation
ARDS: Advance Remote Display System
ARF: Automatic Report Feature

arg: argument
ARGS: Advanced Raster-Graphics System
ARI: Applications Reference Index
Automated Readability Index
ARIES: Automated Reliability Interactive Estimation System
ARIMA: Autoregressive Integrated Moving Average
ARIS: Activity Reporting Information System
Automated Reactor Inspection System
arith: arithmetic
ARL: Average Run Length
ARM: Asynchronous Response Mode
Autoregressive Moving Average
ARMA: Autoregressive Moving Average
ARMAN: Artificial Methods Analyst
ARMM: Automatic Reliability Mathematical Model
ARMMS: Automated Reliability and Maintainability Measurement System
ARO: After Receipt of Order
AROM: Alterable Read-Only Memory
AROS: Alterable Read Only Operating System
ARP: Analogous Random Process
ARPA: Advanced Research Projects Agency
ARPANET: Advanced Research Projects Agency Network
ARPS: Advanced Real-Time Processing System
ARQ: Answer-Return Query
Automatic Repeat Request
Automatic Request for Repetition
ARR: Address Recall Register

ARS: Advanced Record System (of General Services Administration)
Audio Response System
Automatic Route Selection
Automatic Route Setting
ARSTEC: Adaptive Random Search Technique
ART: Actual Retention Time
Authorization and Resource Table
Automated Request Transmission
Average Run Time
ARTS: Audio Response Time-Shared System
Automated Radar Terminal System
ARTS/DB: Analysis of Real-Time Systems/Data Base-Oriented Systems
ARU: Address Recognition Unit
Application Resource Unit
Audio Response Unit
Auxiliary Read-Out Unit
ARX: Automatic Retransmission Exchange
AS: Address Space
Auxiliary Storage
ASA: Acoustical Society of America
American Standards Association (former name of the American National Standards Institute)
American Statistical Association
Asynchronous Adapter
Asynchronous/Synchronous Adapter
Automatic Separation System
Automatic Spectrum Analyzer
ASAP: Advanced Scientific Array Processor
Automated Statistical Analysis Program
Automatic Spooling with Asynchronous Processing
asbl: assemble
assembler
ASC: Adaptive Speed Control
Associative Structure Computer
Automatic System Controller
ASCB: Address Space Control Block
ASCC: Automatic Sequence Controlled Calculator
ASCE: American Society of Civil Engineers
ASCII: American Standard Code for Information Interchange
ASCOM: Association of Telecommunication Services
ASCON: Automated Switched Communications Network
ASCP: Automatic System Checkout Program
ASCU: Association of Small Computer Users
ASCUE: Association of Small Computer Users in Education
ASDA: Accelerate-Stop Distance Available
ASDI: Automatic Selective Dissemination of Information
ASDIC: Association of Information and Dissemination Centers
ASDM: Automated Systems Design Methodology
ASE: Application Support Environment
ASE: Automatic Stabilization Equipment
ASEE: American Society for Engineering Education
ASES: Automated Software Evaluation System
ASF: Active Segment Field
Automatic Sheet Feeder

ASFM: Association of Field Service Managers
ASI: American Standards Institute
American Statistical Index
ASIC: Application Specific Integrated Circuit
ASID: Address Space Identifier
ASIDIC: Association of Information and Dissemination Centers
ASIDP: American Society of Information and Data Processing
ASII: American Science Information Institute
ASIS: American Society for Industrial Security
American Society for Information Science
ASIT: Adaptable Surface Interface Terminal
ASK: Amplitude Shift Keying
ASKS: Automatic Station Keeping System
ASLO: Assembly Layout
aslr: assembler
ASLT: Advanced Solid Logic Technology
asm: assembler
ASM: Algorithmic State Machine
Association for Systems Management
Asynchronous Sequential Machine
asmblr: assembler
ASME: American Society of Mechanical Engineers
ASM/GEN: Assembler Generating System
ASN: Average Sample Number
ASP: Acoustic Signal Processor
Association-Storing Processor
Attached Support Processor
Automated Spooling Priority
ASPEX: Automated Surface Perspectives

ASPI: Asynchronous Synchronous Programmable Interface
ASQ: Analytic Solution to Queues
ASQC: American Society for Quality Control
ASR: Active Status Register
Address Shift Register
Analog Shift Register
Assigned Slot Release
Automatic Send/Receive
Automatic Storage/Retrieval
Available Supply Rate
ASRL: Average Sample Run Length
ASRS: Automatic Storage and Retrieval System
ASSET: Advanced Systems Synthesis and Evaluation Technique
assm: assembler
ASSM: Associative Memory
assmt: assessment
assn: association
assoc: associated
associative
ASSORT: Automatic System for Selection Of Receiver and Transmitter
ASSR: Automated Systems Service Request
AST: Abstract Syntax Tree
Address Synchronizing Track
Asynchronous to Synchronous Transmission Adapter
Automatic Scan Tracking
ASTA: Association of Short-Circuit Testing Authorities
Automatic System Trouble Analysis
ASTAP: Advanced Statistical Analysis Program
ASTC: Australian Science and Technology Council
ASTI: Automated System for Transport Intelligence
ASTM: American Society for Testing Metals (or Materials)

ASTME: American Society of Tool and Manufacturing Engineers
ASTMS: Association of Scientific, Technical and Managerial Staff (UK)
ASTOVL: Advanced Short Take-Off and Vertical Landing
ASTRA: Advanced Structural Analyzer
Automatic Scheduling and Time-dependent Resource Allocation
Automatic Scheduling and Time-integrated Resource Allocation
ASTRAIL: Analog Schematic Translator to Algebraic Language
Assurance and Stabilization Trends for Reliability by Analysis of Lots
ASTROS: Advanced Systematic Techniques for Reliable Operational Software
ASTS: Air to Surface Transport System
ASTUTE: Association of System 2000 Users for Technical Exchange
ASU: Add/Subtract Unit
ASVIP: American Standard Vocabulary for Information Processing
ASVS: Automatic Signature Verification System
ASW: Applications Software
ASYLCU: Asynchronous Line Control Unit
async: asynchronous
asynch: asynchronous
A&T: Assemble and Test
AT: Absolute Title
Address Translator
Anomalous Transmission
Appropriate Technology
Automatic Transmission
ATA: Asynchronous Terminal Adapter
ATAE: Associated Telephone Answering Exchanges
ATAP: Automated Time and Attendance Procedures
ATARS: Automated Travel Agents Reservation Systems
ATAS: Automated Telephone Answering System
ATBM: Average Time between Maintenance
ATC: Advanced Technology Components
Automated Technical Control
Automatic Tool Charger
ATCD: Automatic Telephone Call Distribution
ATD: Actual To Date
ATDE: Advanced Technology Demonstrator Engine
ATDG: Automated Test Data Generator
ATDM: Asynchronous Time-Division Multiplexing
ATE: Automatic Test Equipment
ATEA: Automatic Test Equipment Association
ATEC: Automated Technical Control
Automated Test Equipment Complex
ATEMIS: Automatic Traffic Engineering and Management Information System
ATEV: Approximate Theoretical Error Variance
ATEX: Automatic Test Equipment Conference and Exposition
ATF: Automatic Text Formatter
ATFA: Association of Technicians in Financing and Accounting
ATFC: Automatic Traffic-Flow Control

ATG: Automatic Test Generation
    Automatic Test Generator
ATGF: Automatic Test Generation Facility
ATI: Automatic Track Initiation
    Average Total Inspection
ATIR: Autotransaction Industry Report
ATIS: Automatic Terminal Information Service
    Automatic Transmitter Identification System
ATL: Active Task List
    Analog-Threshold Logic
    Applications Terminal Language
ATLAS: Abbreviated Test Language for Avionics Systems
    Automated Testing and Load Analysis System
    Automatic Tabulating, Listing And Sorting System
ATM: Asynchronous Time Multiplexing
    Automated Teller Machine
    Automatic Teller Machine
ATMAC: Advanced Technology Microelectronic Array Computer
ATMS: Advanced Terminal Management System
    Automatic Transmission Measuring System
ATMSS: Automatic Telegraph Message Switching System
atn: attention
AtoD: Analog to Digital
ATOLS: Automatic Testing On-Line System
ATOMS: Automated Technical Order Maintenance Sequence(s)
atr: attribute
ATR: Angle, Time, Range
ATRAC: Angle Tracking Computer
ATRVAL: Attribute Value
ATS: Analytic Trouble Shooting
    Applications Technology Satellite
    Automated Test System
    Automatic Test System
    Automatic Transfer Service
ATSS: Automatic Telecommunications Switching System
    Automatic Test Support Systems
ATSS-D: Automatic Telecommunications Switching System – Data Services
ATSU: Association of Time-Sharing Users
att: attribute
ATT: Address Translation Table
    Average Total Time
attach: attachment
attn: attention
attr: attribute
ATU: Analysis and Transformation Unit
au: audio
AU: Adder Unit
    Arithmetic Unit
AUD: Asynchronous Unit Delay
AUDDIT: Automatic Dynamic Digital Test System
AUDICS: Auditable Internal Control Systems
audvis: audiovisual
AUT: Advanced User Terminal Assembly Under Test
    Automated Unit Test
AUTODIN: Automatic Digital Network (Western Union)
AUTODOC: Automated Documentation
AUTOFACT: Automated, Integrated Factory of Tomorrow Conference and Exposition
AUTOMAST: Automatic Mathemat-

ical Analysis and Symbolic Translation
AUTOMAT: Automatic Methods And Times
AUTOMEX: Automatic Message Exchange
automtn: automation
AUTONET: Automatic Network Display Program
AUTOPROS: Automated Process Planning System
AUTOSATE: Automated Data Systems Analysis Technique
AUTOSEVOCOM: Automatic Secure Voice Communications (system)
AUTOSPOT: Automatic System for Positioning Tools
AUTOVON: Automatic Voice Network
AUTRAN: Automatic Translation
Automatic Utility Translator
AUTRAX: Automatic Traffic Recording and Analysis Complex
AUW: All-Up-Weight
aux: auxiliary
AUXRC: Auxiliary Recording Control Circuit
av: audiovisual
available
average
AV: Analysis of Variance
Array/Vector
Attribute Value

AVA: Absolute Virtual Address
avail: available
AVC: Automatic Volume Control
AVD: Alternate Voice and Data
ave: average
avg: average
AVHRR: Advanced Very High Resolution Radiometer
AVISAM: Average Index Sequential Access Method
Average Indexed Sequential Access Method
AVM: Automatic Voltage Margin
AVOCON: Automated Vocabulary Control
AVOS: Acoustic Valve Operating System
Advisor Virtual memory Operating System
AVR: Automatic Volume Recognition
AVS: Automated Verification System
Automatic Volume Sensing
AVT: Attribute Value Time
AWAR: Area Weighted Average Resolution
AWC: Association for Women in Computing
AWF: Acceptable Work-Load Factor
AWGN: Additive White Gaussian Noise
AWS: Active Work Space
AXP: Associative Crosspoint Processor
AZAS: Adjustable Zero Adjustable Span

B

b: base
batch
bel
binary
bit
blank
block
boolean
bus
byte
BA: Bus Available
BA/BASIC: Business Applications written in BASIC
BABS: Batch Automated Balancing System
BAC: Bus Adaptor Control
BACIS: Budget Accounting Information System
BACT: Best Available Control Technology
BAIS: Bulletin Articles Information Subsystem
BAK: backup
bal: balance
BAL: Basic Assembly Language
Business Application Language
BALLOTS: Bibliographic Automation of a Large Library Operations using a Time-Sharing System
BALM: Block And List Manipulator
BALUN: Balanced to Unbalanced
BAM: Basic Access Method
Block Allocation Map
BAMP: Basic Analysis and Mapping Program
BAP: Basic Assembly Program
Bus Available Pulse

BAPTA: Bearing and Power Transfer Assembly
BAR: Base Address Register
Buffer Address Register
BARON: Business/Accounts Reporting Operating Network
BARS: Bell Audit Relate System (Telephone Laboratories)
BAS: Bell Audit System (Telephone Laboratories)
Block Automation System
Business Accounting System
BASBOL: Basic Business Oriented Language
BASE: Basic Semantic Element
BASIC: Beginner's All-Purpose Symbolic Instruction Code
BASRM: Basic Analog Simulation System
bat: batch
BAT: Best Available Technology
BATEA: Best Available Technology Economically Achievable
BAUD: Baudot Code
bb: broadband
BB: Begin Bracket
BBAC: Bus-to-Bus Access Circuit
BBC: Broadband Coaxial Cable
Broadband Control
BBL: Basic Business Language
Branch Back and Load
BBS: Business Batch System
BBSP: Building Block Signal Processor
BBU: Battery Backup
BIT Buffer Unit
BC: Basic Control
Binary Code
Bulk Core
Business Computer

BCA: Bisynchronous Communications Adapter
Bit Count Appendage
BCAM: Basic Communication Access Method
BCB: Bit Control Block
BCC: Block-Check Character
Business Computer Center
BCD: Binary-Coded Decimal
BCDIC: Extended Binary Coded Decimal Interchange Code
BCDNAF: Binary Coded Decimal Nonadjacent Form
BCE: Basic Comparison Element
Before Common Era
BCH: Bids per Circuit per Hour
Block Control Header
Bose-Chaudhuri-Hocquenghem (code)
BCI: Basic Command Interpreter
BCIA: Bounded Carry Inspection Adder
BCIU: Bus Control Interface Unit
BCJS: Buffer Control Junction Switch
BCL: Base-Coupled Logic
BCM: Basic Control Memory
BCO: Binary Coded Octal
BCP: Batch Communications Program
BIT Control Panel
Budget Change Proposal
Byte Control Protocol
BCPL: Basic Combined Programming Language
BCR: Badge Card Reader
Byte Count Register
BCS: Basic Communications Support
Basic Control System
Block Check Sequence
British Computer Society
Business Computer System
BCT: Between Commands Testing
BCU: Basic Counter Unit
Block Control Unit
Buffer Control Unit
BCUA: Business Computers Users Association
BD: Blank Display
BDAM: Basic Direct Access Method
BDBE: Basic Data Base Environment
BDC: Binary-Differential Computer
BDCB: Buffered Data and Control Bus
BDE: Basic Data Exchange
BDF: Backwards Differentiation Formulas
Basic Display File
BDFS: Basic Disk Filing System
BDL: Build Definition Language
Building Description Language
BDM: Basic Data Management
BDOS: Basic Disk Operating System
Batch Disk Operating System
BDP: Business Data Processing
BDR: Bi-Duplexed Redundancy
bdry: boundary
BDS: Bulk Data Switching
Business Definition System
BDT: Binary Deck-to-Tape
BDTS: Buffered Data Transmission Simulator
BDU: Basic Device Unit
BDX: Bar Double-X
BE: Back End
Beam Expander
Bus Enable
BEAMOS: Beam Addressed Metal Oxide Semiconductor
BEAMS: Base Engineer Automated Management System
BECS: Basic Error Control System
BEEC: Binary Error-Erasure Channel
BEEF: Business and Engineering Enriched FORTRAN

bel: bell (character)
Bell: Bell System (American Telephone and Telegraph)
BEM: Basic Editor Monitor
BEMA: Business Equipment Manufacturers' Association
BEN: Bus Enable
BER: Bit Error Rate
BERM: Bit Error Rate Monitor
BERT: Bit Error Rate Test
Bit Error Rate Tester
BES: Basic Executive System
BEST: Basic Executive Scheduler and Timekeeper
Business EDP System Technique
BETA: Business Equipment Trade Association
BEU: Basic Encoding Unit
BEX: Broadband Exchange
B/F: Background/Foreground
BF: Blocking Factor
BFAP: Binary Fault Analysis Program
BFAS: Basic File Access System
BFD: Basic Floppy Disk
BFF: Buffered Flip-Flop
BFI: Batch Freeform Input
BFIC: Binary Fault Isolation Chart
BFN: Beam-Forming Network
BFO: Beat Frequency Oscillator
BFPDDA: Binary Floating Point Digital Differential Analyser
BFPR: Binary Floating Point Resistor
BFS: Balanced File Organization Scheme
BFT: Bulk Function Transfer
bg: background
BGS: Basic Graphic System
BHLF: ASCII Subset
BHSI: Beyond Very High Speed Integration
BI: Batch Input
Buffer Index
Bus Interface
BIAS: Broadcast Industry Automation System
BIB: Balanced Incomplete Block
BIBO: Bounded-Input Bounded-Output
BIC: Buffer Interlace Controller
Byte Input Control
BICARSA: Billing, Inventory Control, Accounts Receivable, Sales Analysis
BICEPS: Basic Industrial Control Engineering Programming System
BIE: Boundary-Integral Equation
BIFET: Bipolar combined with J-FET
BILBO: Built-In Logic Block Observer
BIM: Beginning of Information Marker
BIT Image Memory
Bus Interface Module
BIMS: Business Information Management System
bin: binary
BIO: Buffered Input-Output
BIOI: Block Input-Output Input
BIO-L: Bi-phase Level
BIO-M: Bi-phase Mark
BIOO: Block Input-Output Output
BIOR: Business Input-Output Rerun
BIOS: Basic Input-Output System
BIO-S: Bi-phase Space
BIP: BASIC Interpreter Package
Binary Image Processor
BIPS: Billions of Instructions Per Second
BIR: Bus Interface Register
BIRS: Basic Indexing and Retrieval System
BIS: Bureau of Information Science
Business Information System

BISAD: Business Information Systems Analysis and Design
BISAM: Basic Indexed Sequential Access Method
BISYNC: Binary Synchronous Communication Protocl
BIT: Binary Digit
　Built-In-Test
BIU: Basic Information Unit
　Buffer Image Unit
　Bus Interface Unit
BIZMAC: Business Machine Computer
BJF: Batch Job Foreground
BKER: Block Error Rate
bkg: bookkeeping
bkrgd: background
bksp: backspace
bl: blank
　blanking
BL: Block Length
BLA: Binary Logical Association
BLC: Board Level Computer
BLD: Binary Load Dump
BLERT: Block Error Rate Test
BLF: Branch Loss Factor
BLINK: Backward Linkage
BLISS: Basic Language for the Implementation of System Software
　Basic List-Oriented Information Structures System
blk: block
BLL: Base Locator Linkage
　Below Lower Limit
BLM: Basic Language Machine
BLMPX: Block Multiplexer
BLMUX: Block Multiplexer
BLP: Bypass Label Processing
BLU: Basic Link Unit
BLUE: Best Linear Unbiased Estimate
bm: benchmark
BM: Base Machine
　Basic Material
　Bill of Materials
　Buffer Module
　Business Machine
BMC: Block Multiplexer Channel
　Bubble Memory Controller
　Bulk Media Conversion
　Burst Multiplexer Channel
BMD: Benchmark Monitor Display System
　Bubble Memory Device
BMDP: Biomedical Data Processing
BMIS: Bank Management Information System
BML: Basic Machine Language
BMLC: Basic Multiline Controller
BMOM: Base Maintenance and Operational Model
BMP: Batch Message Processing
　Benchmark Program
　Bill of Materials Processor
BMT: Block Mode Terminal Interface
BN: Block Number
BNF: Backus Naur Form
　Backus Normal Form
BNG: Branch No Group
BO: Byte Out
BOA: Basic Ordering Agreement
BOC: Back Office Crunch
　Block-Oriented Computer
　Breach Of Contract
　Byte Output Control
BOCI: Business Organization Climate Index
BOD: Board Of Directors
BOFADS: Business Office Forms Administration Data System
BOG: Board of Governors
BOI: Branch Output Interrupt
BOLD: Bibliographic Online Display
BOM: Bill of Materials
BOMP: Bill Of Material Processor
BOMS: Base Operations Maintenance Simulator
Bool: Boolean

boot: bootstrap
BOP: Bit-Oriented Protocol
BOPA: Basic Operating Programming Aid
BOR: Bureau of Operating Rights
  Bus Out Register
BORAM: Block Organized Random Access Memory
BORSHT: Battery, Overvoltage, Ring, Supervision, Hybrid Test
BOS: Basic Operating System
  Batch Operating System
BOSR: Base Of Stack Register
BOSS: Basic Operating Software System
  Batch Operating Software System
  Business Oriented Software System
BOT: Beginning Of Tape
BP: Batch Processing
  Buffered Printing
BPA: Bandpass Amplifier
BPAM: Basic Partitioned Access Method
BPC: Basic Peripheral Channel
BPE: Basic Programming Extensions
BPF: Bandpass Filter
BPI: Bits Per Inch
  Bytes Per Inch
BPL: Binary Program Loader
  Business Planning Language
  Business Programming Language
BPM: Batch Processing Monitor
BPMM: Bits Per Millimeter
BPPF: Base Program Preparation Facility
BPR: By-Pass Ratio
BPS: Basic Programming Support
  Basic Programming System
  Binary Program Space
  Bits Per Second
  Bytes Per Second
BPSA: Business Products Standards Association
BPSI: Bits Per Square Inch
br: break
BR: Base Register
  Break Request
  Bus Request
BRC: Bit Reversion Circuit
  Bounded Right Context
BRG: Baud Rate Generator
BRM: Binary Rate Multiplier
  Bit Rate Multiplier
BRMC: Business Research Management Center
BROM: Bipolar Read Only Memory
BRS: Break Request Signal
BRTM: Basic Real Time Monitor
BRU: Basic Resolution Unit
BRUCE: Buffer Register Under Computer Edit
BS: Back Space
  Backspace Character
  Back Spread
  Beam Splitter
  Bits per Second
  Block Sale
  British Standard
  Bureau of Ships
  Bureau of Standards
  Business System
BSA: Binary Synchronous Adapter
BSAL: Block Structured Assembly Language
BSAM: Basic Sequential Access Method
  Baltic Steamship Company
BSC: Binary Symmetric Channel
  Binary Synchronous Communication
BSCA: Binary Synchronous Communication Adapter
BSCC: Binary Synchronous Communications Controller
BSCM: Binary Synchronous Communications Macro

BSCS: Binary Synchronous Communication System
BSC/SS: Binary Synchronous Communications/Start-Stop
BSD: Bulk Storage Device
BSELCH: Buffered Selector Channel
BSF: Back Space File
BSI: British Standard Interface
British Standards Institution
BSIE: Banking Systems Information Exchange
BSL: Bit Serial Link
BSM: Basic Storage Module
Batch Spool Monitor
BSP: Business Systems Planning
BSQI: Basic Schedule of Quantified Items
BSR: Back Space Record
Buffered Send/Receive
BSS: Bulk Storage System
BSY: Binary Synchronous
bt: between
BT: Burst Trapping
BTAM: Basic Tape Access Method
Basic Telecommunications Access Method
Basic Terminal Access Method
BTC: Batch Terminal Controller
Block Transfer Controller
BTE: Bi-Directional Transceiver Element
Business Terminal Equipment
BTF: Bulk Transfer Facility
BTL: Business Translation Language

BTM: Basic Transport Mechanism
Batch Time-Sharing Monitor
BTMA: Busy Tone Multiple-Access
BTNS: Basic Terminal Network Support
BTP: Batch Transfer Program
BTS: Batch Terminal Simulation
BTSS: Basic Time Sharing System
Braille Time Sharing System
BTT: Bank Teller Terminal
BTU: Basic Transmission Unit
British Thermal Unit
BU: Base Unit
Bottom Up
BUC: Bus Control
BUDS: Building Utility Design System
BUE: Built-Up-Edge
buf: buffer
BUG: Basic Update Generator
BUIC: Back-Up Interceptor Control
BUMP: Bottom-up Modular Programming
BUR: Backup Register
bus: business
BUS: Basic Utility System
BUSREQ: Bus Request
B&W: Black and White
BW: Bits per Word
BWC: Buffer Word Counter
BWD: Basic Work Data
BX: Base Indexed
BYMUX: Byte Multiplexer
BYP: By Pass
bypro(s): by-product(s)

C

c: capacitance
capacitor
carry
centi
clear
clock
computer
constant
control
controller
counter
C: A low-level general purpose programming language associated with the UNIX operating system
C3: Command Control and Communications
C4: Controlled Collapse Chip Connection
C&A: Classification and Audit
CA: Channel Adapter
Communications Adapter
Connecting Arrangement
Control Area
CAAD: Computer-Aided Architectural Design
CAAIS: Computer-Assisted Action Information System
CAAS: Computer-Aided Approach Sequencing
CABD: Computer-Aided Building Design
CABS: Computer-Aided Batch Scheduling
Computer Augmented Block System
CAC: Computer Acceleration Control
Computer-Aided Classification

CACA: Computer-Aided Circuit Analysis
CACD: Computer-Aided Circuit Design
CACM: Communications of the Association for Computing Machinery
CACS: Computer-Assisted Communication System
Content Addressable Computing System
CACSD: Computer-Aided Control System Design
CA/D: Character Assemble/Disassemble
CAD: Computer-Aided Design
Computer-Aided Detection
Computer-Aided Dispatching
CADA: Computer-Assisted Distribution and Assignment
CADAE: Computer-Aided Design and Engineering
CADAM: Computer-Graphics Augmented Design and Manufacturing
CADAPSO: Canadian Association of Data Processing Service Organizations
CADAR: Computer-Aided Design, Analysis and Reliability
CADAS: Computerized Automatic Data Acquisition System
CADAVRS: Computer-Assisted Dial Access Video Retrieval System
CAD/CAM: Computer-Aided Design/Computer-Aided Manufacturing

CADCOM: Computer-Aided Design for Communications
CADD: Computer-Aided Design and Drafting
CADDIA: Cooperation in the Automation of Data Documentation for Import/Export and Agriculture (EC)
CADE: Computer-Aided Design and Engineering
Computer-Aided Design Evaluation
Computer-Assisted Data Entry
Computer-Assisted Data Evaluation
CADES: Computer-Aided Development and Evaluation System
CADIC: Computer-Aided Design of Integrated Circuits
CADICS: Computer-Aided Design of Industrial Cabling Systems
CADIS: Computer-Aided Design of Information Systems
CADLIC: Computer-Aided Design of Linear Integrated Circuits
CADMAT: Computer-Aided Design Manufacture and Testing
CADO: Computer-Aided Document Origination
CADOCR: Computer-Aided Design of Optical Character Recognition
CADPIN: Customs Automated Data Processing Intelligence Network
CADS: Computer-Aided Design System
Computer-Aided Digitizing System
Computer-Analysis and Design System
Content Addressable File Store
CADSS: Combined Analog-Digital Systems Simulator
CADSYS: Computer-Aided Design System
CADTES: Computer-Aided Design and Test
CAE: Computer-Aided Engineering
Computer-Assisted Estimating
CAF: Computer-Assisted Fraud
CAFC: Computed Automated Frequency Control
CAFRS: Client Accounting and Financial Reporting System
CAFS: Content-Addressable File Store
CAG: Computer-Assisted Guidance
Cooperative Automation Group
CAGD: Computer-Aided Geometric Design
CAI: Computer-Administered Instruction
Computer-Aided Instruction
Computer-Assisted Instruction
CAIC: Computer-Assisted Indexing and Classification
CAINS: Computer-Aided Instruction System
CAIOP: Computer-Analog Input-Output
CAIRS: Computer-Assisted Information Retrieval System
CAIS: Canadian Association for Information Science
Computer-Aided Insurance System
CAIVR: Computer-Assisted Instruction with Voice Response
CAL: Common Assembly Language

Computer-Assisted Learning Conversational Algebraic Language
CALA: Computer-Aided Loads Analysis
CALB: Computer-Aided Line Balancing
calc: calculate
CALRS: Centralized Automated Loop Reporting System
CALSSP: Common Assembly Language Scientific Subroutine Package
CAM: Calculated Access Method
Communications Access Manager
Communications Access Method
Computer-Aided Manufacturing
Content Addressable Memory
Content Addressed Memory
CAMA: Centalized Automatic Message Accounting
Control and Automation Manufacturers Association
CAMAC: Computer-Aided Measurement and Control
Computer Automated Measurement and Control
CAMA-ONI: Centralized Automatic Message Accounting-Operator Number Identification Operator
CAMECEC: Computer-Aided Machine Loading
CAMEL: Computer-Aided Manufacturing Network
CAMELOT: Computerization and Mechanization of Local Office Tasks
CAMP: Central Access Monitor Program

Compiler for Automatic Machine Programming
Controls And Monitoring Processor
CAMPRAD: Computer-Assisted Message Preparation Relay and Distribution
CAMPS: Computer-Assisted Message Processing System
can: cancel
cancellation
canc: cancel
cancellation
CANDE: Command and Edit
Culvert Analysis and Design
CANDO: Computer Analysis of Networks with Design Orientation
CANTRAN: Cancel Transmission
CAOS: Computer-Augmented Oscilloscope System
cap: capacity
CAP: Computer-Aided Planning
Computer-Aided Programming
CAPABLE: Controls And Panel Arrangement By Logical Evaluation
CAPARS: Computer-Aided Placement and Routing System
CAPC: Computer-Aided Production Control
CAPE: Computer-Aided Planning and Estimating
CAPER: Computer-Aided Pattern Evaluation and Recognition
CAPERTSIM: Computer-Assisted Program Evaluation Review Technique Simulation
CAPM: Computer-Aided Production Management

CAPOSS: Capacity Planning and Operation Sequencing System
CAPP: Computer-Aided Part Planning
Computer-Aided Process Planning
Content-Addressable Parallel Processor
CAPRI: Card and Printer Remote Interface
Computerized Analysis for Programming Investments
CAPS: Computer-Aided Planning System
Computer-Aided Problem Solving
CAPTAINS: Character And Pattern Telephone Access Information Network System
CAPUR: Computer-Assisted Programming User Remotes
CAQA: Computer-Aided Quality Assurance
CAR: Carry Register
Channel Address Register
Computer-Aided Retrieval
Current Address Register
CARAD: Computer-Aided Reliability and Design
CARD: Compact Automatic Retrieval Display
CARDA: Computer-Aided Reliability Data Analysis
CARDS: Computer-Aided Reliability Data System
C-ARMS: Commercial-Accounts Routing and Design System
carr: carrier
CARS: Computer-Aided Routing System
Computer-Audit Retrieval System
Computerized Audit and Reporting System
cart: cartridge
CAS: Circuits And Systems
Client Accounting System
Column Address Select
Column Address Strobe
Customer Accounting System
CASA: Computer and Automated Systems Association
CASCADE: Centralized Administrative Systems Control and Design
CAS/CPA: Computer Accounting System/Computer Performance Analysis
CASD: Computer-Aided System Design
CASE: Computer-Aided Software Engineering
Computer-Aided Systems Engineering
Computer-Aided Systems Evaluation
CASH: Computer-Aided Stock Holdings
Computer-Aided System Hardware
CASNET: Casual-Associative Network
CASO: Computer-Assisted System Operation
CASOE: Computer Accounting System for Office Expenditure
CASS: Computer Automatic Scheduling System
CASSM: Context Addressed Segment Sequential Memory
CAST: Computer Applications and Systems Technology
Computer-Assisted Scanning Techniques
CAT: Computer-Aided Testing
Computer-Aided Tomography

Computer-Aided Translation
Computer-Aided Typesetting
Computer-Assisted Teleconferencing
Computer-Assisted Testing
Credit Authorization Telephones
Credit Authorization Terminal
CATC: Computer-Assisted Test Construction
CATE: Computer Automated Translation and Editing
catl: catalog
catlg: catalog
CATLINE: Cataloging On-Line
CATS: Centralized Automatic Test System
Computer-Aided Trouble-Shooting
CATV: Cable Antenna Television
Cable Telecommunications and Video
Cable Television
Community Antenna Television
CATVA: Computer-Assisted Total Value Assessment
CAU: Crypto Auxiliary Unit
CAW: Channel Address Word
CAX: Community Automatic Exchange
CB: Citizen's Band
Communications Buffer
Condition BIT
CBA: Computer-Based Automation
Concrete Block Association
C-BASIC: Commercial BASIC
CBBS: Computerized Bulletin Board Service
CBC: Chain Block Controller
Cipher Block Chaining
Computer Based Conferencing
CBCT: Customer-Bank Communication Terminal

CBE: Computer-Based Education
CBEMA: Canadian Business Equipment Manufacturers Association
Computer and Business Equipment Manufacturers Association
CBFM: Constant Bandwidth Frequency Modulation
CBI: Charles Babbage Institute
Compound Batch Identification
Computer-Based Instruction
CBIE: Computer-Based Information Exchange
CBIS: Computer-Based Information System
CBL: Computer-Based Learning
CBM: Confidence Building Measure
CBMIS: Comprehensive Budget and Management Information System
Computer-Based Management Information System
CBMS: Computer-Based Message Service
Computer-Based Message System
CBOSS: Count, Back Order, and Sample Select
CBT: Computer-Based Terminal
Computer-Based Training
CBX: Computerized Branch Exchange
CC: Channel Controller
Charge-Coupled
Cluster Controller
Command Chain
Communications Computer
Communications Controller
Computer Center
Computerized Conferencing
Condition Code
Control Computer
Control Counter
Cursor Control

CC&A: Computer Control and Auditing
CCA: Channel to Channel Adapter
Common Communication Adapter
CCAID: Charge-Coupled Area Imaging Device
CCAM: Conversational Communication Access Method
CCAP: Communications Control Application Program
CCAS: Communication Control Aid System
CCB: Character Control Block
Command Control Block
Communications Control Batches
Communications Control Block
Configuration Control Board
CCC: Central Communications Controller
Central Computer Center
CCD: Charge Coupled Device
C/CDSB: Command/Control Disable
CCE: Communication Control Equipment
CCEB: Combined Communications Electronics Boards
CCF: Central Computing Facility
Communications Control Field
Complex Coherence Function
Compressed Citation File
CCH: Channel Check Handler
Connections per Circuit per Hour
CCHS: Cylinder-Cylinder-Head Sector
CCIA: Computer and Communications Industry Association
CCIP: Command and Control Information Processing
CCIR: Comite Consultatif International de Radiocommunication (French)
CCIS: Common Channel Interoffice Signaling
Computer-Controlled Interconnect System
CCITT: Comite Consultatif International Telegraphique et Telephonique (International Telegraph and Telephone Consultation Committee) (French)
CCIU: Command Channel Interface Unit
CCL: Common Command Language
Communications Control Language
Concise Command Language
CCM: Communications Control Module
Counter-Countermeasures
CCMD: Continuous Current Monitoring Device
CCMS: Computer Center Management System
CCMSS: Computer Controlled Microform Search System
CCMT: Computer Controlled Machine Tool
CCN: Common-Carrier Network
CCO: Computer Controller Operation
Current Controlled Oscillator
CCP: Certificate in Computer Programming
Certified Computer Programmer
Communication Control Panel
Communication Control Processor
Communications Control Program
Conditional Command Processor
Coordinated Commentary Programming
CCR: Channel Control Reconfiguration

Computer Character Recognition
Computer Controlled Retrieval
Condition Code Register
Customized Communications Routine
CCROS: Card Capacity Read-Only Storage
CC&S: Central Computer and Sequencer
CCS: Common Channel Signaling
Communications Control System
Hundred Call Seconds
CCSA: Common-Control Switching Arrangement
Customer Controlled Switching Arrangement
CCSB: Computer and Communications Standards Board
CCSE: Corporate Communications Switching Equipment
CCSP: Communications Concentrator Software Package
CCST: Center for Computer Sciences and Technology
CCT: Computer Compatible Tape
CCTV: Closed Circuit Cable Television
Closed Circuit Television
CCTV/LSD: Closed Circuit Television/Large Screen Display
CCU: Central Control Unit
Command Chain Unit
Communications Control Unit
Computer Control Unit
Correlation Control Unit
CCV: Common Control Vector
Control Configured Vehicle
CCVS: COBOL Compiler Validation System
CCW: Channel Command Word
Channel Control Word
Counter Clockwise

cd: card
CD: Carrier Detect
Chain Data
Compact Disk
CDA: Command and Data Acquisition
Computer Dealers Association
CDAC: Communications Dual Access Controller
CDB: Common Data Bus
Current Data Bit
CDC: Call Directing Code
Code Directing Character
Computer Display Channel
CDE: Contents Directory Entry
CDEC: Central Data Conversion Equipment
CDF: Combined Distribution Frame
Contiguous-Disk File
CDHS: Comprehensive Data Handling System
CDI: Collector Diffused Isolation
CDL: Compiler Description Language
Computer Description Language
Computer Design Language
Computer Development Laboratory
CDM: Cash Dispensing Machine
Code-Division Multiplexing
CDMA: Cartridge Direct Memory Access
Code-Division Multiple Access
CDMS: Commercial Data Management System
CDN: Corporate Data Network
CDO: Community Dial Office
CDP: Centralized Data Processing
Certificate in Data Processing
Certified Data Processor
Communications Data Processor
CDPA: Certified Data Processing Auditor

CDPS: Computing and Data Processing Society
CDR: Call Detail Recording
Card Reader
Critical Design Review
CDROM: Computer Disk Read-Only Memory
CDS: Case Data System
Central Dynamic System
Comprehensive Display System
Control Data Set
Control Display System
CDSS: Customer Digital Switching System
CDTL: Common Data Translation Language
CDU: Cartridge Disk Unit
Control and Display Unit
CE: Chip Enable
Concurrent Engineering
Critical Examination
Customer Engineer
CEA: Central Electricity Authority
Communications-Electronics Agency
CEC: Computers, Electronics and Control Symposium
CECUA: Confederation of European Computer User Association
CED: Computer Entry Device
CEDA: Communications Equipment Distributors Association
CEDAC: Computer Energy Distribution and Automated Control
CEDAR: Computer-Aided Environmental Design Analysis and Realization
CEECS: Computer Environment Energy Control System
CEGL: Cause Effect Graph Language
CEI: Chip Enable Input
Contract End Item

CELEX: European Community legal database (EC)
CEM: Central Enhancement and Maintenance
CEMAST: Control of Engineering Material, Acquisition, Storage and Transport
CENEL: Comite Europeen de Coordination des Normes Electriques (European Electrical Standards Coordinating Committee) (French) (EC)
CENELEC: Comite Europeen de Normalisation Electrotechnique (European Community for Electrotechnical Standardization) (French) (EC)
CEO: Chip Enable Output
Comprehensive Electronics Office
CEPA: Society for the Advancement of Computers in Engineering, Planning and Architecture
CEPT: Conference Europeenne des administration des Postes et des Telecommunications (European Conference of Postal and Telecommunications Administrations) (French)
CER: Civil Engineering Report
CERC: Computer Entry and Readout Control
CERDEC: Center for Research and Documentation in the European Community (EC)
CER-DIP: Ceramic Dual-In-Line Package
CERE: Computer Entry and Readout Equipment
CERT: Character Error Rate Test
Character Error Rate Tester

Constant Extension Rate Test
CESD: Composite External Symbol Dictionary
CESO: Council of Engineers and Scientists Organizations
CESSE: Council of Engineering and Scientific Society
CET: Console Electric Typewriter
CETIA: Control, Electronics, Telecommunications, Instrument Automation
CEU: Channel Extension Unit
CF: Carried Forward
Commercial FORTRAN
Context Free
Count Forward
CFA: Component Flow Analysis
Computer Family Architecture
CFB: Ciper Feed Back
CFC: Channel Flow Control
CFCF: Central Flow Control Facility
CFE: Contractor Furnished Equipment
CFG: Context Free Grammer
CFIA: Component Failure Impact Analysis
CFL: Context Free Language
CFM: Cubic Feet per Minute
CFMS: Chained File Management System
CFO: Cancel Form Order
Consolidated Functions Ordinary
CFO+: Consolidated Functions Ordinary Support System
CFP: Creation Facilities Program
CFS: Combined File Search
Corporate Financial System
CFSS: Combined File Search System
CFTG: Context Free Transduction Grammer

CG: Color Graphics
Computer Graphics
CGI: Computer-Generated Image
CGL: Computer Generated Letter
CGOS: Computervision Graphics Operating System
CGP: Color Graphics Printer
Computervision Graphics Processor
CGPC: Cellular General Purpose Computer
CGSA: Computer Graphics Structural Analysis
ch: change
channel
character
CHAMP: Character Manipulation Procedures
Communications Handler for Automatic Multiple Programs
chan: channel
char: character
CHAT: Cheap Access Terminal
CHC: Channel Control
CHCU: Channel Control Unit
CHDL: Computer Hardware Definition Language
Computer Hardware Description Language
CHE: Chip Enable
CHECS: Check Handling Executive Control System
chg: charge
CHI: Computer Human Interaction
CHIF: Channel Interface
CHIL: Current Hogging Injection Logic
CHIPS: Clearing House Interbank Payments System
CHIRP: Confidential Human Factors Incident Report
CHITO: Container Handling In Terminal Operations
chk: check
chkpt: checkpoint

chnl: channel
CHOL: Common High Order Language
CHP: Channel Processor
chr: character
CHR: Channel Reconfiguration Hardware
CHRT: Coordinated Human Resource Technology
CHT: Collection, Holding, and Transfer
CI: Carry In
Communications Interface
Computer Industry
Configuration Item
Current-awareness Information
CIA: Computer Industry Association
CIB: Channel Interface Base
Command Input Buffer
CIC: Corporate Information Center
Custom-Integrated Circuit
CICA: Construction Industry Computing Association
CICI: Confederation of Information Communication Industries (EC)
CICP: Communication Interrupt Control Program
CICS: Customer Information Control System
CICS/VS: Customer Information Control System/Vertical Storage
CID: Charge-Injection Imaging Device
Communication Identifier
Component Identification Number
CIDA: Channel Indirect Data Addressing
CIDF: Control Interval Definition Field
CIDS: Comprehensive Industry Distribution System
CIE: Computer Interrupt Equipment
CIF: Central Information File
Computer-Integrated Factory
Customer Information File
CIL: Computer Interpreter Language
Current Injection Logic
CILA: Casualty Insurance Logistics Automated
CILOP: Conversion In Lieu Of Procurement
CIM: Communications Interface Monitor
Computer Input Microfilm
Computer Integrated Manufacturing
Console Interface Module
CIMC: Communications Intelligent Matrix Control
CIMS: Computer Installation Management System
Computer Integrated Manufacturing System
Countermeasures Internal Management System
CINV: Control Interval
CIO: Central Input-Output
CIOCS: Communications Input-Output Control System
CIOU: Central Input-Output Unit
CIP: Communications Interrupt Program
Complex Information Processing
CIPS: Canadian Information Processing Society
CIR: Color Infrared
Current Instruction Register
CIRC: Centralized Information Reference and Control
CIRCA: Computerized Information Retrieval and Current Awareness
CIRCAL: Circuit Analysis

CIRCUS: Circuit Simulator
CIRT: Conference on Industrial Robot Techology
CIS: Central Information System
Commercial Instruction Set
Control Indicator Set
Current Information Selection
Custom Integrated System
Customer Information System
CISAM: Compressed Index Sequential Access Method
CISC: Complex Instruction Set Computing
CISD: Corporate Information Service Department
CISS: Conference on Information Science and Systems
Consolidated Information Storage System
CITA: Commercial Industrial Type Activities
CITCA: Committee of Inquiry into Technological Change in Australia
CITS: Central Integrated Test System Multiplex
CIU: Central Interface Unit
Channel Interface Unit
Communications Interface Unit
Computer Interface Unit
CJB: Cold Junction Box
ck: clock
CKD: Count-Key-Data Device
cl: centiliter
CL: Command Language
Compiler Language
Control Leader
Control Line
CLA: Carry Lookahead
Communications Line Adapter
Computer Law Association
CLAD: Cover Layer Automated Design
CLAIMS: Class Codes, Assigned, Index, Method, Search
CLAIMS/CLASS: Class Codes, Assigned, Index, Method, Search/Classification
CLAIMS/GEM: Class Codes, Assigned, Index, Method, Search/General, Electrical, Mechanical
CLAMP: Computer Listing and Analysis of Maintenance Programs
CLASP: Circuit Layout, Automated Scheduling and Production
CLASS: Capacity Loading and Scheduling System
Closed Loop Accounting for Stores Sales
CLAT: Communications Line Adapter for Teletype
CLB: Central Logic Bus
Clear Both
CLC: Communication Line Control
Communications Line Controller
Communications Link Controller
Current Leading Components
CLCM: Communication Line Concentrator Module
cld: cancelled
cleared
CLD: Current-Limiting Device
CLE: Conservative Logic Element
CLEAR: Closed Loop Evaluation And Reporting
CLEAT: Computer Language for Engineers and Technologists
CLEO: Clear Language for Expressing Orders
CLEOS: Conference on Laser and Electro-Optical Systems

CLI: Command Language Interpreter
CLIC: Command Language for Interrogating Computers
Computer Layout of Intergrated Circuits
Conversational Language for Interactive Computing
CLIMATE: Computer and Language Independent Modules for Automatic Test Equipment
CLIO: Conversational Language for Input-Output
CLIP: Cellular Logic Image Processor
Computer Layout Installation Planner
CLIRA: Closed Loop In-Reactor Assembly
CLISP: Conversational LISP
clk: clock
CLKIN: Clock In
CLKOUT: Clock Out
CLM: Clinical Library Master
Communications Line Multiplexer
CLOB: Core Load Overlay Builder
CLODS: Computerized Logic-Oriented Design System
CLOG: Computer Logic Graphics
CLP: Communication Line Processor
Current Line Point
clr: clear
CLR: Combined Line and Recording
CLS: Communications Line Switch
CLT: Communications Line Terminals
CLUE: Compiler Language Utility Extension
CLUSAN: Cluster Analysis
cm: centimeter
CM: Central Memory
Communications Multiplexer
Control Memory
Control Module
Core Memory
Corrective Maintenance
CMA: Communications Managers Association
Computer Management Association
Computer Monitor Adapter
Computerized Management Account
CMAP: Central Memory Access Priority
CMAR: Control Memory Address Register
CMARS: Cable Monitoring and Rating System
CMAS: Construction Management Accounting System
CMB: Corrective Maintenance Burden
CMC: Communications Management Configuration
Communications Mode Control
Comparison Measuring Circuit
CMCA: Character Mode Communications Adapter
CM/CCM: Countermeasures/ Counter Countermeasures
cmd: command
CMDIS: Computer Management Distributed Information Software
CME: Central Memory Extension
Computer Measurement and Evaluation
CMF: Comprehensive Management Facility
Constant Magnetic Field
CMG: Computer Measurement Group
CMI: Computer-Managed Instruction
CMIS: Common Manufacturing Information System

Computer-oriented Management Information System
Corporate Management Information System
CML: Common Mode Logic
Current Mode Logic
CMM: Communications Multiplexer Module
Coordinate Measuring Machine
cmnd: command
CMOS: Complementary Metal-Oxide Semiconductor
CMP: Console Message Processor
CMPM: Computer-Managed Parts Manufacture
CMR: Code Matrix Reader
Common Mode Rejection
CMRR: Common Mode Rejection Ratio
CMS: Circuit Maintenance System
Compiler Monitor System
Computer Management System
CMT: Cassette Magnetic Tape
Change Management Tracking
Computer-Managed Training
Computer Mediated Teleconferencing
Construction Materials Testing
CMU: Control Maintenance Unit
CMX: Character Multiplexer
Customer Multiplexer
CN: Communications Network
Contract Number
Coordination Number
CNA: Communications Network Architecture
CNC: Computer Numerical Control
cncl: cancel
cncld.: cancel
CNDP: Communication Network Design Program
CNE: Communications Network Emulator

CNEP: Cable Network Engineering Program
CNET: Centre National d'Etudes et de Recherches de Telecommunications (French) Communications Network
cnl: cancel
cancellation
CNM: Communication Network Manager
CNMI: Communications Network Management Interface
CNOP: Conditional NonOperation
CNP: Communications Network Processor
CNS: Communications Network Simulator
Communications Network System
cnt: count
cntl: control
cntr: counter
cntrl: control
CO: Carry Out
Console Output
COADS: Conference on Application Development Systems
COAMP: Computer Analysis of Maintenance Policies
COAX: Coaxial Cable
COBLOS: Computer Based Loans System
COBOL: Common Business-Oriented Language
COC: Character Oriented Communications Controller
COCOL: COBOL Compiler-Oriented Language
COCR: Cylinder Overflow Control Record
COCS: Container Operating Control System
CODAP: Comprehensive Occupational Data Analysis Program

CODAS: Customer Oriented Data System
CODASYL: Conference on Data Systems Language (EC)
CODEC: Coder-Decoder
Coding-Decoding Device
CODEM: Coded Modulator-Demodulator
CODEST: European Development of Science and Technology (EC)
CODEX: Coder-Decoder
CODIL: Content Dependent Information Language
CODILS: Commodity Oriented Digital Input Label System
COFAD: Computerized Facilities Design
COGAP: Computer Graphics Arrangement Program
COGENT: Compiler and Generalized Translator
COGO: Coordinate Geometry
COINS: Computer and Information Sciences
Coordinated Inventory Control System
col: column
COL: Communications Oriented Language
Computer Oriented Language
coll: collator
Collat: collateral
COM: Cassette Operating Monitor
Center Of Mass
Computer Output Microfiche
Computer Output Microfilm
Computer Output Microfilmer
Computer Output Microfilming
Computer Output Micrographics
COMAC: Continuous Multiple Access Collator
COMAT: Computer-Assisted Training
comb: combination
COMET: Computer Message Transmission
COMFOR: International Computer Forum and Exposition
COMFORT: Commercial FORTRAN
COMICS: Computer-Oriented Managed Inventory Control System
COMMANDS: Computer Operated Marketing, Mailing and News Distribution System
COMMEND: Computer-aided Mechanical Engineering Design
COMM-STOR: Communications Storage Unit
Comp: compatible
composite
computer
computerization
computerize
computerized
COMPARE: Computer Oriented Method of Program Analysis, Review and Evaluation
COMPAS: Computer Acquisition System
COMPASS: Central Office Maintenance Printout Analysis and Suggestion System
Computer Assisted Classification and Assignment System
COMPCON: Computer Conference
COMPEC: Computer Peripherals and Small Computer Systems Trade Exhibition
COMPENDEX: Computerized Engineering Index

COMPETA: Computer and Peripherals Equipment Trade Association
COMPROC: Command Processor
COMPSAC: Computer Software and Applications Conference
compu: computable
computability
computer
computerized
COMRADE: Computer Aided Design Environment
COMS: Computer-based Operations Management System
COMSAT: Communications Satellite Corporation
COMSYL: Communications Systems Language
COMTEC: Computer Micrographics Technology
COMTEX: Communications Oriented Multiple Terminal Executive
COMX: Communications Executive
cond: condition
conf: conference
CONIO: Console Input-Output
CONIT: Connector for Networked Information Transfer
CONMAN: Console Manager
const: constant
cont: controller
conv: conversion
convertible
COP: Communication Output Printer
COPE: Cassette Operating Executive
COPICS: Communications Oriented Production Information and Control System
COPS: Calculator Oriented Processor System
CORDIC: Coordinate Rotation Digital Computer
CORREGATE: Correctable Gate
CORS: Canadian Operational Research Society
COS: Cassette Operating System
Commercial Operating System
Communications Operating System
Communications Oriented Software
COSAM: COBOL Shared Access Method
COSATI: Committee on Scientific and Technical Information
COSCL: Common Operating System Control Language
COSMIC: Computer Software Management and Information Center
COSTI: Committee on Scientific and Technical Information
COSY: Compressed Symbolic
COT: Customer Oriented Terminal
COUPLE: Communications Oriented User Programming Language
CP: Call Processor
Card Punch
Central Processor
Character Printer
Command Processor
Communications Processor
Condition Precedent
Control Part
Control Program
Correspondence Printer
Critical Path
CPA: Critical Path Analysis
CPB: Channel Program Block
Critical Path Bar (chart)
CPC: Card Programmed Calculator
Computer Power Center
Computer Production Control

Computerized Production Control
CPCEI: Computer Program Contract End Item
CPCI: Computer Program Configuration Item
CPU Power Calibration Instrument
CPCS: Check Processing Control System
CPDAMS: Computer Program Development and Management System
CPDP: Computer Program Development Plan
CPDS: Computer Program Design Specification
CPE: Central Processing Element
Computer Performance Evaluation
Customer Premises Equipment
CPEUG: Computer Performance Evaluation Users Group
CPF: Control Program Facility
CPFSK: Continuous Phase Frequency Shift Keying
CPG: COBOL Program Generator
CPH: Characters Per Hour
CPI: Characters Per Inch
Conference Papers Index
CPIN: Computer Program Identification Number
CPIS: Computerized Personnel Information System
CPL: Common Program Library
Computer Program Library
Conversational Programming Language
CPL1: Checkout PL/1
CPM: Cards Per Minute
Cards Processed per Minute
Computer Performance Management
Computer Performance Monitor
Continuous Processing Machine
Control Program for Microcomputers
Critical Path Method
Current Processor Mode
CP/M: Control Program Microcomputer
CPMA: Central Processor Memory Address
Computer Peripherals Manufacturers Association
CPN: Computer Product News
CPO: Commodity Pool Operator
Concurrent Peripheral Operations
CPODA: Contention Priority-Oriented Demand Assignment
CPOL: Communications Procedure-Oriented Language
CPP: Critical Path Plan
Current Purchasing Power
CPPS: Critical Path Planning and Scheduling
CP-R: Control Program – Real Time
CP&R: Card Punch and Reader
CPR: Constant Percentage Resolution
Cost Performance Report
CPS: Cards Per Second
Central Processor Subsystem
Characters Per Second
COBOL Programming System
Computerized Publishing System
Control Program Support
Controlled Path System
Conversational Programming System
Cycles Per Second
CPSK: Coherent Phase-Shift Keying
CPSS: Computer Power Support System

CPT: Chief Programmer Team
Continuous Performance Test
CPT&E: Computer Program Test and Evaluation
CPTO: Chief Programmer Team Organization
CPU: Central Processing Unit
CP-V: Control Program - Five
CQA: Computer-aided Question Answering
CQMS: Circuit Quality Monitoring System
CR: Card Reader
Carriage Return
Carry Register
Command Register
Communications Register
Control Register
Critical Ratio
CRA: Catalog Recovery Area
Computer Retailers Association
CRAM: Card Random Access Memory (Method)
Computerized Reliability Allocation Method
CRAMM: Coupon Reading and Marking Machine
CRAR: Control ROM Address Register
CRB: Complementary Return to Bias
CRBE: Conversational Remote Batch Entry
CRC: Carrier Return Character
Cyclic Redundancy Check
CRCC: Cyclic Redundancy Check Character
CRD: Computer Read-out Device
CREDIT: Cost Reduction Early Decision Information Techniques
CREF: Cross References
CREST: Comite de Recherche Scientifique et Technique (Committee of Scientific and Technological Research) (French) (EC)
CRF: Context Roll Rile
Cross Reference File
CR-HI: Channel Request–High Priority
CRIS: Current Research Information System
CRISP: Computer Resources Integrated Support Plan
CRJE: Conversational Remote Job Entry
CR-LO: Channel Request–Low Priority
CRM: Computer Resources Management
CR-MED: Channel Request Medium Priority
CROM: Control Read-Only Memory
CRONOS: Community Statistical Office computerized economic data bank (EC)
CROS: Capacitor Read Only Storage
CR/P: Card Reader/Punch
CRP: Combined Refining Process
Counter-Rotation Platform
CRQ: Console Reply Queueing
CRT: Cathode Ray Tube
Computer Remote Terminal
CRTC: Carthode Ray Tube Controller
CRU: Card Reader Unit
Communications Register Unit
Control and Reporting Unit
CS: Chip Select
Communications System
Computer Science
Condition Subsequent
Constructor Syntax
Control Store
C/S: Certificate of Service
CSA: Canadian Standards Association

Common Service Area
Computer Services Association
CSAM: Circular Sequential Access Memory
CSAR: Communication Satellite Advanced Research
Control Store Address Register
CSB: Communication Scanner Base
CSCC: Cumulative Sum Control Chart
CSCS: Cost, Schedule, and Control System
CSD: Circuit Switched Data
Closed System Delivery
Computerized Standard Data
CSDD: Computer Subprogram Design Document
CSDF: Computer System Development Facility
CSDL: Conceptual Schema Definition Language
CSDM: Continuous Slope Delta Modulation
CSDR: Control Store Data Register
CSE: Computer Science and Engineering
CSECT: Control Section
CSERB: Computer, Systems, and Electronics Requirements Board (UK)
CSF: Critical Success Factor
CSG: Context Sensitive Grammer
CSI: Command String Interpreter
Cosmic Scale Integration
CSL: Context-Sensitive Language
Control and Simulation Language
Current Switch Logic
CSM: Computer System Manual
CSMA: Communications Systems Management Association
CSMP: Continuous System Moduling Program

CSMS: Computerized Specification Management System
CSN: Card Security Number
CSO: Central Statistical Office
CSOS: Complementary Silicon On Sapphire
C/SP: Communications/Symbiont Processor
CSP: Commercial Subroutine Package
CSPC: Cost and Schedule Planning and Control
CSR: Control Status Register
Customer Service Representative
CSROEPM: Communication, System, Results, Objectives, Exception, Participation, Motivation
CSS: Character Start-Stop
Computer Scheduling System
Computer Systems Simulator
Continuous System Simulation
CSSL: Continuous System Simulation Language
CST: Code Segment Table
Consolidated Schedule Technique
CSTR: Current Status Register
CSTS: Computer Sciences Teleprocessing System
CSU: Channel Service Unit
Circuit Switching Unit
Communications System User
Customer Set Up
CSV: Circuit Switched Voice
CSW: Channel Status Word
C&T: Classification and Testing
ct: counter
CT: Cable Transfer
Cassette Tape
Change Ticker
Communications Terminal
Computerized Tomography

CTAB: Commerce Technical Advisory Board
CTB: Code Table Buffer
Concentrator Terminal Buffer
CTC: Centralized Traffic Control
Channel To Channel
Counter Timer Circuit
CTCA: Channel-To-Channel Adapter
CTCC: Central Terminal Computer Controller
CTCM: Computer Timing and Costing Model
CTCS: Component Time Control System
CTD: Charge Transfer Device
CTE: Computer Telex Exchange
Customer Terminal Equipment
CTFC: Central Time and Frequency Control
CTI: Charge Transfer Inefficiency
ctl: control
CTL: Cassette Tape Loader
Compiler Target Language
Complementary Transistor Logic
CTLR: Control Register
CTM: Communications Terminal Module
Composite-Tape Memory
CTMC: Communications Terminal Multiplex Cabinet
CTOS: Cassette Tape Operating System
C/TP: Control/Test Panel
ctr: counter
CTR: Current Transfer Ratio
ctrl: control
CTRS: Computerized Test-result Reporting System
CTS: Clear To Send
Coaxial Terminal Switch
Communications Technology Satellite

Communications Terminal Synchronous
Computer Telegram System
Conversational Time Sharing
CTSS: Compatible Time Sharing System
Computer Time Sharing Service
CTV: Cable Television
cu: cubic
CU: Control Unit
Correlation Unit
Customer Use
CUA: Circuit Unit Assembly
Computer Users Association
CUAG: Computer Users Associations Group
CUDN: Common User Data Network
CUE: Computer Updating Equipment
Correction-Update-Extension
CUESTA: Communications User Emulated System for Traffic Analysis
CUG: Closed User Group
CUM: Central-Unit Memory
CUP: Communications User Program
CUPID: Create, Update, Interrogate and Display
CUTS: Cassette User Tape System
Computer Users Tape System
CUV: Current Use Value
CVC: Carrier Virtual Circuit
CVIS: Computerized Vocational Information System
CVM: COBOL Virtual Machine
CVR: Computer Voice Response
Continuous Video Recorder
CVS: Constant Volume Sampling
Conversational System

CVSD: Continuously Variable Slope Delta Modulation
CVT: Communications Vector Table
Constant Voltage Transformer
cw: clockwise
CW: Command Word
Continuous Wave
Control Word
CWA: Control Word Address
CWD: Clerical Work Data
CWM: Clerical Work Measurement
CWP: Communicating Word Processor
Current Word Pointer
CWPS: Communicating Word Processing System
CWS: Compiler Writing System
CXA: Central Exchange Area
CXR: Carrier Detector
cxy: carrier
cy: carry
currency
cycle
cyl: cylinder

D

d: data
datum
deci
decimal
density
depth
destination
digit
digital
displacement
domain
double
1D: One Dimensional
2D: Double Density
Two Dimensional
2 1/2D: 2 1/2Dimensional
3D: Three Dimensional
Triple Diffused
da: deka
DA: Data Administrator
Data Available
Demand Assignment
Design Automation
Destination Address
Direct Action
Directory Assistance
Disk Action
Display Adapter
D/A: Digital to Analog (converter)
DAA: Direct Access Arrangement
DAB: Display Attention BITs
DABS: Discrete Address Beacon System
DAC: Data Accepted
Data Acquisition and Control
Data Analysis and Control
Demand Assignment Controller
Design Augmented by Computer
Digital-to-Analog Converter
DACBU: Data Acqusition Control and Buffer Unit
DACC: Design Assertion Consistency Checker
DACE: Data Acqusition and Control Executive
DACL: Diablo Application Compiler Language
DACOR: Data Correction
DACOS: Data Communication Operating System
DACS: Data Acquisition and Conversion System
DADB: Data Analysis Data Base
DADEC: Design And Demonstration Electronic Computer
DADEE: Dynamic Analog Differential Equation Equalizer
DADIOS: Direct Analog to Digital Input-Output System
DADS: Data Acquisition and Display System
DADSM: Direct Access Device Space Management
DAF: Data Acquisition Facility
Destination Address Field
DAFA: Data Accounting Flow Assessment
DAFC: Digital Automatic Frequency Control
DAFM: Direct Access File Manager
DAFT: Digital-to-Analog Function Table
DAG: Directed Acyclic Graph
DAI: Direct Access Information
DAIS: Direct Access Intelligence Systems

47

DAISY: Decision Aiding Information System
DAL: Data Access Line
Data/Address Line
DAM: Data Addressed Memory
Descripter Attribute Matrix
Diagnostic Acceptability Measure
Direct Access Method
DAMA: Demand Assigned Multiple Access
DAME: Digital Automatic Measuring Equipment
DAMOS: Data Moving System
DAMS: Direct Access Management System
DAP: Data Access Protocol
Distributed Array Processor
DAPS: Direct Access Programming System
Distributed Application Processing System
DAPU: Data Acqusition and Processing Unit
DAR: Damage Assessment Routine
Data Access Register
DARC: Direct Access Radar Channel
DARDO: Direct Access to Remote Data Bases Overseas
DARPA: Defense Advanced Research Projects Agency
DARS: Data Acquisition and Reduction System
DART: Daily Automatic Rescheduling Technique
Design Automation Routing Tool
Detection, Action and Response Technique
DARTS: Distributors Automated Real-Time System
DAS: Data Access Security
Data Acquisition System
Data Administration System
Data Analysis System
Data Automation System
Design Analysis System
DASD: Direct Access Storage Device
Direct Access Storage Drive
DASDI: Direct Access Storage Device Initialization
DASDL: Data and Structure Definition Language
DASDR: Direct Access Storage Dump Restore
DASEL: Data Analysis and Statistical Experimental Language
DASF: Direct Access Storage Facility
DASH: Dual Access Storage Handling
DASL: Data Access System Language
DASM: Direct Access Storage Media
DASP: Datapoint Attached Support Processor
DAT: Data Abstract Tape
Desk-top Analysis Tool
Digital Audio Tape
Disk Allocation Table
Dynamic Address Translation
DATACOM: Data Communication
DATACOMM: Data Communications
DATACON: Systems/Data Processing Conference
DATACOR: Data Correction
DatAn: Data Analysis
DataNet: Data Network
DATAR: Digital Automatic Tracking and Ranging
DATAS: Data in Associative Storage
DATEL: Data Telecommunication
DATICO: Digital Automatic Tape Intelligence Checkout
DatIn: Data Inserter
DaTran: Data Transmission

DAU: Data Access Unit
Data Adapter Unit
DAV: Data Above Voice
Data Available
Data Valid
db: decibel
DB: Data Bank
Data Base
Data BIT
Data Bus
DBA: Adjusted Decibels
Data-Base Administration
Data-Base Administrator
DBAAM: Disk Buffer Area Access Method
DBAM: Data Base Access Method
DBC: Data Base Computer
DBCB: Data Base Control Block
DBCCP: Data Base Command and Control Processor
DBCL: Data Base Command Language
DBCS: Data Base Control System
DBCTG: Data Base Concepts Task Group
DBD: Data Base Description
Data Base Design
Data Base Directory
DBDA: Data Base Design Aid
DB/DC: Data Base/Data Communication
DBDD: Data Base Design Document
DBDE: Data Base Design Evaluator
DBDGEN: Data Base Description Generation
DBDL: Data Base Definition Language
DBDNAME: Data Base Description Name
DBE: Data Bus Enable
DBG: Data Base Generator
DBI: Double Byte Interleaved
DBIN: Data Bus In
DBIOC: Data Base Input/Output Control

dbl: double
DBL: Data Base Language
DBM: Data Base Machine
Data Base Management
Data Base Manager
Data Base Module
Decibels Referenced to One Milliwatt
Direct Branch Mode
DBMC: Data Base Management Computer
DBML: Data Base Management Language
DBMS: Data-Base Management Software
Data-Base Management Subsystem
Data-Base Management System
DBOMP: Data Base Organization and Maintenance Processor
DBOS: Disk Based Operating System
DBP: Data Base Processor
DBPROTOTYPE: Data Base Prototype
DBR: Data Base Representation
Data Base Retrieval
Descriptor Base Register
DBRN: Decibels Above Reference Noise
DBRNC: Decibels Away from the Reference Noise when Measured With a C-Message Filter
DBS: Data Base Service
Data Base System
Direct Broadcast System
DBX: Digital Branch Exchange
DC: Data Cartridge
Data Cassette
Data Channel
Data Classifier
Data Code
Data Communication

Data Counter
Decimal Classification
Device Control
Device Controller
Digital Computer
Direct Current
Disk Controller
Double Column
DCA: Data Communications Administrator
Digital Computer Association
DC-AC: Direct Current to Alternating Current
DCAM: Data Collection Access Method
DC&AS: Digital Control and Automation System
DCB: Data and Control Bus
Data Control Block
Device Control Block
DCC: Data Circuit Concentrator
Data Collection Center
Data Communications Controller
Device Cluster Controller
Direct Control Channel
DCCH: Disk Cartridge Channel
DCCS: Distributed Capability Computing System
DCCU: Data Communications Control Unit
DCD: Data Carrier Detect
Data Correlation and Documentation System
DC/DC: Direct Current to Direct Current
DCDS: Digital Control Design System
DCE: Data Circuit Equipment
Data Communications Equipment
DCF: Disk Controller/Formatter
Document Composition Facility
DCH: Data Channel
DCI: Direct Channel Interface

DCIA: Digital Card Inverting Amplifier
DCIO: Direct Channel Interface Option
DCIU: Data Channel Interface Unit
dcl: declaration
DCM: Data Communications Multiplexer
Display Control Module
DCMS: Dedicated Computer Message Switching
DCN: Distributed Computer Network
DCNA: Data Communication Network Architecture
DCOS: Data Collection Operating System
DCP: Data Collection Program
Data Communications Program
DCPC: Dual Channel Port Controller
DCPCM: Differentially Coherent Pulse Code Modulation
DCPP: Data Communications Preprocessor
DCPSK: Differentially Coherent Phase Shift Keying
DCR: Data Collection Routine
Design Change Request
Digital Cassette Recorder
DCRABS: Disk Copy Restore and Backup System
DCS: Data Center Scheduler
Data Collection System
Data Communication System
Data Control System
Diagnostic Control Store
Distributed Computing System
Document Control System
DCSL: Deterministic Context Sensitive Language
DCT: Data Communications Terminal
Device Characteristics Table

DCTL: Direct Coupled Transistor Logic
DCU: Data Communications Unit
Data Control Unit
Device Control Unit
Disk Control Unit
DCVG: Display Control Vector Generator
DCW: Data Control Word
DD: Data Dictionary
Data Division
Double Deck
DDA: Digital Differential Analyzer
DDAM: Dynamic Design-Analysis Method
DDAS: Digital Data Acquisition System
DDC: Direct Digital Control
DDD: Direct Distance Dialing
DDL: Data-Description Language
Digital Data Link
DDName: Data-Definition Name
DDP: Distributed Data Processing
DDR: Dynamic Device Reconfiguration
DDS: Dataphone Digital Service
Digital Data System
DD Statement: Data-Definition Statement
DDT&E: Design, Development, Test, and Evaluation
DE: Data Entry
dec: decimal
decoder
decrement
DECA: Descent Engine Control Assembly
deck: deque
DEE: Digital Evaluation Equipment
def: definition
DFU: Data File Utility
del: delete
DEL: Delete (character)
Direct Exchange Line
dem: demand

DEMA: Data Entry Management Association
DEMS: Digital Electronic Message Service
DES: Data Encryption Standard (National Bureau of Standards)
Design and Evaluation System
DeTab: Decision Table
DETRAN: Decision table Translator
DEU: Data Exchange Unit
D&F: Determination and Findings
DF: Data Field
Destination Field
Device Flag
DFC: Data-Flow Control
DFL: Design For Manufacturability
DFR: Decreasing Failure Rate
DFT: Diagnostic Function Test
Digital Facility Terminal
dh: deadhead
DH: Design Handbook
DHS: Data Handling System
DI: Device Independence
Discrete Input
DIAL: Draper Industrial Assembly Language
DIAN: Digital Analog
DIANE: Direct Information Access Network for Europe (EC)
DIANESGUIDE: Online guide to European database producers, hosts, databases and databanks (EC)
DIBOL: Digital Business Oriented Language
DIC: Digital Incremental Computer
Digital Integrating Computer
dict: dictionary
DI/DO: Data Input/Data Output
DIDS: Decision Information Distribution System
Digital Information Display System

dig: digit
digital
DIMS: Data Information and Manufacturing System
DIN: Data Identification Number
DIOS: Distributed Input/Output System
DIP: Dual In-line Package
dir: directory
DIRAC: Direct Access
DISLAN: Display Language
DIV: Data In Voice
DIVA: Digital Inquiry-Voice Answerback
DL: Data Language
Data Link
Data List
DLC: Data-Link Control (character)
DLD: Deadline Date
DLE: Data-Link Escape (character)
DLP: Dynamic Limit Programming
DLS: Debt Liquidation Schedule
DLT: Data-Loop Transceiver
Decision Logic Table
dm: decimeter
DM: Data Management
Data Manager
Design Manual
DMA: Direct Memory Access
Drum Memory Assembly
DMAC: Direct Memory Access Channel
DME: Distance Measuring Equipment
DML: Data Manipulating Language
DMO: Data Management Officer
dmp: dump
DMR: Data Management Routines
DMS: Data Management System
Data Multiplexer
DMU: Data Management Unit
DN: Data Name
DNC: Direct Numerical Control
DNIC: Data Network Identification Code
DNL: Do Not Load

DOB: Disbursed Operating Base
DOC: Direct Operating Costs
DODC: Double (Dual) Overhead Camshaft
DOES: Direct Order Entry System
DOF: Degree Of Freedom
DO/IT: Digital Output/Input Translator
DOLARS: Disk On-line Accounts Receivable System
DOMINA: Distribution-Oriented Management Information Analyzer
DOP: Developing Out Paper
DORACE: Design Organization, Record, Analyze, Charge, Estimate
DOS: Disk Operating System
DOSES: Development of Statistical Expert Systems
DOS/VS: Disk Operating System with Virtual Storage
DOT: Designated Order Turnaround
Double-B: Double-Banked
DP: Data Processing
Data Processor
Distribution Point
Dynamic Program
Dynamic Programming
DPC: Data Processing Center
DPE: Data Processing Equipment
DPMA: Data Processing Management Association
DPS: Data-Processing Station
DPSK: Differential Phase-Shift Keying
dr: divisor
DR: Data Report
DRA: Digital Read-in Assembly
DRAM (D-RAMS): Dynamic Random Access Memory (chip)
DRAW: Direct Read After Write
DRCS: Dynamically Redefinable Character Set

DREAM: Design Realization, Evaluation and Modelling Digital Recording and Measurement
DRO: Digital Read-Out
DRON: Data Reduction
DS: Data Set
Data Structure
DSBAM: Double SideBand Amplitude Modulation
DSCB: Data-Set Control Block
DSDD: Double-Sided Double-Density
DSDT: Data-Set Definition Table
DSE: Data-Switching Exchange Distributed Systems Environment
DSECT: Dummy Control Section
dsk: disc (disk)
DSN: Data-Set Name
DSP: Digital Signal Processing Distributed System Program
DSP Chip: Digital Signal Processing Chip
dspl: display
DSR: Data Set Ready
DSS: Decision Support System Distribution Scheduling System
Dynamic Support System
DSSD: Double-Sided Single-Density
DSU: Data Service Unit

DT: Data Table
Data Terminal
Dial Tone
DTAS: Data Transmission And Switching (System)
DTC: Desk Top Computer
DTE: Data-Terminal Equipment
DTG: Date-Time Group
DTR: Data Terminal Ready
DTUPC: Design-to-Unit Production Cost
DUNS: Data Universal Numbering System (Dun's Number)
dup: duplicate
DUP: Disk Utility Program
DUT: Device Under Test
DUV: Data Under Voice
DV: Dependent Variable
dvc: device
DVCDN: Console Command–Device Down
DVCUP: Console Command–Device Up
DVP: Delivery Versus Payment
DVST: Direct View Storage Tube
DW: Daisy Wheel
Double-Word
DXC: Data Exchange Control
DYNAMIT: Dynamic Allocation of Manufacturing Inventory and Time
DYSTAL: Dynamic Storage Allocation

E

e: empty
 enable
 error
 execute
 execution
 expended
 exponent
 expression
 voltage
EA: Effective Address
 Element Activity
 Energy Analysis
 Environment Analysis
 Environmental Analysis
EAD: Equipment Allowance Document
 Estimated Availability Date
EADAS: Engineering and Administration Data Acquisition System
EAE: Extended Arithmetic Element
EAM: Electrical Accounting Machine
EAN: European Article Numbering
EAP: Emulator Application Program
 Extended Arithmetic Processor
EAPROM: Electrically Alterable Programmable Read-Only Memory
EAR: Extended Address Register
EARL: Easy Access Report Language
EAROM: Electrically Alterable Read-Only Memory
EASAL: Easy Application Language
EASY: Exception Analysis System

EAU: Extended Arithmetic Unit
EAX: Electronic Automatic Exchange
EBAM: Electron Beam Addressable Memory
EBC: Electronic Business Communications
EBCD: Extended Binary-Code Decimal
EBCDIC: Extended Binary-Coded Decimal Interchange Code
E BEAM: Electronic Beam
EBES: Electron Beam Exposure System
EBM: Extended Branch Mode
EBR: Electron Beam Recording
EBV: Extended Binary Vectors
EC: Electronic Computer
 Engineering Change
 Error Correcting
 European Community
 Extended Control
ECA: Electronics Control Assembly
ECAM: Extended Content-Addressable Memory
ECAP: Electronic Circuit Analysis Program
ECB: Event Control Block
ECC: Error Check and Control
 Error Checking and Correction
 Error Correction Code
 Error Correction Control
ECCM: Electronic Counter Counter Measures
ECCNP: European Conference on Computer Network Protocols
ECD: Estimated Completion Date

55

ECDIN: Environmental Data and Information Network on Chemicals (EC)
ECE: Executive Communications Exchange
ECI: European Cooperation in Informatics
Export Consignment Identifying number
ECIF: Electronic Components Industry Federation
ECL: Emitter-Coupled Logic
Executive Control Language
ECM: Electric Coding Machine
Electronic Counter Measures
Extended Core Memory
ECMA: European Computer Manufacturers' Association
ECN: Engineering Change Notice
ECO: Engineering Change Order
ECOM: Electronic Computer-Originated Mail
ECOMA: European Computer Measurement Association
ECON: Extended Console System
ECOS: Extended Communications Operating System
ECP: Emulator Control Program
ECPS: Extended Control Program Support
ECR: Electronic Cash Register
Embossed Character Reader
ECREEA: European Conference of Radio and Electronic Equipment Association
ECS: Extended Control Storage
Extended Core Store
ECSA: European Computing System Simulator
ECSS: Extendable Computer System Simulator
ECSW: Extended Channel Status Word
ECT: Earliest Completion Time
Environment Control Table
Estimated Completion Time

ECTA: Error Correcting Tree Automata
ECTEL: European Telecommunications and Professional Electronics Industry
ECTL: Emitter Coupled Transistor Logic
ed: editor
extra
ED: Encryption Device
E/D: Encode/Decode
EDA: Electronic-Design-Automation
EDAC: Error Detection and Correction
EDBMS: Engineering Data Base Management System
EDBS: Educational Data Base Management System
EDC: Electronic Digital Computer
Estimated Date of Completion
Extended Device Control
External Disk/Drum Channel
EDD: Envelope Delay Distortion
Expert Data base Designer
EDFM: Extended Disk File Management System
EDGAR: Electronic Data Gathering And Retrieval
edi: editor
EDI: Electronic Document Interchange
EDINET: Educational Instruction Network
EDIS: Engineering Data Information System
edit: editor
EDL: Emulation Design Language
EDM: Electrical Discharge Machining
Event Driven Monitor
EDMA: Extended Direct Memory Access
EDMS: Extended Data Base Management System
EDOS: Extended Disk Operating System

EDP: Electronic Data Processing
EDPE: Electronic Data Processing Equipment
EDPEP: Electronic Data Processing Education Program
EDPM: Electronic Data-Processing Machine
EDPS: Electronic Data Processing System
EDS: Electronic Data Switching
Electronic Data System
Engineering Data System
Exchangeable Disk Store
EDSAC: Electronic Delay Storage Automatic Computer
edt: editor
EDT: Engineering Design Text
EDVAC: Electronic Discrete Variable Automatic Computer
EDX: Event Driven Executive
EE: Electrical Engineer
Errors Excepted
E-E: End-to-End
EEA: Electronic Engineering Association
EECA: European Electronic Component Manufacturers Association
EECL: Emitter to Emitter Coupled Logic
EEI: Essential Elements of Information
EEIC: Elevated Electrode Integrated Circuit
EEP: Electronic Evaluation and Procurement
Electronic Event Programmer
EE-PROMs: Electrically Erasable, Programmable Read-Only Memories
EF: Execution Function
Extended Facility
External Flag
EFA: Extended Finite Automation
EFF: Expandable File Family

effect: effective
EFL: Emitter-Follower Logic
Error Frequency Limit
EFOP: Expanded Function Operator Panel
EFS: Error Free Seconds
External Function Store
EFT: Electronic Financial Transaction
Electronic Funds Transfer
EFTPOS: Electronic Funds Transfer at Point Of Sale
EFTS: Electronic Funds Transfer System
E/GCR: Extended Group Coded Recording
EGM: Enhanced Graphics Module
EHCN: Experimental Hybrid Computer Network
EHF: Extra High Frequency
EHP: Effective HorsePower
EHPM: Electro-Hydraulic Pulse Motor
EHV: Extra High Voltage
EI: Enable Interrupt
Error Indicator
EIA: Electronic Industries Association
EIA-J: Electronic Industries Association of Japan
EIC: Equipment Identification Code
EIEMA: Electrical Installation Equipment Manufacturers Association
EIES: Electronic Information Exchange System
EIN: European Informatics Network
EIOS: Extended Input/Output System
EIRENE: European Information Researchers Network (EC)
EIRP: Effective Isotropic Radiated Power
EIS: Executive Information System
Extended Instruction Set

EIT: Emplacement, Installation, and Test(ing)
EITS: Express International Telex Service
EL: End of the Line
External Link
ELA: Equipment Leasing Association
Extended Line Adapter
ELAN: Error Logging and Analysis
elem: element
ELF: Extensible Language Facility
Extra Low Frequency
ELINT: Electronic Intelligence
ELP: Electronic Line Printer
ELR: Error Logging Register
ELS: Entry Level System
ELSI: Extremely Large Scale Integration
elt: element
EM: Electronic Mail
End-of-Medium (character)
Extended Memory
EMA: Extended Memory Area
EMAD: Engine Maintenance, Assembly, and Disassembly
EMB: Emulator Board
EMC: Electromagnetic Compatibility
Emitter Coupled Logic
External Multiplexer Channel
EMF: Electromagnetic Interference
EMI: Electromagnetic Interference
EMIND: European Modular Interactive Network Designer
EML: Emulator Machine Language
EMMS: Electronic Mail and Message System
EMOD: Erasable Memory Octal Dump
EMP: Electromagnetic Pulse
EMPL: Extensible Microprogramming Language
EM&S: Equipment Maintenance and Support
EMS: Electronic Mail System
Electronic Message Service
Extended Main Store
EMSS: Electronic Message Service System
EMT: Emulator Trap
EMU: Electromagnetic Unit
Extended Memory Unit
EMUG: European Manufacturing Automation Protocol Users' Group (EC)
ENALIM: Evolving Natural Language Information Model
enbl: enable
end: endorsement
ENDOC: Directory of environmental information and documentation centers (EC)
ENDS: Euratom Nuclear Documentation System (EC)
ENFIA: Exchange Network Facilities for Interstate Access
ENIAC: Electronic Numerical Integrator And Calculator (Computer)
ENLG: Enable Level Group
ENN: Expand Nonstop Network
enq: enquiry
ENS: Extended Network Services
ENT: Equivalent Noise Temperature
EO: Enable Output
Engineering Order
EOA: Effective On (Or) About
End-Of-Address
EOB: End-Of-Block
EOC: End-Of-Character
End-Of-Conversion
EOD: End-Of-Data
Entry-On-Duty
E&OE: Errors and Omissions Excepted
EOE: End-Of-Extent
EOF: End-Of-File
EOI: End-Of-Inquiry

EOJ: End-Of-Job
EOL: End-Of-Line
EOLM: End-Of-Line Marker
EOM: End-Of-Medium
   End-Of-Message (code)
EON: End-Of-Number
EOP: End-Of-Page
EOQ: End-Of-Query
EOR: End-Of-Record
   Exclusive OR
EOS: Electronic Office System
   End-Of-Screen
   End-Of-Segment
   End-Of-Sequence
   End-Of-Step
EOST: Electrical Output Storage Tube
EOT: End-Of-Tape
   End-Of-Test
   End-Of-Text
   End-Of-Transmission (character)
EOV: End-Of-Volume
EOW: End-Of-Word
EP: Emulator Program
EPA: Estimated Profile Analysis
   Extended Performance Analysis
EPBX: Electronic Private Branch Exchange
EPC: Editorial Processing Center
EPCI: Entry Point Control Item
EPIC: Exchange Price Information Computer
EPL: Electronic Switching Systems Programming Language
   Encoder Programming Language
EPLANS: Engineering, Planning and Analysis Systems
EPO: Emergency Power Off
EPOS: Electronic Point-of-Sale
EPR: Error Pattern Register
EPROM: Electrically Programmable Read-Only Memory

EPS: Electronic Payments System
   Even Parity Select
EPSCS: Enhanced Private Switched Communications Service
EPT: Execution Processing Unit
   Executive Process Table
eq: equal (to)
eql: equal
eqpt: equipment
equ: equal
EQUATE: Electronic Quality Assurance Test Equipment
equip: equipment
equiv: equivalent
er: error
ER: Established Reliability
   Exponent Register
E-R: Entity-Relationship
ERA: Electronic Representatives Association
ERCC: Error Checking and Correction
ERCR: Electronic Retina Computing Reader
EREP: Environmental Recording, Editing, and Printing
ERJE: Extended Remote Job Entry
ERMA: Electronic Recording Machine Accounting
EROM: Erasable Read-Only Memory
ERP: Effective Radiated Power
   Error Recovery Procedures
err: error
ERRC: Expandability, Recoverability, Repairability Cost
ERT: Expected Run-Time
ERU: External Run Unit
ES: Expert System
   External Store
ESA: Externally Specified Address
ESB: Electrical Standards Board
esc: escape
ESCS: Emergency Satellite Communications System

ESD: Electrostatic Discharge
External Symbol Dictionary
ESDS: Entry Sequenced Data Set
ESE/VM: Expert System Environment/VM
ESF: Extended Spooling Facility
ESI: Externally Specified Index
ESL: European Systems Language
ESN: External Segment Name
ESP: Electrosensitive Paper
ESPL: Electronic Switching Programming Language
ESPRIT: European Strategic Program for Research and Development in Information Technology (EC)
ESR: Electronic Send/Receive
Equivalent Series Resistance
ESS: Electronic Switching System
Event Scheduling System
est: estimated
EST: Earliest Start Time
ESTV: Error Statistics by Tape Volume
ESU: Electrostatic Unit
ESV: Error Statistics by Volume
ET: Eastern Time
Emerging Technology
End of Text
ETB: End-of-Transmission-Block
ETC: Estimated Time of Completion
ETD: Estimated Time of Departure
ET/GTS: Electronic Text and Graphics Transfer System
E-TIME: Execution Time
ETLG: Enable This Level Group
ETLT: Equal To or Less Than
ETMF: Elapsed Terminal Measurement System
ETOS: Extended Tape Operating System
ETP: Electrical Tough Pitch
ETR: Expected Time of Response
ETRO: Estimated Time of Return to Operation

ETS: Electronic Translator System
Electronic Typing System
Engine Test Stand
ETSI: European Telecommunications Standards Institute (EC)
ETSPL: Extended Telephone Systems Programming Language
ETSS: Entry Time-Sharing System
Experimental Time-Sharing System
ETT: Expected Test Time
ETV: Educational Television
ETX: End-of-Text
End-of-Transmission
ETX/ACK: End of Text/Acknowledge
EU: End-User
Execution Unit
EUCLID: Easily Used Computer Language for Illustration and Drawing (EC)
EUDG: European Datamanager User Group
EUF: End User Facility
EUROCOMP: European Computing Congress
EUROCON: European Conference on Electronics
EURODICAUTOM: Online terminology databank (EC)
EUROMICRO: European Association for Microprocessing and Microprogramming (EC)
EURONET: European Information Network (EC)
EURONET DIANE: Direct Information Access Network for Europe (EC)
EV: End Vector
EVA: Error Volume Analysis

EVDS: Electronic Visual Display Subsystem
EVFU: Electronic Vertical Format Unit
evid: evidence
EVIL: Extensible Video Interactive Language
EVM: Extended Virtual Machine
EVMA: Expanded Virtual Machine Assist
EVR: Electronic Video Recording
EWOS: European Workshop for Open Systems (EC)
ex: execute
executor
EXCP: Execute Channel Program
exctr: executor
EXD: External Device
EXDAMS: Extendable Debugging and Monitoring System
exec: execute
executive
EXF: External Function
EXLST: Exit List
EXOR: Exclusive OR
exp: exponent
express
expression
ExPlan: Exercise Plan
EXPLOR: Explicit Patterns, Local Operations, and Randomness
expo: exposition
expr: expression
ext: external
EXTM: Extended Telecommunications Module
EXTRAN: Expression Translator
EXTRN: External Reference

F

f: false
farad
fetch
file
fixed
flag
fraction
fractional
frequency
full
function
functional
FA: Facilitating Agency
Factory Automation
Field Address
Full Adder
fac: facsimile
factual
FAC: File Access Channel
Floating Accumulator
FACE: Field Alterable Control Element
FACES: FORTRAN Automatic Checkout System
FACS: Financial Accounting and Control System
FACT: Facility for Automation, Control and Test
Factor Analysis Chart Technique
Factory Automation, Control, and Test Facility
Fully Automatic Compiling Technique
FacTs: Facsimile Transmission
FADP: Federal Automatic Data Processing
FADPUG: Federation Automatic Data Processing users Group
FADS: Force Administration Data System
FORTRAN Automatic Debugging System
FAL: File Access Listener
FAM: Fast Auxiliary Memory
File Access Manager
FAMHEM: Federation of Associations of Materials Handling Equipment Manufacturers
FAMIS: Financial And Management Information System
FAMOS: Floating-gate Avalanche-injection Metal-Oxide Semiconductor
FAMS: Forecasting and Modeling System
FAP: Failure Analysis Program
FAPRS: Federal Assistance Program Retrieval System
FAPS: Financial Application Preprocessor System
FAQ: Fair Average Quality
FAQS: Fast Queuing System
FAR: File Address Register
FASB: Financial Accounting Standards Board
FASCIA: Fixed Asset System Control Information and Accounting
FASR: Forward Acting Shift Register
FAST: Fast Access Storage Technology
File Analysis and Selection Technique
Forecasting and Assessment in the field of Science and Technology (EC)

63

FASTER: Filing and Source Data Entry Techniques for Easier Retrieval
FATAR: Fast Analysis of Tape and Recovery
FATS: Fast Analysis of Tape Surfaces
FAVER: Fast Virtual Export/Restore
fax: facsimile
FB: File Block
Fixed Block
F/B: Foreground/Background
FBA: Fixed-Block Architecture
FBD: Full Business Day
FBM: Foreground and Background Monitor
FC: Flow Controller
Flux Change
Font Change
Front End Computer
Function Code
FCA: Functional Configuration Audit
FCB: File Control Block
Forms Control Buffer
FCBA: Fair Credit Billing Act
FCCFF: First Check Character Flip Flop
FCCTS: Federal COBOL Compiler Testing Service
FCFO: Full Cycling File Organization
FCFS: First Come, First Serve(d)
FCI: Flux Changes Per Inch
FCIM: Farm, Construction and Industrial Machinery
FCL: Format Control Language
Functional Capabilities List
FCM: Firmware Control Memory
FCP: File Control Processor
File Control Program
FCPI: Flux Changes Per Inch
FC/PM: Facility Control/Power Management
FCPU: Flexible Central Processing Unit

FCRAM: File Create And Maintenance
FCS: Finance Communication System
Financial Control System
Fixed Control Storage
Frame Check Sequence
FCSC: Federal Conversion Support Center
fct: function
FCTS: Federal Compiler Testing Service
FCU: File Control Unit
FCVS: FORTRAN Compiler Validation System
FD: File Definition
File Description
Flexible Disk
Floppy Disk
Full Duplex
FDB: Field Descriptor Block
File Data Block
FDC: Floppy Disk Controller
Fully Distributed Costs
FDCS: Functionally Distributed Computing System
FDCT: Factory Data Collection Terminal
FDD: Flexible Disk Drive
Floppy Disk Drive
FDDL: File Data Description Language
FDEP: Formatted Data Entry Program
FDL: Forms Description Language
FDM: Frequency Division Multiplex
FDMA: Frequency Division Multiple Access
FDMI: Function Management Data Interpreter
FDOS: Floppy Disk Operating System
FDR: Fast Dump Restore
File Data Register
FDS: Flexible Disk System
Floppy Disk System

FDSR: Floppy Disk Send/Receive
FDT: Functional Description Table
FDU: Form Description Utility
FDX: Full Duplex
F&E: Facilities and Equipment
FE: Field Editor
 Field Engineering
 Format Effector
 Framing Error
 Front End
FEAT: Frequency of Every Allowable Term
FEC: Forward Error Correction
 Front-End Computer
FECP: Front End Communications Processor
FEDNET: Federal Information Network
FEDS: Fixed/Exchangeable Disk Store
FEDSIM: Federal Computer Performance Evaluation and Simulation Center
FED-STD: Federal Standard
FEFO: First-Ended, First-Out
FEM: Finite Element Modeling
FEMA: Foundry Equipment Manufacturers Association
FEP: Front End Processor
FERST: Freight and Equipment Reporting System for Transportation
FES: Forms Entry System
FET: Field-Effect Transistor
FETE: FORTRAN Execution Time Estimator
FEX: Foreign Exchange
FEXT: Far-End Cross Talk
FF: Fast Forward
 Flip-Flop
 Form-Feed
FFMED: Fixed Format Message Entry Device
FFN: Full Function Node
FFP: Fast FORTRAN Processor
FFPI: Flip-Flop Position Indicator
FFS: Formatted File System

fg: foreground
FGS: FORTRAN Graphics Support
FGT: Foreground Table
FH: Field Handler
 File Handler
 Fixed Head
FHD: Fixed Head Disk
FHDS: Fixed Head Disk/Drum Store
FHF: Fixed Head File
FHSF: Fixed Head Storage Facility
FI: Format Identifier
 Front End Processor Interface
FIB: File Information Block
FIC: First-In-Chain
FICON: File Conversion
FICS: Factory Information Control System
 Financial Information and Control System
 Forecasting and Inventory Control System
FID: Forecasts-In-Depth
 Format Identification
FIDAC: Film Input to Digital Automatic Computer
FIDAS: Forms-Oriented Interactive Data Base System
FIF: Family Information Facility
FIFO: First In, First Out
FIGS: Figures Shift
FILEX: File Exchange
FILO: First In, Last Out
FILSYS: File System
FILU: Four-Bit Interface Logic Unit
FIMS: Financial Information Management System
 Functionally Identification Maintenance System
FINAC: Fast Interline Non-active Automatic Control
FINAR: Financial Analysis and Reporting
FINMAN: Financial Management
Finstat: Financial Times database of key statistical information

FINUFO: First In Not Used First Out
FIO: For Information Only
FIP: Finance Image Processor
FIPS: Federation Information Processing Standard
FIPS-O: General Description of the Federal Information Processing Standards Register
FIR: File Indirect Register
FIRM: Financial Information for Resource Management
FIS: Feasible Ideal System Floating (point) Instruction Set
FISSL: Finite State Specification Language
FIST: Feasible Ideal System Target
FIT: File Inquiry Technique Functional Industrial Training
FITAL: Financial In Terminal Application Language
FITCE: Federation des Ingenieurs des Telecommunications de la Communaute Europeenne (Federation of Telecommunications Engineers in the European Community) (French) (EC)
FIU: Federation of Information Users
FIXBLK: Fixed Blocked
FIXUNB: Fixed Unblocked
FJA: Functional Job Analysis
FL: Field Length
F/L: Fetch/Load
FLAG: FORTRAN Load and Go
FLAP: Flow Analysis Program
FLCN: Field Length Condition Register
fld: field
FLEE: Fast Linkage Editor
FLEXIMIS: Flexible Management Information System
flg: flag

FLIC: FORTRAN Language Industrial Control
FLIH: First-Level Interrupt Handler
FLIM: Fast Library Maintenance
FLIT: Fault Location by Interpretive Testing
FLOP: Floating-Point Operation per second
FLOWGEN: Flowchart Generator
FLP: Floating Point
FLPAU: Floating Point Arithmetic Unit
FLR: Flag Register
FLT: Fault Locating Test
FLTS: FASTER Language Translation System
FLTSATCOM: Fleet Satellite Communications System
FLV: Finite Logical View
FM: Facilities Management
File Management
File Manager
Format Manager
Frequency Modulation
FMA: Fabricating Machinery Association
FMD: Function Management Data
FMFB: Frequency Modulation Feedback
FML: File Manipulation Language
FMLF: File Management Loading Facility
FMPP: Flexible Multipipeline Processor
FMPS: Functional Mathematical Programming System
FMR: Facility Management Reporting
FMS: File Management System
Flexible Manufacturing System
FN: Functional Network
FNB: File Name Block
FNF: First Normal Form
FNP: Front End Network Processor

FNPA: Foreign Numbering Plan Area
FNR: File Next Register
FNS: Feedback Node Set
FNT: File Name Table
FOC: Fiber Optics Communications
FOCAL: Formula Calculator
FOCH: Forward Channel
FOCIS: Fiber Optic Communication and Information Society
Financial On-line Central Information System
FOCUS: Forum of Control Data Users
FOD: Function Operational Design
fol: folio
following
FOL: Function Of Lines
FOM: Fiber-Optic Modem
FOOF: Fanout-Observed Output Function
FOPC: First Order Predicate Calculus
FOPIC: Fiber Optic Modem
FOPS: Forecast Operating System
FOQ: Free On Quay
FORBLR: FORTRAN Assembler
FORDAP: FORTRAN Debugging Aid Program
FOREM: File Organization Evaluation Model
FORGE: File Organization Generator
FORGO: FORTRAN Load and Go
FORIMS: FORTRAN-Oriented Information Management System
FORMAC: Formula Manipulation Compiler
FORMS: Forms Management System
FORT: Formula Translation
FORTRAN
FORTE: File Organization Techniques
FORTRAN: Formula Translation
FORTUNE: FORTRAN Tuner
FOS: Function Operational Specification

FOSDIC: Film Optical Scanning Device for Input to Computers
FOSE: Federal Office Systems Expo
FOTS: Fiber-Optic Transmission System
FP: Faithful Performance
File Processor
Floating Point
Frame Pointer
Function Processor
FPA: Floating Point Arithmetic
Free of Particular Average
FPAL: Floating Point Arithmetic Library
FPB: Floating Point Board
FPC: Functional Processor Cluster
FPGA: Field Programmable Gate Array
FPLA: Field-Programmable Logic Array
FPM: File Protect Memory
FPP: Fixed-Path Protocol
Floating-Point Package
Floating-Point Processor
FPPU: Floating Point Processor Unit
FPR: Floating Point Register
FPROM: Field Programmable Read-Only Memory
FPS: Frames Per Second
FPU: File Processing Unit
Floating Point Unit
FQL: Formal Query Language
FQR: Formal Qualification Review
FQT: Formal Qualification Test
FR: File Register
Final Report
Final Request
Floating Point Register
Functions of Reads
F/R: Failure and Recovery
FRACA: Failure Reporting, Analysis and Corrective Action
fract: fraction
FRD: Functional Requirements Document

FRED: Front End for Databases
freq: frequency
FRIMP: Flexible Reconfigurable Interconnected Multiprocessor System
FRL: Frame Representation Language
FRM: Functional Requirements Model
FROM: Fusable Read-Only Memory
FRR: Functional Recovery Routines
FRSS: Financial Results Simulator System
FRU: Field Replaceable Unit
FRUMP: Fast Reading and Understanding Memory Program
FS: Field Separator
Field Service
File Separator
Finite State
Full Scale
Function Select
FSA: Finite State Automation
FSC: Federal Supply Code
FSCB: File System Control Block
FSCM: Federal Supply Code for Manufacturers
FSCR: Field Select Command Register
FSD: Full Scale Deflection
Functional Sequence Diagram
FSEC: Federal Software Exchange Center
FSF: Forward Space File
FSIM: Functional Simulation
FSK: Frequency-Shift Keying
FSL: Formal Semantic Language
FSM: Finite State Machine
FSOS: Free Standing Operating System
FSP: Full-Screen Processing
FSR: Feedback Shift Register
Forward Space Record
Full Scale Range

FSS: Flying Spot Scanner
FSSA: Flight Service Station Automation
FST: File Status Table
FSU: Facsimile Switching Unit
Field Select Unit
ft: feet
FT: Format Type
Frequency and Time
FTA: Fault Tree Analysis
FTC: Fault Tolerant Computer
FTF: Factory Terminal Facility
File To File
FTI: Fixed Time Interval
FTL: Fast Transient Loader
FTN: FORTRAN
FTP: File Transfer Program
File Transfer Protocol
FTPI: Flux Transitions Per Inch
FTS: Federal Telecommunication System
Free Time System
FTSC: Federal Telecommunications Standards Committee
FTT: Financial Transaction Terminal
FU: Field Unit
Functional Unit
func: function
FUS: FORTRAN Utility System
F-V: Frequency to Voltage
FVU: File Verification Utility
fw: firmware
FW: First Word
FWA: First Word Address
fwd: forward
fwdg: forwarding
FWP: First Word Pointer
FWT: Flexible Working Time
FXPALU: Fixed Point Address Arithmetic Logic Unit
FY: Fiscal Year
FYI: For Your Information
FYIG: For Your Information and Guidance

G

g: gain
giga-
gram
graph
group
GA: General Average
Global Address
Graphic Adapter
GaAs: Gallium Arsenide Chips
GAB: Graphic Adapter Board
GAC: General Access Copy
GAD: Graphic Active Device
GADS: Geographical Analysis and Display System
GAGS: General Application Guidance System
GAIC: Gallium Arsenide Integrated Circuit
GAL: Generalized Assembly Language
GALPAT: Galloping Pattern
GAM: Graphic Access Method
GAP: Graphics Application Program
GAPM: Generalized Access Path Method
GAS: Global Address Space
Graphics Application Program
GASP: General Activity Simulation Program
Generalized Audit Software Package
GASPAN: Gamma Spectral Analysis
GAT: Generalized Algebraic Translator
Greenwich Apparent Time
GATS: General Acceptance Test Software
GAUGE: General Automation Users Group Exchange
gb: GigaBIT
Gigabyte
GB: General Business
GBF: Geographic Base File
GBIT: GigaBIT
GBMP: General Benchmark Program
GBS: General Business System
GBTS: General Banking Terminal System
g-byte: gigabytes
gc: gigacycle
GC: Garbage Collection
GCB: General Circuit Breaker
GCCA: Graphic Communications Computer Association
GCD: Greatest Common Divisor
GCE: Ground Communication Equipment
gch: gigacharacters
GCI: Generalized Communication Interface
GCLA: Group Carry Look-Ahead
GCOS: General Comprehensive Operating Supervisor
GCR: Group Coded Recording
GCS: Graphics Compatibility System
GCSC: Guidance Control and Sequencing Computer
GCT: Graphics Communications Terminal
Greenwich Civil Time
GD: Global Data
Graphics Display
GDA: Global Data Administrator
GDB: Global Data Base
GDBMS: Generalized Data Base Management System
GDBS: Global Data Base System
GDC: Guidance Display Computer

GDD: General Design Document
GDDL: Graphical Data Definition Language
GD/DS: Generalized Dictionary/Directory System
GDE: Generalized Data Entry
GDF: Group Distribution Frame
GDG: Generation Data Group
GDI: Generalized Data Base Interface
GDL: Graphic Display Library
GDM: Global Data Manager
GDMS: Generalized Data Management Systems
GDP: Generalized Data Base Processor
Goal Directed Programming
GDS: Graphic Data System
Graphic Design System
GDSDF: Generalized Data Structure Definition Facility
GDU: Graphic Display Unit
GEDIT: General Purpose Text Editor
GEL: General Emulation Language
GEMCOS: Generalized Message Control System
gen: general
generate
generation
GENIE: General Information Extractor
GENISYS: Generalized Information System
GENTRAS: General Training System
GERT: Graphical Evaluation and Review Technique
GERTS: General Remote Terminal System
GET: Gross Error Test
GETMA: GET from local Manufacturer
GFI: Guided Fault Isolation
GFM: Government-Furnished Material
GFP: Generalized File Processor

GFS: General Financial System
GGG: Gadolinium Gallium Garnet
GHC: Gating Half-Cycle
ghz: gigahertz
GIC: General Input/Output Channel
GICS: Graphic Input/Output Command System
GIDEP: Government Industry Data Exchange Program
GIGO: Garbage In, Garbage Out
GIL: General Purpose Interactive Programming Language
GIM: Generalized Information Management
GIMIC: Guard Ring Isolated Monolithic Integrated Circuit
GINO: Graphical Input and Output
GIOP: General Purpose Input/Output Processor
GIPSY: General Information Processing System
GIRL: Generalized Information Retrieval Language
GIRLS: Graphical Data Interpretation and Reconstruction in Local Satellite
GIRS: Generalized Information Retrieval System
GIS: Generalized Information System
Guidance Information System
GJ: Graphic Job (processor)
GJP: Graphic Job Processor
GL: General Ledger
GL/FICS: General Ledger/Financial Information and Control System
GM: General Macroassembly
Graphic Machine
Group Mark
GMAP: General Macroassembly Program
Generalized Macroprocessor
GMAT: Greenwich Mean Astronomical Time
GMIS: Generalized Management Information System

Government Management Information Sciences
GML: Generalized Mark-up Language
Graphic Machine Language
GMR: General Modular Redundancy
GMS: General Maintenance System
GMSS: Graphical Modeling and Simulation System
GMT: Generalized Multitasking
Greenwich Mean Time
gnd: ground
GO: General Operations
General Order
Generated Output
GOES: Geo-Stationary Operational and Environmental Satellite
GOL: Goal Oriented Language
GOMAC: Government Microcircuit Applications Conference
GOR: General Operations Requirement
GOS: Grade Of Service
Graphics Operating System
GP: General Purpose
Grace Periods
Graphic Package
Graphic Processor
GPA: General Purpose Array
GPAC: Graphics Package
GPACK: General Utility Package
GPC: General Peripheral Controller
General-Purpose Computer
GPCA: General Purpose Communications Adapter
GPCB: General Purpose Communications Base
GPCF: General Purpose Computing Facility
GPC/P: General Purpose Controller/Processor
GPD: General Protocol Driver
GPDC: General-Purpose Device Controller

General-Purpose Digital Computer
GPDS: General-Purpose Discrete Simulator
General-Purpose Display System
GPIA: General Purpose Interface Adapter
GPIB: General Purpose Interface Bus
GPIBA: General Purpose Interface Bus Adapter
GPIC: General Purpose Intelligent Cable
GPIO: General Purpose Input/Output
GPL: General Purpose Language
GPLAN: Generalized Plan
GPM: General Purpose Macrogenerator
General Purpose Module
Gross Processing Margin
GPOS: General Purpose Operating System
GPP: General Purpose Processor
GPR: General-Purpose Register
GPS: General Problem Solver
General Programming Subsystem
GPSCS: General Purpose Satellite Communications System
GPSN: General Purpose Packet Satellite Network
GPSS: General Purpose Simulation System
General-Purpose Systems Simulator
GPU: General Processing Unit
GR: General Records
General Register
GRAD: Generalized Remote Access Data Base
GRAIN: Graphics-Oriented Relational Algebraic Interpreter
GRANADA: Grammatical Nonalgorithmic Data Description

GRANIS: Graphical Natural Inference System
GRASP: Generalized Read and Simulate Program
Generalized Remote Acquisition and Sensor Processing
Graphics Subroutine Package
GRF: Geographic Reference File
GRG: Graphical Rewriting Grammar
GRINDER: Graphical Interactive Network Designer
GRIP: Graphics Interactive Programming
grnd: ground
GRS: General Records Schedule
General Register Stack
General Reporting System
GRT: Greater Than
GRTS: General Remote Terminal Supervisor
GS: Graphics System
Group Separator
GSAM: Generalized Sequential Access Method
GSC: Group Switching Center
GSE: Ground Support Equipment
GSI: Grand Scale Integration
GSIU: Ground Standard Interface Unit
GSM: Graphics System Module
GSP: Graphics Subroutine Package
GSR: Global-Shared Resources
GSS: Graphic Support Software
GSTDN: Ground Spacecraft Tracking and Data Network
GSVC: Generalized Supervisor Call
GT: Gas Turbine Engine
Graphics Terminal
Greater Than
G/T: Gain-to-noise-Temperature ratio
GTDPL: Generalized Top-Down Parsing Language
GTF: Generalized Trace Facility
Greater Than Flag
GTP: Graphic Transform Package

H

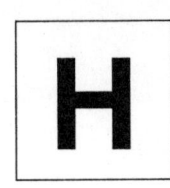

h: hardware
head
hecto
hierarchy
home
horizontal
host
hour
H: Half-Adder
Home Address
HA: Half-Adder
Hazard Analysis
HAB: Home Address Block
HAC: Hierarchical Abstract Computer
HAD: Herein After Described
HAG: Home Address Gap
HAL: Highly Automated Logic
HAM: Hierarchical Access Method
HAMT: Human-Aided Machine Translation
hand: handling
HAPUB: High Speed Arithmetic Processing Unit Board
HAR: Home Address Register
HARDMON: Hardware Monitor
hardwr: hardware
HASQ: Hardware Assisted Software Queue
HATRS: High Altitude Transmit/Receive Satellite
HAU: Horizontal Arithmetic Unit
Hybrid Arithmetic Unit
hb: handbook
hybrid
HBAR: Head Bar Address Register
HBEN: High Byte Enable
HBS: High Byte Strobe
HC: Held Covered
Host Command
Host Computer
HCF: Host Command Facility
HCI: Host Computer Interface
Hybrid Computer Interface
HCMTS: High-Capacity Mobile Telecommunications System
HCP: Hard Copy Printer
High Speed Channel Processor
Host Communications Processor
HCR: Hardware Check Routine
HCRST: Hardware Clipping, Rotation, Scaling and Translation
HCS: Hard Copy System
Hundred Call Seconds
H/D: Head/Disk
HD: Half-Duplex
Hierarchical Direct
High Density
HDA: Head/Disk Assembly
HDAM: Hierarchical Direct Access Method
HDAS: Hybrid Data Acquisition System
HDC: High Speed Data Channel
HDDR: High Density Digital Recording
HDF: High Density Flexible
HDLA: High Level Data Link Control Adapter
HDLC: High-level Data-Link Control
HDLM: High Level Data Linkage Module
HDLR: Hexadecimal Symbolic Loader
HDM: Hierarchical Development Methodology

73

HDMR: High Density Multitrack Recording
HDOS: Hard Disk Operating System
hdr: header
HDR: High Density Recording
HDS: Hybrid Development System
HDT: High Density Tape
HDTV: High-Definition Television
hdw: hardware
HDX: Half-Duplex
HEMT: High-Electron-Mobility Transistors
HER: Human Error Rate
hex: hexadecimal
HEXCALC: Hexadecimal Calculator
HF: High Frequency
HFDF: High-Frequency Distribution Frame
HFE: Human Factors Engineering
H/H: Host to Host
hi: high
HIC: Hybrid Integrated Circuit
HICS: Hierarchical Information Control System
HIDAM: Hierarchical Indexed Direct Access Method
HIDM: High Information Delta Modulation
HIFT: Hardware Implemented Fault Tolerance
HIM: Hardware Interface Module Hierarchy of Interpretive Modules
HINIL: High-Noise-Immunity Logic
HIP: Host Interface Processor
HIPO: Hierarchy, Input, Process, Output
hir: hierarchy
HI-RES: High-Resolution
HIS: Homogeneous Information Sets
HISAM: Hierarchical Indexed Sequential Access Method
HISDAM: Hierarchical Indexed Sequential Direct Access Method
HIT: High Isolation Transformer
HI-TECH: High Technology
HL: High Level Host Language
HLA: High Speed Line Adapter
HLAF: Higher Level Arithmetic Function
HLAIS: High Level Analog Input Subsystem
HLDA: Hold Acknowledge
HLDTL: High Level Diode Transistor Logic
HLI: Host Language Interface
HLL: High-Level Language
HLML: High Level Microprogramming Language
HLMPL: High Level Microprogramming Language
HLPI: High Level Programming Interface
HLQL: High Level Query Language
HLR: High Level Representation
hlt: halt
HLT: Highly Leveraged Transaction
HLTA: Halt Acknowledge
HLTU: Hierarchized Threshold Logic Unit
HM: Hypothetical Machine
HMI: Hardware Monitor Interface
HMLC: High Speed Multiline Controller
HMM: Hardware Multiply Module
HMO: Hardware Microcode Optimizer
HMOS: High Performance Metal Oxide Semiconductor
HMPL: High Level Microprogram Language
HMPY: Hardware Multiplier
HMR: Hybrid Modular Redundancy
HN: Host to Network
HNA: Hierarchical Network Architecture
HNIL: High-Noise-Immunity Logic
HNPA: Home Numbering Plan Area
HNPL: High Level Network Processing Language

HO: High Order
HOL: High-Order Language
HOLDET: Higher Order Language Development and Evaluation Tool
HOLWG: High Order Language Working Group
hor: horizontal
HOS: Higher Order Software
HP: High Power
  Horse Power
  Host Processor
HPA: Heuristic Path Algorithm
  High Power Amplifier
HPAA: High Performance Antenna Assembly
HPCA: High Performance Communications Adapter
HPF: High Pass Filter
  Host Preparation Facility
HPGS: High Performance Graphics System
HPPL: Host Program Preparation Facility
HPT: Head Per Track
hr: hour
HR: Hit Ratio
  Holding Register
HRM: Hardware Read-In Mode
HRMR: Human Read/Machine Read
HRN: Highest Response-Ratio Next
HRNES: Host Remote Node Entry System
HRPM: High Resolution Permanent Magnet
HRSS: Host Resident Software System
HS: Half-Subtracter
  Hierarchical Sequential
HSAM: Hierarchical Sequential Access Method
HSB: High Speed Buffer
HSBA: High Speed Bus Adapter
HSC: High Speed Concentrator
HSDB: High Speed Data Buffer
HSDMS: Highly Secure Database Management System
HSE: High Speed Signal Control Equipment
HSEL: High Speed Selector Channel
HSLC: High Speed Single Line Controller
HSM: Hierarchical Storage Manager
  High-Speed Memory
HSP: High-Speed Printer
HSR: High-Speed Reader
HSS: Hierarchical Service System
H/T: Head per Track
HT: Hand-held Terminal
  Horizontal Tabulation (character)
HTB: Hexadecimal To Binary
HTC: Hybrid Technology Computer
HTL: High Threshold Logic
HTS: Head, Track, and Sector
  Host To Satellite
HU: Horizontal Arithmetic Unit
Human Eng: Human Engineering
HumInt: Human Intelligence
HUT: High Usage Intertoll Trunk
HV: High Voltage
HVR: Hardware Vector to Raster
HVTS: High Volume Time-Sharing
hw: hardware
HWI: Hardware Interpreter
hz: hertz

I

i: current
immediate
indirect
information
input
instruction
interrupt
I&A: Indexing and Abstracting
IA: Immediately Available
Instruction Addresss
Integrated Adapter
IAB: Interrupt Address to Bus
IAC: Integration, Assembly, Checkout
Interactive Array Computer
International Association for Cybernetics
IACP: International Association of Computer Programmers
IAD: Initial Address Designator
Integrated Automatic Documentation
IADR: Instruction Address
IAF: Interactive Facility
IAL: International Algebraic Language
IALE: Instrumented Architectural Level Emulation
IAM: Innovation Access Method
IAMACS: International Association for Mathematics and Computers in Simulation
IANET: Integrated Access Network
IAP: Image Array Processor
IAPS: International ASCII Publication Standard
IAR: Instruction Address Register
Interrupt Address Register
IAS: Immediate Access Storage
Interactive Application System
IASC: International Association for Statistical Computing
IASTED: International Association of Science and Technology for Development
IATA: International Airline Telecommunications Association
IAU: Interface Adaptor Unit
IAW: In Accordance With
IB: Identifier Block
Input Bus
Instruction Bus
Interface Bus
Internal Bus
Is Between
IBC: Integrated Block Channel
Integrated Broadband Communications
IBF: Input Buffer Full
IBFI: International Business Forms Industry
IBG: Inter Block Gap
IBI: Intergovernmental Bureau for Informatics
IBOL: Interactive Business Oriented Language
IBOLS: Integrated Business Oriented Language Support
IBT: Integrated Business Terminal
I&C: Installation and Checkout
I/C: Instrumentation/Control
IC: Identification Code
Index of Coincidence
Information Circular
Instruction Counter
Instrumentation Control
Integrated Circuit

ICA: Integrated Communications Adapter
Intercomputer Adapter
International Communication Association
ICAD: Integrated Control and Display
ICAE: Integrated Communications Adapter Extension
ICAM: Integrated Computer-Aided Manufacturing
ICB: Information Collection Budget
Internal Common Bus
ICBS: Interconnected Business System
IC&C: Invoice Cost and Charges
ICC: International Conference on Communications
ICCA: Independent Computer Consultants Association
ICCAD: International Center for Computer Aided Design
ICCCM: International Conference on Computer Capacity Management
ICCDP: Integrated Circuit Communications Data Processor
ICCF: Interactive Computing and Control Facility
ICCP: Information, Computer and Communications Policy
Institute for the Certification of Computer Professionals
ICCS: Intercomputer Communications System
ICCU: Intercomputer Communications Unit
Intercomputer Control Unit
ICD: Interface Control Document
International Congress for Data Processing
ICDB: Integrated Corporated Data Base
ICDDB: Internal Control Description Data Base
ICDL: Integrated Circuit Description Language
Internal Control Description Language
ICDLA: Internal Control Description Language Analyzer
ICDR: Inward Call Detail Recording
ICDS: Integrated Circuit Design System
ICE: InCircuit Emulator
ICEA: International Consumer Electronics Association
ICES: Integrated Civil Engineering System
ICEX: Integrated Civil Engineering Executive
ICF: Intercommunication Flip-Flop
ICG: Interactive Computer Graphics
ICI: Intelligent Communications Interface
ICL: Intercommunication Logic
Intercomputer Communication Link
Interpretive Coding Language
ICM: Instruction Control Memory
ICMS: Integrated Circuit and Message Switch
ICMUP: Instruction Control Memory Update Processor
ICN: Integrated Computer Network
ICOS: Interactive COBOL Operating System
IC/P: Intelligent Copier/Printer
ICP: Initial Connection Protocol
Inventory Control Point
ICR: Indirect Control Register
Input Control Register
Interrupt Control Register
ICS: Industrial Control System
Information Collection System
Institute of Computer Science
Interactive Communications Software
International Computer Symposium

Interpretive Computer Simulation
ICST: Institute for Computer Sciences and Technology
ICT: In-Coming Trunk
ICU: Industrial Control Unit
Instruction Control Unit
Interface Control Unit
Interrupt Control Unit
ICV: Initial Chaining Value
ICW: Initial Condition Word
Interface Control Word
Id: identification
identifier
I/D: Instruction/Data
ID: Intelligent Digitizer
Item Descriptor
IDA: Integrated Data Analysis
Intelligent Data Access
Interactive Data Analysis
Interactive Debugging Aid
IDAC: Instant Data Access and Control
IDAM: Indexed Direct Access Method
IDAS: Industrial Data Acquisition System
International Data Base Access Service
IDB: Input Data Buffer
Integrated Data Base
IDBMS: Integrated Data Base Management System
IDBR: Input Data Buffer Register
IDC: Internal Data Channel
IDCA: International Development Cooperation Agency
IDCC: Integrated Data Communications Controller
IDCMA: Independent Data Communications Manufacturers Association
IDD: Integrated Data Dictionary
International Direct Dialing
IDDD: International Direct Distance Dialing
IDDL: Interactive Data Base Design Laboratory
IDDS: International Digital Data Service
IDE: Interactive Data Entry
IDEA: Interactive Data Entry/Access
IDEAS: Integrated Design and Analysis System
Integrated Design and Engineering Automated System
Interactive Data Base Easy Access System
IDEN: Interactive Data Entry Network
ident: identification
IDES: Interactive Data Entry System
IDF: Image Description File
Intermediate Distributing Frame
IDI: Improved Data Interchange
Intelligent Dual Interface
Idl: idle
IDL: Information Description Language
Instruction Definition Language
Intermediate Data Description Language
IDM: Interactive Decision Making
IDMAS: Interactive Data Base Manipulator and Summarizer
IDMH: Input Destination Message Handler
IDMS: Integrated Data Base Management System
IDN: Intelligent Data Network
IDO: Isolated Digital Output
IDOS: Interrupt Disk Operating System
IDP: Integrated Data Processing
Interactive Data Base Processor
International Data Processing

IDPS: Interactive Direct Processing System
IDR: Information Descriptor Record
IDRS: Integrated Data Retrieval System
IDS: Information Display System
Integrated Data Store
Intelligent Display System
Interactive Display System
IDT: Intelligent Data Terminal
Interactive Data Terminal
IDU: Industrial Development Unit
Interactive Data Base Utilities
IDVM: Integrated Digital Voltmeter
IE: Interrupt Enable
IEC: International Electrotechnical Commission
IECI: Industrial Electronics and Control Instrumentation
IEEE: Institute of Electrical and Electronics Engineering
IEEE-488: Digital Interface for Programmable Instrumentation Standard
IEEE-583: Modular Instrumentation and Digital Interface System Standard
IERE: Institution of Electronic and Radio Engineers
IES: Illuminating Engineering Society
If: interface
IF: Instruction Field
Intermediate Frequency
IFA: Information Flow Analysis
IFAC: International Federation of Automatic Control
IFAM: Inverted File Access Method
IFC: Interface Clear
IFI: Interfault Interval
IFIP: International Federation for Information Processing
IFIPS: International Federation of Information Processing Societies
IFM: Interactive File Manager
IFMS: Integrated Financial Management System
IFORS: International Federation of Operations Research Societies
IFP: Integrated File Processor
IFPS: Interactive Financial Planning System
IFR: Interface Register
IFRA: Increasing Failure Rate Average
IFRB: International Frequency Registration Board
IFS: Interactive File Sharing
IFU: Instruction Fetch Unit
IGFET: Insulated Gate Field Effect Transistor
IGL: Interactive Graphics Language
IGS: Information Group Separator
Interactive Graphics System
IGT: Interactive Graphics Terminal
IH: Interrupt Handler
IHF: Inhibit Halt Flip-Flop
IHY: I Heard You
II: Interrupt Inhibit
Inventory and Inspection
IIA: Information Industries Association
IIL: Integrated Injection Logic
IIOP: Integrated Input/Output Processor
IIPACS: Integrated Information Presentation And Control System
IIS: Interactive Instructional System
IITI: International Information Technology Institute
IIU: Instruction Input Unit
IJC: Interjob Communications
IJCAI: International Joint Conference on Artificial Intelligence
IJS: Interactive Job Submission
IKB: Intelligent Keyboard
il: idle

IL: Instruction List
Intermediate Language
ILA: Insurance Logistics Automated
Intelligent Line Adapter
Intermediate Level Amplifier
ILB: Initial Load Block
ILC: Instruction Length Code
Instruction Location Counter
ILD: Intersection Loop Detection
ILE: Interface Latching Element
ILM: Intermediate Language Machine
ILO: Individual Load Operation
ILOC: Internal Location
ILP: Intermediate Language Program
ILPS: Interactive Linear Programming System
ILS: International Line Selector
ILTMS: International Leased Telegraph Line Switching Service
IM: Index Marker
Information Management
Instruction Memory
Instrumentation and Measurement
Integrated Modem
Interrupt Mask
IMA: Input Message Acknowledgment
Institute for Manufacturing Automation
Invalid Memory Address
IMACS: International Association for Mathematics and Computers in Simulation
IMARS: Information Management and Retrieval System
IMB: Intermode Bus
IMC: Information Management Concepts
Integrated Multiplexer Channel
Interactive Module Controller
International Micrographics Congress
IMCS: Interactive Manufacturing Control System
IMDR: Intelligent Mark Document Reader
IME: International Microcomputer Exposition
IMG: International Mailgram
IMI: Intermediate Machine Instruction
IMIS: Integrated Management Information System
IML: Information Manipulation Language
Initial Microcode (Microprogram) Load
Intermediate Machine Language
Imm: immediate
IMM: Intelligent Memory Manager
IMMM: International (Conference on) Microcomputer Minicomputers Microprocessors
IMOS: Interactive Multiprogramming Operating System
IMP: Information Management Package
Integrated Manufacturing Planning
Interface Message Processor
Inventory Management Package
IMPAC: Industrial Multilevel Process Analysis and Control
Information for Management Planning Analysis and Coordination
IMPACT: Integrated Management Planning and Control Techniques
IMPL: Initial Microcode (Microprogram) Load
IMPROVE: Inventory Management, Product Replenishment and Order Validity Evaluation

IMPS: Integrated Modular Pushbutton Switch
IMR: Interrupt Mask Register
IMRADS: Information Management, Retrieval and Dissemination System
IMS: Information Management System
Integrated Manufacturing System
Inventory Management System
IMSI: Information Management System Interface
IMSP: Integrated Mass Storage Processor
IMS/VS: Information Management System/Virtual Storage
IMT: Intelligent Microimage Retrieval Terminal
IMTS: Improved Mobile Telephone Service
IMU: Increment Memory Unit
Instruction Memory Unit
IMX: In-Line Multiplexer
Inquiry Message Exchange
in: inch
increase
input
IN: Index Number
Interconnecting Network
Internal Node
INA: Integrated Network Architecture
inc: increment
INCA: Inventory Control and Analysis
incl: including
inclusive
INCOS: Integrated Control System
incr: increment
incre: increment
ind: indicator
industry
INDAC: Industrial Data Acquisition and Control

info: inform
information
informational
INFO: International Information Management Exposition and Conference
INFOL: Information Oriented Language
INFONET: Information Network
INFOR: Information Network and File Organization
INFOTEX: Information Via Telex
INFRAL: Information Retrieval Automatic Language
INFUT: Information Utility
INGA: Interactive Graphic Analysis
INGRES: Interactive Graphic and Retrieval System
init: initialize
inj: injunction
inp: input
INP: Integrated Network Processor
Intelligent Network Processor
INSAR: Instruction Address Register
INSPEC: Information Service in Physics, Electrotechnology and Control
inst: instant
instruction
instrument
INSTINET: Institutional Networks Corporation
instr: instruction
INSYD: Instantaneous Systems Display
int: integer
internal
interrupt
INTA: Interrupt Acknowledge
INTE: Interrupt Enable
INTELCOM: International Telecommunications Exposition
INTELEC: International Telecom-

munications Energy
Conference
INTELSAT: International Telecommunications Satellite Consortium
inten: intensity
INTERMAG: International Magnetics (conference)
intermed: intermediate
INTERNEPCON: International Electronics Production Conference
interp: interpreter
INTERTEST: Interactive Test Controller
INTFU: Interface Unit
INTGEN: Interpreter-Generator
INTI: Industrial and Technological Information
INTIP: Integrated Information Processing
intl: international
intr: interrupt
INTR: Interrupt Register
Interrupt Request
INTREX: Information Transfer Experiments
intro: introduction
INTRQ: Interrupt Request
INWATS: Inward Wide Area Telecommunications Service
INWG: International Network Working Group
INX: Index Character
IO: Immediate Order
I/O: Input/Output
IOA: Input/Output Adapter
IOAU: Input/Output Access Unit
IOB: Input/Output Block
Input-Output Buffer
IOC: Initial Operational Capacity
Input-Output Channel
Input-Output Controller
IOCS: Input/Output Control System
IOCU: Input/Output Control Unit

IOD: Input/Output Device
IOF: Input/Output Front End
IOFU: Instruction and Operand Fetch Unit
IOGEN: Input-Output Generation
IOIH: Input/Output Interrupt Handler
IOLA: Input/Output Link Adapter
IOLC: Input/Output Link Control
IOM: Input/Output Microprocessor
Input/Output Module
Input/Output Multiplexer
IOMS: Input/Output Management System
IOP: Input/Output Processor
Institute of Packaging
IOPS: Input-Output Processing System
Input-Output Program System
IOQ: Input/Output Queue
IOR: Input-Output Read
Input-Output Register
Institute for Operational Research
IORC: Input-Output Read Control
IORS: Input-Output Request Subroutine
IORT: Input-Output Remote Terminal
IOS: Input-Output Supervisor
Input-Output System
Interactive Operating System
IOSA: Input-Output Systems Association
IOSYS: Input/Output System
IOT: Input/Output Transfer
Input/Output Trap
Interoffice Trunk
IOU: Input/Output Unit
IOW: Input/Output Wire
Input/Output Write
IOWQ: Input/Output Wait Queue
IOX: Input-Output Executive
ip: input

IP: Impact Printer
Information Processor
Initial Permutation
Initial Phase
Input/Output Processor
Instruction Pointer
Interchangeable Parts
Interface Processor
IPA: Integrated Peripheral Adapter
Integrated Printer Adapter
Intermediate Power Amplifier
IPARS: International Passenger Programmed Airlines Reservation System
IPB: Industrial Process Control
Integrated Processor Board
Interprocessor Buffer
IPC: Industrial Process Control
Integrated Peripheral Channel
Interprocess Controller
Interprocess Coupler
IPCS: Interactive Problem Control System
IPD: Information Processing Department
IPE: Industrial Plant Equipment
IPF: Information Processing Facility
Information Productivity Facility
IPI: Intelligent Printer Interface
IPIC: Initial Production and Inventory Control
IPICS: Initial Production and Inventory Control System
IPL: Information Processing Language
Initial Program Load
Initial Program Loader
Interrupt Priority Level
IPM: Inventory Policy Model
IP/MP: Inphase/Midphase
IPO: Input, Process, and Output
Installation Productivity Option

IPO/E: Installation Productivity Option/Extended
IPOT: Inductive Potentiometer
IPPF: Instruction Preprocessing Function
IPR: Imposter Pass Rate
IPS: Index Participation
Information Processing System
Installation Performance Specifications
IPSB: Interprocessor Signal Bus
IPSJ: Information Processing Society of Japan
IPSS: Information Processing System Simulator
IPSX: Interprocessor Switch Matrix
IPSY: Interactive Planning System
IPT: Improved Productivity Techniques
Improved Programming Techniques
IPTC: International Press Telecommunications Council
IPU: Instruction Processing Unit
Integrated Processor Unit
Interprocessor Unit
IQ: Information Quick
IQA: Institute of Quality Assurance
IQE: Interruption Queue Element
IQF: Interactive Query Facility
IQL: Interactive Query Language
IQMH: Input Queue Message Handler
IQRP: Interactive Query and Report Processor
I&R: Information and Retrieval
Ir: infrared
IR: Independent Research
Index Register
Informal Report
Information Retrieval
Inspection Report
Instruction Register
Interim Report
Interrupt Request

IRA: Information Resource Administration
Instruction Register, Address Portion
IRAM: Indexed Random Access Method
IRAN: Inspection and Repair As Necessary
IRAR: Integrated Random Access Reservation
IRB: Interruption Request Block
IRC: International Record Carrier
IR&D: Independent Research and Development
IRD: Internal Research and Development
IRED: Infrared Emitting Diode
IREP: Internal Representation
IRF: Input Register Full
IRFITS: Infrared Fault Isolation Test System
IRG: InterRecord Gap
IRH: Inductive Recording Head
IRI: Industrial Research Institute
Interreference Interval
IRIG: Interrange Instrumentation Group
IRJE: Interactive Remote Job Entry
IRL: Information Retrieval Language
IRM: Information Resources Management
Inspection, Repair and Maintenance
Intelligent Remote Multiplexer
Interim Research Memorandum
IRN: Internal Routing Network
IROS: Increased Reliability of Operational Systems
IRP: Inventory and Requirements Planning
IRQ: Interrupt Request
IRR: Internal Rate of Return
Interrupt Return Register

Irreg: irregular
IRS: Information Retrieval System
Inquiry and Reporting System
IRT: Index Return (character)
IRTU: Intelligent Remote Terminal Unit
IRUC: Intermediate Resource Usage Condition
IRV: Interrupt Request Vector
IRW: Indirect Reference Word
IRX: Interactive Resource Executive
IS: Indexed Sequential
Information Science
Information Separator
Information System
International Standard
ISAL: Information System Access Line
ISAM: Indexed Sequential Access Method
ISAR: Indirect Scratchpad Address Register
Information Storage And Retrieval
ISARL: Indirect Scratchpad Address Register Upper
ISBL: Information System Base Language
ISBN: International Standard Book Number
ISC: Ideal Standard Cost
ISD: Information Structure Design
Intermediate Storage Device
International Subscriber Dialing
ISDN: Integrated Services Digital Network
ISDOS: Information System Design and Optimization System
ISDS: Instruction Set Design System
Integrated Software Development System

ISE: Institute for Software Engineering
Insystem Emulator
Interrupt System Enable
ISEM: Improved Standard Electronic Module
ISEP: International Standard Equipment Practice
I-SEQ: Indexed Sequential
ISF: Individual Store and Forward
ISFD: Integrated Software Functional Design
ISFM: Indexed Sequential File Manager
ISFMS: Indexed Sequential File Management System
ISFSM: Incompletely Specified Finite State Machine
ISG: InterSubblock Gap
ISI: Information Structure Implementation
Instrument Systems Installation
Internally Specified Index
Intersymbol Interference
ISIC: International Standard Industrial Classification
ISIS: Integrated Software Invocation System
ISK: Instruction Space Key
ISL: Interactive Simulation Language
Intersatellite Link
Intersystem Link
ISMEC: Information Service in Mechanical Engineering
ISMH: Input Source Message Handler
ISMM: International Society for Mini and Microcomputers
ISMS: Image Store Management System
ISN: Initial Sequence Number
Input Sequence Number
Internal Sequence Number
ISNOT: Is Not Equal To

ISO: Information Systems Office
International Standards Organization (International Organization for Standardization)
ISOC: Individual System/Organization Cost
ISP: Instruction Set Processor
ISPC: International Sound Program Center
ISPICE: Interactive Simulation Program with Integrated Circuit Emphasis
IS&R: Information Storage and Retrieval
ISR: Information Storage and Retrieval
Interrupt Service Routine
ISRAD: Integrated Software Research and Development
ISRM: Information Systems Resource Manager
ISS: Integrated Support System
Intelligent Support System
Ionosphere Sounding Satellite
ISSCC: International Solid-State Circuits Conference
ISSMB: Information Systems Standards Management Board
ISSN: International Standard Serial Number
ISSR: Information Storage, Selection, and Retrieval
ISSS: Integrated Support System Sort
ISSUE: Information System and Software Update Environment
IST: Internal Standard
ISTA: International Society for Technology Assessment
ISTAB: Information Systems Technical Advisory Board
ISTR: Indexed Sequential Table Retrieval

ISU: Instruction Storage Unit
Interface Sharing Unit
ISZ: Increment and Skip on Zero
IT: Indent Tab (character)
Information Technology
Input Terminal
Inspection Tag
Intelligent Terminal
Inventory Transfer
Inventory Turnover
ITA: Interface Test Adapter
ITAM: Interdata Telecommunications Access Method
ITAVS: Integrated Testing, Analysis and Verification System
ITB: Intermediate Text Block
Internal Transfer Bus
ITC: Installation Time and Cost
Integrated Transaction Controller
Intelligent Transaction Controller
Interdata Transaction Controller
International Telemetering Conference
ITDF: Interactive Transaction Dump Facility
ITDM: Intelligent Time Division Multiplexer
ITDNS: Integrated Tour Operating Digital Network Service
ITDS. Integrated Technical Data Systems
ITEM: Integrated Test and Maintenance
Interactive Technique for Effective Management
ITEMS: Incoterm Transaction Entry Management System
ITF: Integrated Test Facility
ITI: Interactive Terminal Interface
I-TIME: Instruction Time
itin: itinerary
ITL: Intermediate Transfer Language

ITM: Indirect Tag Memory
ITN: Integrated Teleprocessing Network
ITOS: Interactive Terminal-Oriented Software
ITP: Integrated Transaction Processor
Interactive Terminal Protocol
Interactive Transactional Program
ITPS: Interactive Text Preparation System
ITRA: Interdata Transaction Controller
ITRAC: Interdata Transaction Controller
ITS: Institute for Telecommunication Science
Interactive Terminal Support
Invitation To Send
ITT: Intertoll Trunk
ITU: International Telecommunication Union
ITV: Instructional Television
IU: Information Unit
Input Unit
Instruction Unit
Interface Unit
IUB: Instruction Used BIT
IURP: Integrated Unit Record Processor
IUS: Information Unit Separator
Interchange Unit Separator
IV: Independent Validation
Independent Verification
Interface Vector
IVA: Inventory Valuation Adjustment
IVDTS: Integrated Voice/Data Terminal
IVESS: Interactive Vehicle Scheduling System
IVG: Interrupt Vector Generator
IVM: Interface Virtual Machine

IVP: Installation Verification Procedure
IVT: Integrated Video Terminal
IV & V: Independent Verification and Validation
IWDS: Interactive Wholesale Distribution System
IWGDE: Interlaboratory Working Group for Data Exchange
IWP: International Word Processing Association
IWPA: International Word Processing Association
IWS: Instruction Work Stack
Interactive Work Station
IX: Index Register
IXC: Interexchange Channel
IXM: Index Manager
IXU: Index Translation Unit

J

j: job
   judgment
JA: Job Analysis
JAB: Job Analysis and Billing
JACC: Joint Automatic Control Conference
JACM: Journal of the Association for Computing Machinery
JAF: Job Accounting Facility
JAI: Job Accounting Interface
jam: jammed
JAR: Jump Address Register
JARS: Job Accounting Report System
JAS: Job Analysis System
JASIS: Journal of the American Society for Information Science
JAT: Job Accounting Table
JBS: Japanese Broadcast Satellite
JCB: Job Control Block
JCC: Job Control Card
JCIT: Jerusalem Conference on Information Technology
JCL: Job Control Language
JCLGEN: Job Control Language Generation
JCLPREP: Job Control Language Preprocessor
JCM: Job Cylinder Map
JCN: Jump on Condition
JCP: Job Control Processor
   Job Control Program
JCS: Job Control Statement
JCT: Job Control Table
JDL: Job Description Library
JDS: Job Data Sheet
JE: Job Entry
JECL: Job Entry Control Language

JEDEC: Joint Electronic Device Engineering Council
JEF: Japanese Processing Extended Feature
JEIDA: Japan Electronic Industry Development Association
JEMC: Joint Engineering Management Conference
JEPS: Job Entry Peripheral Services
JES: Job Entry System
JESSI: Joint European Submicron Silicon (EC)
JET: Journal Entries Transfer
JETS: Job Executive and Transport Satellite
JFCB: Job File Control Block
JFET: Junction Field Effect Transistor
JFN: Job File Number
JIC: Joint Information Center
JIRA: Japanese Industrial Robot Association
JIS: Japanese Industrial Standard
   Japanese Institute for Standards
   Job Information System
   Job Input Station
JISC: Japanese Industrial Standards Committee
JJ: Josephson Junction
JL: Job Library
   Job Lot
JM: Job Memory
   Job Mix
JMEM: Job Memory
jmp: jump
JMSX: Job Memory Switch Matrix
JOBDOC: Job Documentation
JOBLIB: Job Library

89

JOC: Job Order Costing
JOL: Job Organization Language
JOMO: Job Mix Optimization
JOVIAL: Jules' Own Version of International Algorithmic Language
JP: Job Processor
JPA: Job Pack Area
JPL: Jet Propulsion Laboratory
JPM: Joint Profit Maximization
JPU: Job Processing Unit
JR: Job Rotation
Joint Return
JSA: Japanese Standards Association
JSCS: Job Shop Control System
JSF: Job Services File
JSIA: Japan Software Industry Association
JSL: Job Specification Language
JSME: Japan Society of Mechanical Engineers
JSWAP: Job Swapping Memory
JT: Job Table
JTIDS: Joint Tactical Information Distribution System
JTPS: Job and Tape Planning System
JUG: Joint Users Group
JUN: Jump Unconditionally

K

k: kelvin
key
keyboard
kiloBIT
kilobyte
K: Measured Computer Storage Capacity
ka: kiloampere
kb: keyboard
kiloBIT
kilobyte
kbd: keyboard
KBE: Keyboard Entry
KBI: Key Buying Influence
kbit: kiloBIT
KBL: Keyboard Listener
KBPS: KiloBITs Per Second
kbs: kilobyte
kc: kilocycle
kch: kilocharacter
kchr: kilocharacter
KCL: Keystation Control Language
KCS: Kilocharacters Per Second
KCS/SO: Keyboard Class Select/Statistics Output
KCU: Keyboard Control Unit
KD: Key Definition
Keyboard and Display
KDE: Keyboard Data Entry
KDEM: Kurzweil Data Entry Machine
KDOS: Key Display Operating System
Key to Disk Operating System
KDP: Keyboard, Display, and Printer
KDS: Key Display System
Key-to-Diskette System
KDSS: Key to Disk Subsystem
KDT: Key Data Terminal
KEG: Key Gap
KEP: Key Entry Processing
keybd: keyboard
KF: Key Field
KFAS: Keyed File Access System
kg: kilogram
KGM: Key Generator Module
kh: kilohour
khz: kilohertz
KIC: Kernal Input Controller
KICU: Keyboard Interface Control Unit
KIL: Keyed Input Language
kilopac: kilopackets
KIM: Keyboard Input Matrix
KIPS: Knowledge Information Processing Systems
Thousands of Instructions Per Second
KIS: Keyboard Input Simulation
KISS: Keyed Indexed Sequential Search
KIST: Korea Institute of Science and Technology
KL: Key Length
klooj: kludge
km: kilometer
KMON: Keyboard Monitor
KOBOL: Key Station On-line Business-Oriented Language
KOPS: Thousands of Operations Per Second
KORSTIC: Korea Science and Technological Information Center
kp: keypunch
KPC: Keyboard/Printer Control
KPR: Keypunch Replacement

KR: Key Register
KRL: Knowledge Representation Language
KSAM: Keyed Sequential Access Method
KSDS: Key Sequenced Data Set
KSH: Key Strokes Per Hour
KSR: Keyboard Send/Receive
KSR/T: Keyboard Send/Receive Terminal
KST: Known Segment Table
KT: Key Tape
KTDS: Key-to-Disk Software
KTL: KEY-EDIT Terminal Language
KTM: Key Transport Module
kv: kilovolt
KVA: Kilovolt-Ampere
kw: kilowatt
kiloword
KWH: Kilowatt Hour
KWIC: Key Word In Context
KWOC: Keyword Out of Context
KXU: Keyword Transformation Unit

L

l: inductance
language
left
length
link
local
low
LA: Line Adapter
Local Address
Logical Address
LADDER: Language Access to Distributed Data with Error Recovery
LADS: Local Area Data Set
LAMA: Local Automatic Message Accounting
LAMP: Logic Analysis for Maintenance Planning
LAN: Local Area Network
LAP: Link Access Procedure
LAP-A: Byte-Oriented Link Access Procedure
LAP-B: BIT-Oriented Link Access Procedure
LAR: Limit Address Register
LARPS: Local and Remote Printing Station
LAS: Local Address Space
LASCOT: Large Screen Color Television
LASER: Light Amplification by Stimulation of Emitted Radiation
LASL: Los Alamos Scientific Laboratory
LASP: Local Attached Support Processor
LASS: Logistics Analysis Simulation System
LATA: Local Access and Transport Areas
LATS: Low Altitude Target Satellite
LAU: Line Adapter Unit
LAVA: Look Ahead Variable Acceleration
LB: Line Buffer
Logical Block
Lower Bound
LBA: Linear Bounded Automation
Local Bus Adapter
LBC: Left Bounded Context
Local Bus Controller
LBEN: Low Byte Enable
lbl: label
LBMI: Lease Base Machine Inventory
LBO: Line Build-Out
lbr: librarian
LBR: LASER Beam Recorder
LBS: Line Buffer System
LC: Line Concentrator
Line Control
Location Counter
Lower Case
L/C: Line Control
LCA: Line Control Adapter
Low Cost Automation
LCB: Line Control Block
Link Control Block
Logic Control Block
LCBX: Large Computerized (Private) Branch Exchange
LCC: Ledger Card Computer
Life Cycle Costs
LCCPMP: Life Cycle Computer Program Management Plan

LCD: Least Common Denominator
Liquid Crystal Display
LCDS: Low Cost Development System
LCES: Least Cost Estimating and Scheduling
LCF: Least Common Factor
Logical Channel Fill
LCFS: Last-Come, First Served
LCH: Logical Channel
LCHILD: Logical Child
LCL: Less than Carload Lot
Limited Channel Logout
Lower Control Limit
LCM: Large Core Memory
Least Common Multiple
Line Concentrator Module
Line Control Module
LCNTR: Location Counter
LCP: Language Conversion Program
Link Control Procedure
Local Control Point
Logical Construction of Programs
LCR: Least Cost Routing
LCS: Large Core Storage
LCSP: Logical Channels Switching Program
LCT: Latest Completing Time
Line Control Table
Logical Channel Termination
Low Cost Technology
LC/TC: Line Control/Task Control
LCU: Line Control Unit
Level Converter Unit
Local Control Unit
LCW: Line Control Word
LD: Logical Design
Long Distance
LDA: Local Data Administrator
Local Display Adapter
Logical Device Address
LDB: Large Data Base
Logical Data Base
LDBS: Local Data Base System

LDC: Local Display Controller
Low Density Center
Low Speed Data Channel
LDCS: Long Distance Control System
LDD: Local Data Distribution
LDL: Logical Data Base Level
LDLA: Limited Distance Line Adapter
LDM: Limited Distance Modem
Linear Delta Modulation
Local Data Manager
LDMS: Laboratory Data Management System
LDMX: Local Digital Message Exchange
LDO: Logical Device Order
LDT: Language Dependent Translator
LDU: Line Drive Unit
LDX: Long Distance Xerox
LE: Leading Edge
Less than or Equal (to)
LEAD: Learn, Execute, and Diagnose
LEADS: Law Enforcement Automated Data System
LED: Light-Emitting Diode
LEF: Line Expansion Function
LEM: Logic Enhanced Memory
Logical End of Media
len: length
LEQ: Less than or Equal (to)
let: letter
lev: level
LEVTAB: Level Table
LEX: Line Exchanger
LF: Line Feed
Low Frequency
LFC: Local Form Control
LFD: Local Frequency Distribution
LFF: Limited Fanout-Free
LFM: Local File Manager
LFN: Logical File Name
LFS: Local Format Storage

LFSR: Linear Feedback Shift Register
lft: left
LFU: Least Frequently Used
lg: large
LG: Line Generator
LGI: Linear Gate and Integrator
LGN: Logical Group Number
LHC: Left Hand Chain
LHF: List Handling Facility
LHS: Left-Hand Side
LIA: Laser Industry Association
Laser Institute of America
Loop Interface Address
Low Speed Input Adapter
lib: librarian
LIB: Line Interface Base
Line-Item Budget
LIBE: Library Editor
LIBEDIT: Library Editor
LIBMAN: Library Management
LIB/OL: LIBRARIAN/Online
libr: librarian
LIBRIS: Library Information System
LIDO: Logic In, Documents Out
LIED: Linkage Editor
LIF: Line Interface Feature
LIFER: Language Interface Facility with Ellipsis and Recursion
LIFO: Last In, First Out
LIH: Line Interface Handler
LILO: Last In, Last Out
LIM: Language Interpretation Module
Line Interface Module
Linear-Induction-Motion engine
LIMA: Logic-In-Memory Array
LIMIT: Lot-size Inventory Management Interpolation Technique
LIML: Linear Propagation Time Immediate Language
LINDI: Line to Disk
LINED: Line Editor
LINUS: Logical Inquiry and Update System
LIOCS: Logical Input/Output Control System
LIOP: Local Input/Output Processor
Low Speed Input/Output Processor
LIPID: Logical Page Identifier
LIPS: Laboratory Interconnecting Programming System
LIQT: Liquid Transient
liquid: liquidation
LIRS: Library Information Retrieval System
LISA: Linked Index Sequential Access
LISH: Last In, Still Here
LISP: List Processing
lit: literal
LIU: Line Interface Unit
LJE: Local Job Entry
LKM: Low Key Maintenance
LL: Leased Line
Local Line
Local Loopback
LLA: Leased Line Adapter
Long Line Adapter
Low Speed Line Adapter
LLBA: Language and Language Behavior Abstracts
LLG: Logical Line Group
LLI: Low Level Interface
LLIB: Load Module Librarian
LLL: Lawrence Livermore Laboratory
LLM: Low Level Multiplexer
LLN: Line-Link Network
LLRR: Log-Likelihood Ratio Representation
LM: Link Manager
Local Memory
Logic Module
Loop Multiplexer
LMB: Left Most BIT

LMBI: Local Memory Bank Interface
Local Memory Bus Interface
LMCSS: Letter Mail Code Sort System
LMI: Local Memory Image
LML: Logical Memory Level
LMOS: Loop Maintenance Operations System
LMS: List Management System
LMT: Local Mean Time
Logical Mapping Table
LMU: Line Monitor Unit
LMX: Local Multiplexer
ln: line
LN: Link Number
LNA: Low-Noise Amplifier
LNB: Local Name Base
LNE: Local Network Emulator
LNG: Liquefied Natural Gas
LNM: Logical Network Machine
LNN: Linear Nearest Neighbor
LNR: Low Noise Receiver
lo: low
LO: Local Oscillator
LOA: Low Speed Output Adapter
LOAP: Length of Adjacency Process
loc: local location
LOC: Location Counter
Location Dependent
LOF: Look Ahead on Fault
LOFAR: Low Frequency Analysis Recording
LOGFED: Log File Editor
LOGIK: Logical Organizing and Gathering of Information Knowledge
LOP: Line Oriented Protocol
LOR: Level Of Repair
Look Ahead on Request
LOS: Line Of Sight
Loss Of Signal
LOSR: Limit Of Stack Register
LOT: Light Operated Typewriter

LOTIS: Logic, Timing and Sequencing
LOTS: Low Overhead Time-Sharing System
LOWL: Low-Level Language
LP: Lead Programmer
Light Pen
Line Printer
Line Protocol
Linear Programming
Logic Probe
LPA: Link Pack Area
LPC: Linear Predictive Coding
LPCM: Linear Phase Code Modulation
LPE: Layer Primitive Equation
LPF: Low Pass Filter
LPI: Lines Per Inch
LPID: Logical Page Identifier
LPL: List Processing Language
Local Processor Link
LPM: Lines Per Minute
LPN: Logical Page Number
LPP: Latest Precedence Partition
LPS: Language for Programming-in-the-Small
Linear Programming System
Lines Per Second
LPT: Largest Processing Time First
Line Printer
LPTTL: Low Power Transistor-Transistor Logic
LPTV: Low Power Television service
LPU: Language Processor Unit
Line Printer Unit
Line Processing Unit
LPVT: Large Print Video Terminal
LR: Left to Right
Limit Register
Limited Response
Logical Record
L-R: Left to Right
LRA: Logical Record Access
LRAC: Long Run Average Cost curve

LRBC: Left-Right Bounded-Context
LRC: Longitudinal Redundancy Check
LRCC: Longitudinal Redundancy Check Character
LRCR: Longitudinal Redundancy Check Register
LRECL: Logical Record Length
LREP: Left-Bracketed Representation
LRIC: Long Run Incremental Costing
LRIP: Low Rate Initial Production
LRL: Linking Relocating Loader
 Logical Record Length
 Logical Record Location
LRR: Loop Regenerative Repeater
LRSP: Long Range Strategic Planning
LRU: Least Recently Used
LS: Least Significant
 Local Store
 Low Speed
LSA: Line-Sharing Adapter
 Lump-Sum Appropriation
LSAR: Local Storage Address Register
LSB: Least Significant Bit
 Lock, Stock and Barrel
LSC: Loop Station Connector
 Low Speed Concentrator
 Low Speed Interface Control
LSD: Language for Systems Development
 Least Significant Difference
 Least Significant Digit
 Line Signal Detector
LSDB: Launch Support Data Base
LSDR: Local Store Data Register
LSFR: Local Storage Function Register
LSI: Large-Scale Integration
LSIC: Large Scale Integrated Circuit (Circuitry)
LSID: Local Session Identification
LSL: Ladder Static Logic
 Link and Selector Language
LSM: Letter Sorting Machine
 Line Select Module
LSMA: Low Speed Multiplexer Arrangement
LSMLC: Low Speed Multiline Controller
LSP: Local Store Pointer
LSPTP: Low Speed Paper Tape Punch
LSQA: Local System Queue Area
LSR: Local Shared Resources
 Local Storage Register
 Low Speed Reader
LSS: Language for Symbolic Simulation
LST: Landing Ship Tank
 Landing Ship Transport
 Latest Starting Time
 Local Standard Time
LSTTL: Low Power Schottky Transistor Transistor Logic
LS/TTL: Low Power Schottky Transistor Transistor Logic
LSU: Least Significant Unit
 Library Storage Unit
 Line-Sharing Unit
 Load Storage Unit
 Local Storage Unit
LSUP: Loader Storage Unit Support Program
LSX: LSI-UNIX System
L&T: Language and Terminal
LT: Less Than
 Line Terminator
LTA: Logical Transient Area
LTB: Logical Twin Backward Pointer
LTBL: Level Table
LTC: Line Time Clock
 Local Terminal Controller
LTD: Line Transfer Device
LTF: Logical Twin Forward Pointer
LTH: Logical Track Header

LTM: Leverage Transaction Merchant
Long Term Memory
LTOC: Lowest Total Overall Cost
LTPD: Lot Tolerance Percent Defective
ltr: letter
LTRS: Letters Shift
LTS: Line Transient Suppression
LTT: Long-Term Trend
LTU: Line Termination Unit
LU: Logical Unit
LUB: Logical Unit Block
LUE: Link Utilization Efficiency
LUF: Limiting System Utilization Factor
LU-LU: Logical Unit to Logical Unit
LUN: Logical Unit Number
LUSVC: Logical Unit Services Manager
L/V: Loader/Verifier
LVA: Line Voltage Analyzer
Local Virtual Address
LW: Last Word
LWA: Last Word Address
LWB: Lower Bound
LWC: Loop Wiring Connector
LXMAR: Load External Memory Address Register

M

m: machine
   magnetization
   mantissa
   master
   mega
   memory
   meter
   milli
   mode
   modem
   monitor
   multiplier
ma: milliampere
M&A: Maintenance and Administration
MA: Manufacturing Assembly
   Memory Address
MAB: Macroaddress Bus
mac: macro
MAC: Machine Aided Cognition
   Maintenance Allocation Chart
   Memory Access Controller
   Message Authenticator Code
   Multiaccess Computing (Computer)
   Multiple Access Control
MACC: Micro Asynchronous Communications Controller
MACDAC: Man Communication and Display to Automatic Computer
MACE: Management Applications in a Computer Environment
mach: machine
   machinery
maclib: macrolibrary
macp: macroprocessor
macro: macroassembler
   macroprocessor

macrol: macrolanguage
MACS: Monitoring and Control Station
   Multiline Automatic Calling System
MACSYM: Measurement and Control System
MAD: Mean Absolute Deviation
MADCAP: Mathematical Problems and Set Operations
MADR: Microprogram Address Register
MAE: Memory Address Extension
MAFIA: Multiaccess Executive with Fast Interrupt Acceptance
mag: macrogenerator
   magnetic
MAGEN: Matrix and Report Generator
MAGPIE: Machine Automatically Generating Production Inventory Evaluation
MAHR: Milliampere Hour
MAI: Machine Aided Indexing
   Multiple Access Interface
maint: maintenance
MAJSR: Major State Register
MAL: Maximal Acceptable Load
   Memory Access Logic
   Meta Assembly Language
MAM: Memory Allocation Manager
   Multiapplication Monitor
MAMS: Manufacturing Applications Management System
man: manual
   manufacture
MANDATE: Multiline Automatic Network Diagnostic and Transmission Equipment

_manf: manufacture
    manufacturer
    manufacturing
MANIAC: Mathematical Analyzer Numerical Integrator And Computer
    Mechanical And Numerical Integrator And Computer
MANMAN: Manufacturing Management
manuf: manufacture
    manufacturing
MANUPACS: Manufacturing Planning and Control System
MAOS: Metal Alumina Dielectric Oxide Semiconductor
MAP: Macroassembly Program
    Maintenance Analysis Procedures
    Management Analysis and Projection
    Memory Allocation and Protection
    Microprogrammed Array Processor
MAPD: Maximum Allowable Percent Defective
MAPGEN: Map Generator
MAPI: Machinery and Allied Products Institute
MAPICS: Manufacturing, Accounting, and Production Information Control System
MAPS: Management Analysis and Planning System
    Manufacturing and Production System
    Multivariate Analysis, Participation, and Structure
MAR: Macroaddress Register
    Memory Address Register
    Microprogram Address Register

MARC: Machine Readable Catalog
marg: margin
    marginal
MART: Maintenance Analysis and Review Technique
    Mean Active Repair Time
mas: macroassembler
MAS: Management (Managerial) Appraisal System
MASCOT: Modular Approach to Software Construction Operation and Test
MASER: Microwave Amplification by Stimulated Emission of Radiation
MASIS: Management and Scientific Information System
MASK: Multiple Amplitude Shift Keying
MASM: Meta Assembler
MASS: Multiple Access Switching System
MASTER: Multiple Access Shared-Time Executive Routines
MAT: Medial Axis Transformation
    Memory Address Test
MATE: Modular Automatic Test Equipment System
MATEX: Macrotext Editor
MATLAN: Matrix Manipulation Language
MATR: Management Access To Records
MATS: Multiple-Access Time Sharing
MATV: Master Antenna Television System
MAU: Memory Access Unit
    Multiple Access Unit
max: maximum
mb: megaBIT
    megabyte
MB: Memory Buffer
    Memory Bus

MBC: Memory Bus Controller
  Multiple Basic Channel
MBCD: Modified Binary Coded Decimal
MBD: Magnetic Bubble Domain Device
MBE: Molecular Beam Epitaxy
MBF: Monotonic Boolean Function
MBI: Memory Bank Interface
MBIO: Microprogrammable Block Input/Output
mbit: megaBIT
MBM: Magnetic Bubble Memory
mbr: member
MBR: Memory Base Register
  Memory Buffer Register
MBU: Memory Buffer Unit
m-byte: megabyte
mc: megacycle
MC: Magnetic Card
  Master Control
  Memory Control
  Memory Controller
MCA: Multiprocessor Communications Adapter
MCAR: Machine Check Analysis and Recording
MCB: Microcomputer Board
MCBF: Mean Characters Between Failures
  Mean Cycles Between Failure
MCC: Micro CPU Chip
  Miscellaneous Common Carrier
  Multichannel Communications Controller
  Multichip Carrier
MCCD: Message Cryptographic Check Digits
MCCU: Multiple Channel Control Unit
MCD: Monitor Console Routine Dispatcher
MCDBSU: Master Control and Data Buffer Storage Unit

MCDS: Management Control Data System
MCEL: Machine Check Extended Logout
MCF: Magnetic Card File
mch: megacharacter
MCH: Machine Check Handler
MCHB: Maintenance Channel Buffer Register
MCHC: Maintenance Channel Command Register
mchr: megacharacter
MCHTR: Maintenance Channel Transmit Receiver Register
MCI: Machine Check Interruption
MCIC: Machine Check Interruption Code
  Multichannel Interface Controller
MCIS: Maintenance Control Information System
  Map and Chart Information System
  Materials Control Information System
MCL: Microprogram Control Logic
  Monitor Control Language
MCLA: Microcoded Communications Line Adapter
MCLK: Master Clock
MCM: Memory Control Module
MCMC: Multiple-Channel/Multiple-Choice
MCMS: Multichannel Memory System
MCOS: Microprogrammable Computer Operating System
MCP: Marginal-Cost Pricing
  Master Control Program
  Message Control Program
MCPG: Media Conversion Program Generator
MCPU: Multiple Central Processing Unit

MCR: Magnetic Card Reader
Master Control Register
Master Control Routine
Memory Control Register
MCRR: Machine Check Recording and Recovery
MCS: Maintenance Control System
Management Control System
Master Control System
Megacycles per Second
Message Control Supervisor
Message Control System
Microcomputer System
Microprogram Certification System
Multichannel Communications Support
Multiple Console Support
MCST: Magnetic Card Selectric Typewriter
MCU: Maintenance Control Unit
Management Control Unit
Master Control Unit
Memory Control Unit
Microprocessor Control Unit
Microprogram Control Unit
Multiprocessor Communications Unit
Multisystem Communications Unit
MCUSR: Memory Control Unit Special Register
mcz: mechanized
MD: Memory Data Register
Memory Decrement
MDA: Multidimensional Access
MDAC: Multiplying Digital to Analog Converter
MDAP: Machining and Display Application Program
MDB: Master Data Bank
MDC: Memory Disk Controller
Microcomputer Development Center
Multiple Device Controller
MDC&R: Management Data Collection and Reporting
MDCU: Magnetic Disk Control Unit
Multidisplay Control Unit
MDD: Magnetic Disk Drive
MDES: Multidata Entry System
MDF: Main Distributing Frame
Microcomputer Development Facility
MDL: Macrodata Language
Maintenance Diagnostic Logic
Microprocessor Development Lab
MDLC: Multiple Data Link Controller
MDM: Multiplexer/Demultiplexer
MDNF: Minimal Disjunctive Normal Form
MDP: Main Data Path
Microdisplay Processor
MDPS: MICR Document Processing System
MDQS: Management Data Query System
MDR: Memory Data Register
Minimum Daily Requirement
Miscellaneous Data Record
MDS: Maintenance Data System
Management Decision System
Management Display System
Microcomputer Development System
Microprocessor Development System
Modular Data System
Multipoint Distribution Service
MDSS: Microprocessor Development Support System
MDT: Mean Down Time
Merchant Deposit Transmittal
MDU: Maintenance Diagnostic Unit
ME: Memory Element

MEA: Memory Inspection Ending Address
MEB: Modem Evaluation Board
MECO: Measurement and Control
meg: megabyte
MEGAFLOP: One Million Floating-Point Operations Per Second
MELCU: Multiple External Line Control Unit
mem: memorandum
memory
ME/ME: Multiple Entry/Multiple Exit
MEMR: Memory Read
MEMSEL: Memory Select
MEMW: Memory Write
MEP: Microfiche Enlarger Printer
MERLIN: Machine Readable Library Information
MERM: Multilateral Exchange Rate Model
MES: Metal Semiconductor
Multiple Earning Statement
MESA: Modularized Equipment Storage Assembly
mesg: message
MET: Management Engineering Team
MEU: Memory Expansion and Protection Unit
MEWT: Matrix Electrostatic Writing Technique
mf: microfarad
MF: Master File
Medium Frequency
MFCA: Multifunction Communications Adapter
MFCM: Multifunction Card Machine
M&FCS: Management and Financial Control System
MFCU: Multifunction Card Unit
mfd: manufactured
MFD: Master File Directory

MFDSUL: Multifunction Data Set Utility Language
MFE: Multifunction Equipment
Multifunction Executive
MFF: Match Flip Flop
mfg: manufacturing
MFG: Message Flow Graph
MFLD: Message Field
MFLOPS: Million Floating Point Operations Per Second
MFLP: Multifile Linear Programming
MFM: Modified Frequency Modulation
MFP: Multiform Printer
MFPC: Multifunction Protocol Converter
MFPE: Minimum Final Prediction Error
mfr: manufacture
manufactured
manufacturer
MFR: Multifrequency Receiver
MFS: Message Format Services
MFSK: Multiple Frequency Shift Keying
MFSL: Mathematical and Functional Subroutine Library
mfst: manifest
MFT: Mutiprogramming with a Fixed Number of Tasks
mg: milligram
MG: Motor Generator
MGG: Matrix Generator Generator
MGP: Multiple Goal Programming
mgr: manager
mgt: management
MH: Materials Handling
Message Handler
MHD: Moving Head Disk
MHE: Materials Handling Equipment
MHI: Materials Handling Institute
MHP: Message Handling Processor
MHS: Multiple Host Support

MHSDC: Multiple High Speed Data Channel
mhz: megahertz
mi: microinstruction
MI: Machine-Independent Maintenance Interface
Maskable Interrupt
Memory Input Register
Memory Interface
MIA: Multiplex Interface Adapter
MIACS: Manufacturing Information and Control System
MIAR: Microaddress Register
MIARS: Maintenance Information Automated Retrieval System
MIAS: Management Information and Accounting System
MIAT: Mean Interarrival Time
MIB: Microinstruction Bus
MICA: Macroinstruction Compiler Assembler
MICALL: Microprocedure Call
MICOT: Minimum Completion Time
MICR: Magnetic Ink Character Recognition
micro: microcomputer
microprocessor
MICROM: Microinstruction Read Only Memory
micron: micrometer
MICROSIM: Microinstruction Simulator
MICS: Management Information and Control System
micsim: microsimulator
MID: Message Input Description
MIDAR: Microdiagnostics for Analysis and Repair
MIDAS: Digital Stimulated Analog Computing program
Management Interactive Data Accounting System
Memory Implement Data Acquisition Systems
Microprogrammable Integrated Data Acquisition System
MIDDLE: Microprogram Design and Description Language
MIDEF: Microprocedure Definition
MIDMS: Machine Independent Data Management System
MIDS: Management Information and Decision System
Mode Indicator Levels
Multimode Information Distribution System
MIF: Master Index File
MIGET: Miniature Interface General Purpose Economy Terminal
MIH: Missing Interruption Handler
Multiplex Interface Handler
MIKADOS: Mini Instant Keyboard Assembler, Debug and Operating System
mil: One thousandth of an inch
MIL: Microimplementation Language
Module Interconnection Language
MIM: Modem Interface Module
MIMD: Multiple Instruction, Multiple Data
MIMI: International Symposium and Exhibition of Mini and Microcomputers and their Applications
MIMOLA: Machine Independent Microprogramming Language
min: minimum
minority
minute
MIND: Modular Interactive Network Designer
MINDD: Minimum Due Date
mini: minicomputer
MINI: Minicomputer Industry National Interchange
MINIT: Minimum Idle Time

MINOS: Modular Input/Output System
MINSD: Minimum Planned Start Date
MINSOP: Minimum Slack Time Per Operation
MIO: Multiple Input/Output
MIOP: Multiplexer Input/Output Processor
MIOS: Metal Insulator Oxide Silicon
Modular Input/Output System
MIP: Material In Process
Mixed Integer Programming
Multipurpose Information Processor
MIPAS: Management Information Planning and Accountancy Service
MIPS: Million Instructions Per Second
MIR: Memory Input Register
Microinstruction Register
MIRAC: Master Index Remote Access Capability
MIRR: Material Inspection and Retrieval Report
MIS: Management Information Service
Management Information System
Metal-Insulator-Semiconductor
MISAM: Multiple Index Sequential Access Method
MISD: Multiple Instruction, Single Data
MISE: Mean Integrated Square Error
MISER: Minimum Size Executive Routines
MIS-MDS: Multiple Instruction Streams - Multiple Data Streams
MISP: Microelectronics Industry Support Program (UK)
MIS-SDS: Multiple Instruction Streams - SIngle Data Streams
MISSION: Manufacturing Information System Support Integrated Online
MISTI: Multipurpose International Securities Trading Information
MIT: Master Instruction Tape
Modular Intelligent Terminal
MITA: Microcomputer Industry Trade Association
MITE: Microprocessor Industrial Terminal
MITI: Ministry of International Trade and Industry (Japan)
MITS: Management Information and Text System
MIU: Modem Interface Unit
MIW: Microinstruction Word
MIX: Microprogram Index Register
MJD: Management Job Description
MJMT: Mean Job Mill Time
mk: mask
MKH: Multiple Key Hashing
mkr: maker
MKS: Meter-Kilogram-Second
mkt: market
ml: multileaving
ML: Machine Language
Maximum Likelihood
Memory Location
Microprogramming Language
MLA: Matching Logic and Adder
Multiple Line Adapter
MLB: Multilayer Board
MLC: Magnetic Ledger Card
Microprogram Location Counter
Multilayer Ceramic
Multiline Controller
MLCI: MULTILINK Channel Interface
MLCP: Multiline Communications Processor

MLCU: Magnetic Ledger Card Unit
MLD: Machine Language Debugger
MLE: Maximum Likelihood Estimate (Estimation)
MLFS: Master Library File System
MLI: Machine Language Instruction
Multileaving Interface
MLIA: Multiplex Loop Interface Adapter
MLIM: Matrix Login-In Memory
MLM: Multileaving Line Manager
MLP: Machine Language Program
MLPA: Modified Link Pack Area
MLR: Minimum Lending Rate
MLRTP: Multileaving Remote Terminal Processor
MLS: Machine Literature Searching
Microprocessor Line Set
MLTA: Multiple Line Terminal Adapter
MLU: Memory Logic Unit
Multiple Logical Unit
mm: millimeter
MM: Main Memory
Maintenance Manual
Mass Memory
Materials Measurement
Memory Module
MMA: Major Maintenance Availability
Multiple Module Access
MMAR: Main Memory Address Register
MMAS: Manufacturing Management Accounting Systems
MMB: Multiport Memory Bank
MMC: Main Memory Controller
Multiport Memory Controller
MMCA: Message-Mode Communications Adapter
MMCC: MultiMini Computer Compiler
MMDDYY: Designation of six character date field (month, day, and year)

MMDS: Multichannel Multipoint Distribution Service
MMF: Magnetomotive Force
MMH/OH: Maintenance Man-Hours per Operating Hour
MMI: Main Memory Interface
Man-Machine Interface
Multimessage Interface
Multiport Memory Interface
MMIS: Maintenance Management Information System
MMIU: Multiport Memory Interface Unit
MMM: Main Memory Module
Man/Machine Model
Monolithic Main Memory
Multiport Memory Multiplexer
MMOS: Message Multiplexer Operating System
MMP: Main Microprocessor
Multiple Microprocessors
MMPS: Manufacturing Material Planning System
MMPU: Memory Management and Protection Unit
MMR: Main Memory Register
Memory Management Register
Multiple Match Resolver
MMS: Man-Machine System
Memory Management System
MMSE: Minimum Mean-Squared Error
MMU: Main Memory Unit
Memory Management Unit
Memory Mapping Unit
mn: mnemonic
MN: Message Number
MNA: Multishare Network Architecture
MNCS: Multipoint Network Control System

MNDP: Multinational Data Processing
mne: mnemonic
MNET: Measuring Network
MNF: Multisystem Networking Facility
mnfrs: manufacturers
MNOS: Metal-Nitride Oxide Semiconductor
MNR: Maximum Number of Records
mo: microoperation
month
MO: Manually Operated
Memory Output
MOAT: Methods Of Appraisal and Test
MOC: Management-Oriented Computing
mod: model
modification
modulate
MOD: Message Output Description
MODAC: Modular Data Acquisition
MODACS: Modular Data Acquisition and Control Subsystem
MODE: Merchant-Oriented Data Entry
MODEM: Modulator-Demodulator
MODI: Modular Optical Digital Interface
MODUS: Modular One Dynamic User System
MOE: Measure Of Effectiveness
MOHOL: Machine-Oriented Higher Order Language
MOL: Machine Oriented Language
MOLE: Market Odd-Lot Execution system
MOM: Maintenance Of Membership
mon: monitor
MONGEN: Monitor Generator
MONITOR: Strategic Analyses, Forecasting and Evaluation in Matters of Research and Technology (EC)
MOPP: Mechanization of Planning Processes
MOPS: Mechanization Outside Plant Scheduling System
Million Operations Per Second
MOR: Management by Objectives and Results
Memory Output Register
MORIF: Microprogram Optimization Technique Considering Resource Occupancy and Instruction Formats
MOS: Management Operating Systems
Manufacturing Operating Systems
Margin Of Safety
Memory Oriented System
Metal-Oxide Semiconductor
Metal-Oxided Silicon
Microprogram Operating System
Multiprogramming Operating System
MOSFET: Metal Oxide Semiconductor Field Effect Transistor
MOS ROM: Metal-Oxide Semiconductor Read-Only Memory
MOSS: Market Oversight Surveillance System
MOST: Management Operation System Technique
Modular Office System Terminal
MOUTH: Modular Output Unit for Talking to Humans
mp: microprocessor
microprogram
multiprocessing
multiprocessor
MP: Mathematical Programming

MPA: Multiple Peripheral Adapter
MPACT: Microprocessor Application to Control-Firmware Translator
MPAR: Microprogram Address Register
MPC: Microprogram Control
  Microprogram Counter
  Modular Peripheral Interface Converter
MPCC: Microprogrammable Communications Controller
  Multiprotocol Communications Controller
MPCI: Multiport Programmable Communications Interface
MPCM: Microprogram Control Memory
MPCR: Microprogram Count Register
MPD: Missing Pulse Detector
MPDS: Message Processing and Distribution System
MPE: Maximum Permitted Error
  Memory Parity Error
MPES: Multiprogramming Executive System
MPF: Manufacturing Progress Function
MPGS: Microprogram Generating System
MPI: Microprocessor Interface
MPL: Macroprocedure Language
  Message Processing Language
  Microprogramming Language
  Multischedule Private Line
mplx: multiplexer
mplxr: multiplexer
MPM: Microprogram Memory
  Multiprogramming Monitor
MPMC: Microprocessor Memory Controller
MPMCU: Microprogram Memory Control Unit
MPMI: Multiport Memory Interface
MPN: Most Probable Number
MPO: Memory Protect Override
MPOS: Multiprogramming Operating System
MPP: Message Processing Program
  Multiple-Product Pricing
  Multiprogrammable Processor
  Multiprogrammable Processor Port
MPR: Microprogram Register
MPROM: Mask Programmed Read Only Memory
MPS: Macroprocessing System
  Mathematical Programming System
  Microprocessing System
  Multiprocessing System
  Multiprogramming System
MP/SCM: Multiport Semiconductor Memory
MPSK: Multiple Phase Shift Keying
MPSS: Multipurpose System Simulator
MPSX: Mathematical Programming System Extended
mpt: multipoint
MPT: Memory Processing Time
MPU: Memory Protection Unit
  Microprocessing Unit
  Microprocessor Unit
mpx: multiplexer
MPX: Multiprogramming Executive
mpy: multiplier
MQ: Multiplier-Quotient
MQE: Message Queue Element
MQL: Mean Queue Length
M&R: Maintainability and Reliability
  Maintainability and Repairs
  Maintenance and Repair
MR: Maintenance Report
  Mask Register
  Master Reset
  Memorandum Report
  Memory Reclaimer
  Modular Redundancy
  Multiple Register
  Multiple Regression

MRA: Materials Requirement Analysis
MRB: Modification Review Board
MRC: Machine Readable Code
Memory Request Controller
MRCS: Multiple Report Creation System
MRCU: Mini-Remote Control Unit
MRD: Memory Read
MRDF: Machine Readable Data File
MRDOS: Mapped Real-Time Disk Operating System
MRDY: Message Ready
MRE: Memory Register Exponent
MREGAD: Multiplexer Regenerator Address
MRH: Magnetoresistive Recording Head
MRI: Memory Reference Instruction
MRIO: Multiregional Input/Output
MRJE: Multileaving Remote Job Entry
MRJE/WS: Multileaving Remote Job Entry/Work Station
MRL: Machine Representation Language
MRO: Maintenance, Repair and Operating (Operational)
MROM: Macroread Only Memory
MRP: Manufacturing Resources Planning
Material Requirements Planning
MRPC: Multiregional Processing Center
MRR: Multiple Response Resolver
MRS: Management Reporting System
MRST: Master Reset
MRT: Maximum-Repair-Time
Mean-Repair-Time
MRU: Minimum Resolvable Unit
ms: millisecond
M&S: Materials and Services
MS: Main Storage
Maintenance and Service
Management Science
Manufacturing System
Margin of Safety
Mass Storage
Master - Slave
Material Specification
Metric System
MSA: Mass Storage Adapter
MSB: Most-Significant Bit
MSBR: Maximum Storage Bus Rate
MSBY: Most Significant Byte
MSC: Mass Storage Control
Mass Storage Controller
Message Switching Concentration
Multisystem Coupling
msch: microscheduler
MSCTC: Mass Storage Control Table Create
MSCU: Modular Store Control Unit
MSCW: Marked Stack Control Word
MSD: Modem Sharing Device
Most Significant Digit
MSDB: Main Storage Data Base
MSDS: Message Switching Data Service
MSDTR: Multispeed Digital Tape Recorded
MSE: Mean Square Error
msec: millisecond
MSEL: Master Scenario Events List
MSF: Mass Storage Facility
msg: message
MSGFLG: Message Flag
Mshp: Machine Shop
MSHP: Maintain System History Program
MSI: Medium Scale Integration
MSIO: Mass Storage Input-Output
MSIS: Multistate Information System
MSK: Minimal Shift Keying
MSL: Machine Specification Language
Mathematical Subprogram Library
MSM: Memory Storage Module

MSNF: Multisystem Networking Facility
MSO: Multistage Operations
MSOS: Mass Storage Operating System
MSP: Manual Switching Position
Modular System Program
MSR: Magnetic Send-Receive
Mark Sense Reading
Mechanized Storage and Retrieval
MSS: Mass Storage System
Multispectral Scanner
MSSC: Mass Storage System Communicator
mssg: message
MST: Master Station
Mean Service Time
Minimal Spanning Tree
Mountain Standard Time
mstr: master
MSU: Mass Storage Unit
Memory Storage Unit
MSV: Mass Storage Volume
Multiservice Vendor
MSVC: Mass Storage Volume Control
MSYN: Master Synchronization
mt: multitasking
multithreading
MT: Machine Translation
Magnetic Tape
Maximum Total
Measured Time
Mountain Time
MTB: Maximum Theoretical Bandwidth
MTBCD: Mean-Time-Between-Confirmed-Defects
MTBCF: Mean-Time-Between-Component-Failure
MTBD: Mean-Time-Between-Defects
MTBE: Mean-Time Between-Errors
MTBF: Mean-Time-Between-Failures
MTBI: Mean-Time-Between Interrupts

MTBM: Mean-Time-Between-Maintenance
MTBO: Mean-Time-Between-Overhauls
MTBR: Mean-Time-Between-Repairs
MTBSE: Mean-Time-Between-Software Errors
MTBSF: Mean-Time-Between-Significant-Failures
MTBUM: Mean-Time-Between Unscheduled-Maintenance
MTBUR: Mean-Time-Between Unscheduled-Removal
MTC: Magnetic Tape Channel
Magnetic Tape Controller
Maintenance Time Constraint
Message Transmission Controller
MTCA: Multiple Terminal Communications Adapter
MTCS: Minimum Teleprocessing Communications System
MTCU: Magnetic Tape Control Unit
MTD: Month To Date
MTE: Multiple Terminal Emulator
MTEL: Macrotime Event List
MTEX: Multithreading Executive
MTF: Mean-Time-to-Failure
Modulation Transfer Function
MTH: Magnetic Tape Handler
MTI: Mission Time Improvement
MTIF: Mission Time Improvement Factor
MTIRA: Machine Tool Industry Research Association
MTL: Merged Transistor Logic
MTM: Methods-Time Measurement
Modification Transmittal Memorandum
MTO: Made-To-Order
Master Terminal Operator
MTOS: Magnetic Tape Operating System
Multitasking Operating System

MTPT: Minimal Total Processing Time
mtr: monitor
MTR: Magnetic Tape Reader
Modular Tree Representation
MTRS: Magnetic Tape Reformatting System
MTS: Manned Teller System
Member-Technical Staff
Message Telecommunication Service
Multiple Terminal System
Multiple Transient System
MTSF: Mean-Time-To-System-Failure
MTSO: Multiprogramming Time-Sharing Operating System
MTST: Magnetic Tape Selectric Typewriter
MTT: Magnetic Tape Terminal
Message Transfer Time
MTTF: Mean-Time-To-Failure
MTTFF: Mean-Time-To-First-Failure
MTTFSF: Mean-Time-To-First-System-Failure
MTTFSR: Mean-Time-To-First System-Repair
MTTOP: Machine Tool Trigger Order Program
MTTR: Maximum Time to Repair
Mean-Time-To-Repair
Mean-Time-To-Restore
MTTS: Multitask Terminal System
MTTSF: Mean-Time-To-System-Failure
MTU: Magnetic Tape Unit
Memory Transfer Unit
Modem Transfer Unit
MTUR: Mean-Time-To-Unscheduled-Replacement
MTX: Multitasking Executive
Multiterminal Executive

mu: multiuser
MU: Machine Unit
Memory Unit
Multiple Unit
MUBUS: Microprocessor Bus
MUD: Master User Directory
MUEXEC: Multiuser Executive
MUF: Material Unaccounted For
Maximum Usable Frequency
MUIR: Microinstruction Register
mul: multiplexer
MUL: Master Urgency List
mult: multiple
multiplier
multi: multiple
MUM: Methodology for Unmanned Manufacturing
Multiuser Monitor
MUR: Multiuse Register
MURTS: Multiple User Remote Terminal Supervisor
MUS: Multiprogramming Utility System
MUSIL: Multiprogramming Utility System Interpretive Language
MUST: Multipurpose User-Oriented Software Technology
MUTEX: Multiuser Terminal Executive
MUTT: Multiuse Terminal Translator
mux: multiplexer
mv: millivolt
MV: Mean Variation
MVDS: Modular Video Data System
MVFG: Multivariable Function Generator
MVM: Manager Virtual Machine
MVS: Multiple Virtual Storage
Multiple Virtual System
MVS/SE: Multiple Virtual Storage/System Extensions

MVT: Multiprogramming with a Variable number of Tasks
mw: milliwatt
MW: Man Week
Million Words
mwd: megaword
MWS: Multiwork Station
MXA: Main Exchange Area
MXC: Multiplexer Channel
MXM: Matrix Memory

N

n: nano
  negative
  node
  number
  numeric
  numerical
na: nanoampere
NA: No Action
  No Approval required
  Not Accurate
  Not And
  Not Applicable
  Not Authorized
  Not Available
  Numerical Aperture
N/A: Name and Address
NAA: Noise Analysis Approach
NAABSA: Not Always Afloat But Safe Aground
NAC: Network Access Controller
NACK: Negative Acknowledgment
NAD: No Apparent Defect
NADUG: National Data Manager Users' Group
NAE: National Academy of Engineering
NAED: National Association of Electrical Distributors
NAF: National Association of Independent Computer Companies
  Network Access Facility
NAI: Net Annual Inflow
  No Action Indicated
NAICC: National Association of Independent Computer Companies
NAK: Negative Acknowledge (character)
NAL: New Assembly Language
NAM: Network Access Machine
  Network Access Method
NAN: Network Application Node
NAND: Not-And
NAP: Network Access Protocol
  Noise Analysis Program
NAR: No Action Required
NAT: No Action Taken
NATS: Negative Authorization Terminal System
NAU: Network Addressable Unit
NB: Narrow Band
  Noise Block
NBCD: Natural Bindary Coded Decimal
NBFM: Narrow Band Frequency Modulation
NBFS: New Balanced File Organization Scheme
NBNC: Noted But Not Corrected
NBPM: Narrow Band Phase Modulation
nbr: number
NBS: Numeric Backspace character
NC: Narrow Coverage
  Network Control
  No Connection
  Normally Closed
  Numerical Control
  Numerically Controlled
NCA: Noncontractual Authorization
NCAM: Network Communication Access Method
NCB: Network Control Block
NCC: National Computer Center
  National Computer Conference
  National Control Center
NCCF: Network Communications Control Facility

113

NCD: Network Cryptographic Device
NCDS: Numerical Control Distribution System
NCE: Network Connection Element
NCF: National Communications Forum
NCH: Network Connection Handler
NCI: No Currency Involved
 Non Coded Information
NCL: Network Control Language
NCM: Network Control Module
NCMT: Numerical Control of Machine Tools
NCN: Network Control Node
NCO: Number Controlled Oscillator
NCP: Network Control Processor
 Network Control Program
NCPAS: National Computer Program Abstract Service
NCS: National Communications System
 Network Control System
NCU: Network Control Unit
 Number Crunching Unit
NCV: No Core Value
ND: No Date
 No Defects
 Not Dated
 Not Desirable
NDAC: Not Data Accepted
NDAM: New Disk Access Method
NDBMS: Network Data Base Management System
NDC: Network Diagnostic Control
 Normalized Device Coordinates
NDD: Nondelivery Diagnostic
NDF: No Defect Found
 Nondeterministic FORTRAN
NDIR: Nondispersive Infrared
NDLC: Network Data Link Control
NDMS: Network Design and Management System
NDR: Nondestructive Read
NDRO: Nondestructive Readout
NDS: Network Data Series

NDT: Network Description Table
NE: Not Equal (to)
NEA: National Electronics Association
NEAT: National Electronic Autocoding Technique
NEC: National Electrical Code
 Not Elsewhere Classified
NED: No Expiration Date
NEF: Noise Equivalent Flux
neg: negative
negl: negligence
NEI: Not Elsewhere Indicated
NEMA: National Electronics Manufacturers' Association
net: network
NET: Not Earlier Than
NETA: New England Telecommunications Association
NETCON: Network Control
NETGEN: Network Generation
NETOP: Network Operator Process
NETSET: Network Synthesis & Evaluation Technique
NETT: Network for Environmental Technology Transfer (EC)
NEXT: Near End Cross Talk
NF: Normal Form
NFAIS: National Federation of Abstracting and Indexing Services
NFAM: Network File Access Method
NFAP: Network File Access Protocol
NFC: Not Favorably Considered
NFD: No Fixed Date
NFE: Network Front End
NFEA: National Federated Electrical Association
NFETM: National Federation of Engineers' Tools Manufacturers
NFF: No Fault Found
NFT: Networks File Transfer
NGG: Neadymium Gallium Garnet
NGP: Network Graphics Protocol
NGT: Nominal Group Technique

nhz: nanohertz
NI: Noninhibitable Interrupt
  Normal Information
NIA: No Input Acknowledge
NIB: Node Initialization Block
NIBL: National Industrial Basic Language
NIC: Network Information Center
  Network Interface Control
NICE: National Information Conference and Exposition
NICS: Network Integrity Control System
NIF: Network Information File
NIFs: Not In Files
NIFO: Next-In, First-Out
NIH: Not Invented Here
NILE: Number of Inverters along any Loop is Even
NIM: Network Interface Machine
  Network Interface Monitor
NIMMS: Nineteen Hundred Integrated Modular Management System
NIOPSWL: New Input/Output Program Status Word Location
NIP: Non Impact Printer
  Nucleus Initialization Program
NIS: Network Information Service
  Network Interface System
NIST: National Institute of Standards & Technology
NIT: Network Interface Task
NJCL: Network Job Control Language
NJE: Network Job Entry
NJI: Network Job Interface
NJOBS: Number of Jobs
NL: New-Line (character)
  No Label
NLA: Normalized Local Address
NLC: Network Language Center
NLOS: Natural Language Operating System
NLT: Not Later Than
  Not Less Than

NM: Network Manager
NMA: National Micrographics Association
NMC: Network Management Center
NMF: New Master File
NMI: Nonmaskable Interrupt
NMO: Number of critical Micro-operations
NMOS: N-Channel Metal Oxide Semiconductor
NMR: N-Modular Redundancy
NMRR: Normal Mode Rejection Ratio
NMS: Network Management Services
NMSE: Normalized Mean Square Error
NNA: New Network Architecture
NNBCLA: Negative Negabinary Carry-Look-Ahead Adder
NNI: Next Node Index
NNN: Non-Normalized Number
no: number
NO: Normally Open
NOA: Network-Oriented Analysis and Transformation Unit
No Adv: No Advice
NOC: Not-Carry
  Not Otherwise Classified
NOCP: Network Operator Control Program
NODAL: Network-Oriented Data Acquisition Language
NODAS: Network-Oriented Data Acquisition System
NOIBN: Not Otherwise Indexed By Name
NOMDA: National Office Machine Dealers Association
noncoll: noncollinear
non-cum: noncumulative
non-par: nonparticipating
NO OP: No-Operation (instruction)
NOP: Not Otherwise Provided for
NOPA: National Office Products Association

NOR: Not OR
NORM: Not Operationally Ready due to Maintenance
Not Operationally Ready Maintenance
NORRD: No Reply Received
NORS: Not Operationally Ready due to Supply
Not Operationally Ready Supply
nos: numbers
NOS: Network Operating System
Not Otherwise Specified
NOS/BE: Network Operating System/Batch Environment
NOSP: Network Operating Support Program
N-P: Negative-Positive
NP: New Page
No Parity
NPA: Numbering Plan Area
NPC: Nanoprogram Counter
NPD: Network Protective Device
NPDA: Network Problem Determination Application
NPIU: Numerical Processing and Interface Unit
NPL: New Programming Language
N-P-N: Negative-Positive-Negative
NPNA: No Protest Non-Acceptance
NPP: Network Protocol Processor
NPR: Noise Power Ratio
Nonprocedural Reference
Nonprocessor Request
NPRL: Nonprocedural Referencing Language
NPS: Numerical Plotting System
NPSM: Non-Productive Standard Minute
NPSTN: National Public Switched Telecommunications Network
NPSWL: New Program Status Word Location

NPT: Network Planning Tool
Nonpacket Mode Terminal
NPU: Network Processing Unit
NQR: Nonquadratic Residues
NR: Not Responsible for
NRC: Networking Routing Center
NR/D: Not Required, but Desired
NRDF: Nonrecursive Digital Filter
nretn: nonreturn
NRFD: Not Ready for Data
NRL: Network Restructuring Language
Normal Rated Load
NRM: Normal Response Mode
NRTZ: Nonreturn to Zero
NRU: Network Resource Unit
NRV: Nodal Route Vector
NRX(C): Non-Return-to-Zero (change) Recording
NRZ: Non-Return-to-Zero Recording
NRZ(C): Non-Return-to-Zero (change) Recording
NRZI: Non-Return-to-Change-on-ones Recording
ns: nanosecond
nonsequenced
NS: New Signal
Not Specified
Not Sufficient
NSC: Network Switching Center
Nodal Switching Center
nsec: nanosecond(s)
NSI: Next Sequential Instruction
Nonstandard Item
NSK: Not Specified by Kind
NSL: Nonstandard Label
NSM: Network Security Module
Network Services Manager
NSMB: National Standards Management Board
NSN: National Stock Number
NSNP: No Space, No Print
NSOS: N-Channel Sapphire on Silicon

NSP: Network Service Protocol
  Numeric Space (character)
  Numeric Subroutine Package
NSPF: Not Specifically Provided For
NSR: No Slot Release
  Normal Service Request
NSS: Network Supervisor System
NSTC: Not Subject To Call
NSW: National Software Works
NT: Not True
  Number of Tracks
NTA: National Telecommunications Agency
NTC: National Telecommunications Conference
NTCA: National Telephone Cooperative Association
  Nontutorial Computer Application
NTE: Not To Exceed
NTF: No Trouble Found
NTIA: National Telecommunications and Information Administration
NTIS: National Technical Information Service
NTO: Network Terminal Option
NTP: Network Terminal Protocol
  Network Termination Processor
  Network Transaction Processing
NTPF: Number of Terminals Per Failure
NTR: Next Task Register
NTSC: National Television Standard Code
NTT: Number Theoretic Transform
NTU: Network Terminating Unit
nu: numeral
NU: Nothing Unsatisfactory
NUA: Network User Address
NUBLU: New Basic Logic Unit
NUF: Noise Ulterior Flux
NUI: Network User Identity
nul: null
NUL: No Upper Limit
  Null character
NULS: Net Unit-Load Size
NULT: Null Tuple
num: number
  numeric
numb: number(s)
nv: nanovolt
NVRAM: Nonvolatile Random Access Memory
NVT: Network Virtual Terminal
NWD: Network Wide Directory
NWDS: Network Wide Directory System
NXA: Nodal Exchange Area
NXM: Nonexistent Memory
NY: Net Yield
NZ: Not Zero
NZSG: Non-Zero-Sum Game
NZT: Nonzero Transfer

O

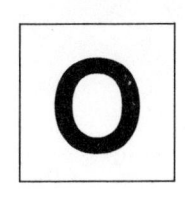

o: official
open
operand
operation
operational
operator
output
OA: Office Automation
Operand Address Register
Operating Assemblies
Operating Authorization
Operational Analysis
OAAU: Orthogonal Array Arithmetic Unit
OABETA: Office Appliance and Business Equipment Trades Association
OAC: Office Automation Conference
Operations Analysis Center
OA/DDP: Office Automation/Distributed Data Processing
OAF: Origin Address Field
OAG: Operand Address Generator
OAIDE: Operational Assistance and Instructive Data Equipment
OA&M: Operation, Administration and Maintenance
OAM: Operand Addressing Mode
OAMP: Optical Analog Matrix Processing
OAP: Orthogonal Array Processor
OAPM: Optimal Amplitude and Phase Modulation
OAR: Operand Address Register
Operations Analysis Report
Operator Authorization Record
Overhaul and Repair

OARS: Opening Automated Report Service
OAS: Output Amplitude Stability
OASYS: Office Automation System
OAT: Operating Acceptance Test
O-A-V: Object-Attribute-Value (triplets)
OB: Official Business
Ordered Back
Output Buffer
Output Bus
OBB: Operation Better Block
OBC: On-Board Computer
OBE: Output Buffer Empty
OBF: Operational Base Facility
obj: object
oblg: obligate
obligation
OBO: Official Business Only
Order Book Official
OBP: On-Board Processor
OBR: Optical Bar Code Reader
Outboard Recorder
OBS: On-Line Business Systems
Optical Beam Scanner
OBV: On-Balance Volume
o/c: overcharge
OC: Office Copy
Official Classification
Open Circuit
Open Collector
Operating Characteristic
Operation Control
Order Card
Output Computer
OCAL: On-Line Cryptanalytic Aid Language
OCB: Override Control BITS
Over-the-Counter Batch
occ: occupation

119

OCC: Operator Control Command
Other Common Carrier
OCCB: Operational Configuration Control Board
OCD: On-Line Communication Driver
OCDMS: On-Board Checkout and Data Management System
OCF: On-Board Computational Facility
Open Channel Flow
Operator Console Facility
OCFP: Operator Command Function Processor
OCG: Optimal Code Generation
OCL: Operation Control Language
Operational Check List
OCM: Oscillator and Clock Module
OCMODL: Operating Cost Model
OCO: One-Cancels-the-Other order
Operations Control Operator
OCP: Operational Control Panel
Output Control Program
OCR: Optical Character Reader
Optical Character Recognition
Output Control Register
OCR-A: Optical Character Recognition - ANSI Standard
OCR-B: Optical Character Recognition - International Standard
OCRE: Optical Character Recognition Equipment
OCRUA: Optical Character Recognition Users Association
OCS: Office Computing System
Optical Character Scanner
Order Communications System
oct: octal
OCU: Operational Control Unit
OD: Original Design
Output Disable
Outside Diameter
ODA: Octal Debugging Aid
Operational Data Analysis
ODB: Output Data Buffer
Output to Display Buffer
ODBR: Output Data Buffer Register
ODC: On-line Data Capture
Operational Document Control
Output Data Control
ODCS: Operational Data Collection System
ODD: Optical Data Digitizer
ODDH: On-Board Digital Data Handling
ODE: Ordinary Differential Equation
ODESY: On-Line Data Entry System
ODG: Off-Line Data Generator
ODM: Outboard Data Manager
ODP: Optical Data Processing
Original Document Processing
ODR: Optical Data Recognition
Original Data Record
Output Definition Register
ODS: Operational Data Summary
Output Data Strobe
ODT: Octal Debugging Technique
On-Line Debugging Techniques
ODU: Output Display Unit
O&E: Operations and Engineering
OE: Office Equipment
Output Enable
OEA: Operator Error Analysis
OEAP: Operational Error Analysis Program
OEC: Organizing, Evaluating, and Coaching
OECQ: Organisation Europeenne pour le Controle de la

Qualite (European Organization for Quality Control) (French)
OEDIT: Octal Editor
OEM: Original Equipment Manufacturer
OEO: Operational Equipment Objective
OEP: Original Element Processor
OER: Original Equipment Replacement
OES: Output Enable Serial
OET: Objective End Time
of: overflow
OF: On File
OFDS: Optimal Financial Decision Strategy
OFI: On-Line Free Form Input
ofl: overflow
OFN: Open File Number
OFR: Open File Report
Ordering Function Register
Over Frequency Relay
OFT: Optical Fiber Tube
og: outgoing
OG: Or Gate
OGW: Overload Gross Weight
oh: overhaul
overhead
OI: Operating Instructions
Output Impedance
OIB: Operation Instruction Book
OIC: Operations Instrumentation Coordinator
Operator's Instruction Chart
OICC: Operations Interface Control Chart
OID: Octal Identifier
Order Initiated Distribution
OIDI: Optically Isolated Digital Input
OIE: Optical Incremental Encoder
OIL: Only Input Lines
Operation Inspection Log
OIOPSWL: Old Input/Output Program Status Word Location

OIP: Operational Improvement Plan
Operational Improvement Program
Optical Image Processor
OIPS: Optical Image Processing System
OIS: Operating Information System
Operational Instrumentation System
Optical Image Sensor
OL: On Line
Open Loop
Operating Location
Operating Log
Operations/Logistics
Or Less
Output Latch
OLAC: Off-Line Adaptive Computer
OLC: On-Line Computer
Open-Loop Control
Operation Load Code
OLCA: On-Line Circuit Analysis
OLCC: Optimum Life Cycle Costing
OLDB: On-Line Data Base
OLDC: On-Line Data Collection
OLDERT: On-Line Executive for Real-Time
OLDS: On-Line Display System
OLG: Open-Loop Gain
OLIFLM: On-Line Image-Forming Light Modulator
OLL: Output Logic Level
OLLS: On-Line Logical Simulation System
OLO: On-Line Operation
OLOE: On-Line Order Entry
OLP: On-Line Programming
OLPS: On-Line Programming System
OLQ: On-Line Query
OLR: Office Loop Repeater
Open Loop Receiver
Open Loop Response
OLRT: On-Line Real Time
OLSC: On-Line Scientific Computer

OLSF: On-Line Subsystem Facility
OLT: On-Line Test
OLTEP: On-Line Test Executive Program
OLTS: On-Line Test System
On-Line Time Share
OLTT: On-Line Teller Terminal
OLX: On-Line Executive
O&M: Operations and Maintenance
Organization and Methods
OM: Office Master
Operating Memorandum
Operating Memory
Operation Manual
Operations Manager
Orthogonal Memory
Output Module
OMA: Operations Monitor Alarm
OMAC: On-Line Manufacturing, Accounting and Control System
OMAP: Object Module Assembly Program
OMAR: Optical Mark Reader
OMC: Operation and Maintenance Center
Operations Monitoring Computer
OMD: Open Macrodefinition
OMEC: Optimized Microminiature Electronic Circuit
OMEF: Office Machines and Equipment Federation
OMEN: Orthogonal Mini-Embedment
OMF: Old Master File
Order Materials For
OMI: Operations Maintenance Instructions
Organization for Microinformation
OMIS: Operational Management Information System
OMPR: Optical Mark Printer
OMR: Optical Mark Reader
Optical Mark Recognition
OMRC: Optical Mark Reader Card
OMRS: Optical Mark Reader Sheet
OMS: Optical Modulation System
ONI: Operator Number Identification
ONLP: On-Line Program Development
ONLY: On-Line Yield
ONS: Off-Normal Switch
O&O: Owned and Operated
Owner and Operator
OOL: Operator-Oriented Language
OOPS: Off-Line Operating Simulator
op: open
operand
operation
operator
optional
output
OP: Open Position
Operation Part
Operation Procedure
Outside Production
OPACK: Operation Acknowledge
OPAL: Operational Performance Analysis Language
OPBU: Operating Budget
OPC: Operation Code
Operations Planning and Control
OPCE: Operator Control Element
OP-COD: Operating Code
OPCODE: Operation Code
OPCOM: Operator Communications
OPCTR: Operations Center
opd: operand
OPDATS: Operational Performance Data System
OPE: Optimized Processing Element
OPECO: Operations Coordinator
oper: operational
OPEVAL: Operational Evaluation
OPEX: Operational Executive
Operational Experience

OPIM: Order Processing and Inventory Monitoring
OPIS: Operational Priority Indicating System
opl: operational
OPL1: Pl/1 Optimizing Compiler
OPM: Operations Per Minute
Operator Master
Operator Programming Method
opnl: operational
OPNML: Operations Normal
opns: operations
OPOL: Optimization-Oriented Language
OPOMP: Overall Planning and Optimization and Machining Process
OPOP: Operator/Operation
opr: operand
operator
OPR: Optical Page Reader
Optical Page Reading
OPRA: Options Price Reporting Authority
OPRAD: Operations Research and Development Management
OPREP: Operational Reporting System
OPREQ: Operation Request
OPRLFT: Operator Fault
oprnl: operational
ops: operations
OPS: On-Line Process Synthesis
OPSCON: Operations Control
OPSCOP: Operations Control Monitor Program
OPSER: Operator Service
OPSREP: Operations Report
OPSTATUSREP: Operations Status Report
OPSWL: Old Program Status Word Location
OPS-X: Operational Teletype Message

OPSYS: Operating System
opt: optimization
optimizer
optional
OPT: Optimized Production Technology
OPTIC: Optical Procedural Task Instruction Compiler
OPTS: On-Line Peripheral Test System
OPU: Operations Priority Unit
OPUR: Object Program Utility Routine
OPUS: Octal Program Updating System
OQC: Outside Quality Control
OQL: On-Line Query Language
Outgoing Quality Level
Outgoing Quality Limit
O&R: Overhaul and Repair
or: overrun
OR: On Return
Operation Record
Operations Research
Ordered Recorded
Over Run
ORA: Output Register Address
ORBIS: Order and Billing System
ORBIT: On-Line, Real-Time, Branch Information
On-Line Reduced Bandwidth Information Transfer
ORC: Operations Research Center
Orthogonal Row Computer
ord: order
ordinary
ordd: ordered
ORDER: On-Line Order Entry System
ORE: Output Register Empty
org: organization
origin
ORGALIME: Organisme de Liaison des Industrie Metaliques

Europeenes (Liaison body for the European engineering and metal industries) (French)
orgl: organizational
orgn: organization
OR/MS: Operations Research/Management Science
ORO: Operations Research Office
OROS: Optical Read-Only Storage
ORR: Operational Ready Rate
ORSA: Operations Research Society of America
ORU: On-Line Replacement Unit
Operational Readiness Unit
os: outstanding
overstocked
OS: Office System
On Schedule
Operating System
Operational Sequence
Optical Scanning
Optimum Size
Order Sheet
OSA: Open Systems Architecture
OSAM: Overflow Sequential Access Method
OSB: Operational Status Bit
osc: oscillator
OSCAR: Optically Scanned Character Automatic Reader
OSCRL: Operating System Command and Response Language
OSD: On-Line System Driver
Optical Scanning Device
OSDP: On-Site Data Processing
On-Site Data Processor
Operational System Development Program
OSE: Operational Support Equipment
OSG: Operand Select Gate
OSHB: One-Sided Height-Balanced

OSI: Open Systems Interconnection
Operating System Interface
Overhead Supply Inventory
OSL: Operand Specification List
Operating System Language
OSM: Operating System Manual
Operating System Monitor
OSML: Operating System Machine Level
OSN: Output Sequence Number
OSP: Outside Purchased
OS/P: Operating Systems for People
OSR: Operand Storage Register
Optical Scanning Recognition
OSS: Operating System Supervisor
Operations Support System
Order Support System
OSSF: Operating System Support Facility
OSSL: Operating Systems Simulation Language
OST: Objectives, Strategies and Tactics
Office of Science and Technology
OSTD: Off-Site Technical Director
OSTF: Operational Suitability Test Facility
OSTP: Office of Science and Technology Policy
OSU: Operational Switching Unit
OS/VS: Operating System/Virtual Storage
OSW: Operational Switching Unit
OSWS: Operating System Workstation
OT: Office of Science and Technology (US)
On Time
On Track
Operating Time
Output Terminal
OTA: Office of Technology Assessment (US)
OTAF: Operating Time At Failure

OTC: Objective, Time, and Cost Operational Test Center
OTCC: Operator Test Control Console
OTCS: Operational Teletype Communications Subsystem
OTDC: Optical Target Designation Computer
OT&E: Operational Test and Evaluation
OTF: Optical Transfer Function
OTG: Option Table Generator
OTIS: Operation, Transport, Inspection, Storage
OTKDF: Other Than Knocked Down Flat
OTL: On-Line Task Loader Operating Time Log
OTM: Office of Telecommunications Management
OTP: Office of Telecommunications Policy (US)
OTRAC: Oscillogram Trace Reader
OTRT: Operating Time Record Tag
OTS: Object Time System
On-Line Terminal System
Operational Time Sync
Orbital Test Satellite
OTSS: Off-The-Shelf System Operational Test Support System
OTU: Operational Test Unit
OU: Operation Unit
Operational Unit
Outlook Unusual
OUD: Operational Unit Data
oupt: output
out: outgoing
output
OUTLIM: Output Limiting Facility
OUTRAN: Output Translator
outstg: outstanding
OUTWATS: Unidirectional WATS with respect to the function of the call organization
ov: overflow
OVD: Optical Video Disk
Optional Valuation Date
ovf: overflow
ovfl: overflow
ovld: overload
ovr: overflow
OWM: Office Work Measurement
oz: ounce

P

p: pair
 parallel
 parity
 patent
 pico-
 picoampere
 pointe
 polynomial
 positive
 power
 procedure
 process
 processor
 program
 punch
P/A: Programmer/Analyst
PA: Pending Availability
 Performance Analysis
 Predictive Analyzer
 Problem Analysis
 Program Access
 Program Address
 Program Analysis
 Program Attention
 Project Analysis
 Public Address
PAAC: Program Analysis Adaptable Control
PABD: Precise Access Block Diagram
PABLI: Online monitor of European Community development projects (EC)
PABX: Private Automatic Branch Exchange
PAC: Performance Analysis and Control
 Planned Availability Concept
 Pneumatic Analog Computer
 Pneumatic Auxiliary Console
 Polled Access Circuit
 Primary Address Code
 Program Authorized Credentials
 Project Analysis and Control
 Pursuant to Authority Contained in
PACE: Packaged Cram Executive
 Performance And Cost Evaluation
 Planned Action with Constant Evaluation
 Planning And Control made Easy
 Precisions Analog Computing Equipment
 Programmed Automatic Communications Equipment
PACER: Process Assembly Case Evaluator Routine
PACM: Pulse Amplitude Code Modulation
PACR: Performance And Compatibility Requirements
PACS: Program Authorization Control System
PACT: Pay Actual Computer Time
 Production Analysis Control Technique
 Program for Automatic Coding Techniques
 Programmable Asynchronous Clustered Teleprocessing
 Programmed Analysis Computer Transfer
 Programmed Automatic Circuit Tester
PACUIT: Packet + Circuit

127

PACX: Private Automatic Computer Exchange
PAD: Packet Assembler/Disassembler
Packet Assembly/Disassembly
Positioning Arm Disk
Preferred Arrival Date
Program Analysis for Documentation
PADEL: Pattern Description Language
PADL: Part and Assembly Description Language
PADLA: Programmable Asynchronous Dual Line Adapter
PADRE: Portable Automatic Data Recording Equipment
PADS: Performance Analysis Display System
Personnel Automated Data System
PAF: Page Address Field
Peripheral Address Field
Production Assembly Facility
PAGAN: Pattern Generation Language
PAGE: Preview And Graphics Editing
PAGES: Program Affinity Grouping and Evaluation System
PAI: Parts Application Information
Prearrival Inspection
Precise Angle Indicator
PAID: Programmers Aid In Debugging
PAIR: Performance And Improved Reliability
Procurement Automated Integrated Requirements
PAL: Pedagogic Algorithmic Language
Precision Artwork Language
Process Assembler Language
Process Audit List
Programmable Array Logic
Programmed Application Library
PALASM: Programmable Array Logic Assembler
PAM: Panel Monitor
Peripheral Adapter Module
Primary Access Method
Profit Analysis Model
Pulse Address Modem
Pulse Amplitude Modulation
PAMA: Pulse-Address Multiple Access
PAM/D: Process Automation Monitor/Disk
PAMS: Plan Analysis and Modeling System
PAMS INFO: Proceedings of the American Society for Information Science
PAN: Personal Account Number
Primary Account Number
PANCAP: Practical Annual Capacity
PANDLCHAR: Pay and Allowances Chargeable
PAP: Phase Advance Pulse
Procurement And Production
PAPA: Probabilistic Automatic Pattern Analyzer
PAPS: Performance Analysis and Prediction Study
Procurement And Production Status System
PAQ: Process Average Quality
par: parameter
P/AR: Peak to Average Ratio
PAR: Page Address Register
Performance And Reliability
Production Automated Riveting
Program Address Register
Program Analysis and Review
param: parameter

PARASYN: Parametric Synthesis
PARD: Precision Annotated Retrieval Display
PARDAC: Parallel Digital to Analog Converter
PAREX: Programmed Accounts Receivable Extra Service
parm: parameter
PARMA: Program for Analysis, Reporting, and Maintenance
part: participating
participation
PART: Production Allocation and Requirements Technique
PARTNER: Proof of Analog Results Through a Numerical Equivalent Routine
PAS: Phase Address System
Phase Array System
Processed Array Signal
PASG: Pulse Amplifier Symbol Generator
PASLA: Programmable Asynchronous Line Adapter
PASS: Planning And Scheduling System
Private Automatic Switching System
Production Automated Scheduling System
PAST: Process Accessible Segment Table
pat: patent
PAT: Prediction Analysis Technique
Production Acceptance Testing
Programmer Aptitude Test
Pseudoadder Tree
patd: patented
PATE: Programmed Automatic Telemetry Evaluator
Programmed Automatic Test Equipment
PATPEND: Patent Pending

PATRIC: Pattern Recognition Interpretation and Correlation
PATS: Preauthorized Automatic Transfer Scheme
patt: patent
pattern
PATT: Partial Automatic Translation Technique
PATX: Private Automatic Telegraph Exchange
PAU: Pattern Articulation Unit
PAUS: Planning and Analysis for Uncertain Situations
PAX: Physical Address Extension
Private Automatic Exchange
PB: Page Buffer
Peripheral Buffer
Program Base
Proportional Band
Push Button
PBA: Permanent Budget Account
PBC: Peripheral Bus Computer
Personal Business Computer
PBD: Precise Block Diagram
PBIC: Programmable Buffer Interface Card
PBM: Program Budget Manager
PBN: Physical Block Number
PBO: Plotting Board Operator
Push-Button Operation
PBP: Point By Point
Push Button Panel
PBS: Push Button Switch
PBSW: Push Button Switch
PBT: Pushbutton Telephone
PBW: Parts By Weight
Proportional Bandwidth
PBX: Private Branch Exchange
pc: percent
percentage
photoconductor
P&C: Purchasing and Contracting
PC: Path Control
Path Controller
Per Cent

Personal Computer
Portable Computer
Printed Circuit
Printed Copy
Production Control
Production Cost
Professional Corporation
Program Counter
Project Control
Pulse Counter
Punched Card
PCA: Physical Configuration Audit
Printed Circuit Assembly
Process Control Analyzer
Protective Connecting Arrangement
Pulse Counter Adapter
PCAM: Partitioned Content Addressable Memory
Punched Card Accounting Machine
PCAP: Process Characterization Analysis Package
PCAS: Punch Card Accounting System
PCB: Page Control Block
Printed Circuit Board
Process Control Block
Program Communication Block
Program Control Block
PCBA: Printed Circuit Board Assembly
PCBS: Printed Circuit Board Socket
PCC: Program Control Counter
Program Controlled Computer
PCCH: Program Control Channel
PCCS: Processor Common Communications System
PCCU: Punched Card Control Unit
PCD: Production Common Digitizer
Program Control Document
PCDI: Per Capita Disposable Income
PCDP: Punched Card Data Processing
PCE: Process Control Equipment
Program Cost Estimate
Punched Card Equipment
PCF: Program Complex File
Program Control Facility
Programmed Cryptographic Facility
PCG: Programmable Character Generator
pch: punch
PCHAR: Printing Character
PCI: Peripheral Controller Interface
Process Control Interface
Program Check Interruption
Program-Controlled Interruption
Programmable Communications Interface
PCIOS: Processor Common Input-Output System
PCK: Phase Control Keyboard
Printed Control Keyboard
PCKB: Phase Control Keyboard
Printed Control Keyboard
PCKT: Printed Circuit
PCL: Print Control Language
Process Control Language
PCLA: Process Control Language
PCLK: Program Clock
PCLR: Parallel Communications Link Receiver
PCLX: Parallel Communications Link Transmitter
PCM: Plug Compatible Mainframe
Plug Compatible Manufacturer
Plug Compatible Memory
Primary Control Program
Pulse Code Modulation
Punch Card Machine
Punched Card Machine
PCMD: Pulse Code Modulation Digital

PCME: Pulse Code Modulation Event
PCMI: Photo-Chromic-Microimage
PCMS: Punched Card Machine System
PCO: Program Controlled Output
P-CODE: pseudocode
PCOS: Process Control Operating System
PCP: Peripheral Control Pulse
Preliminary Cost Proposal
Primary Control Program
Process Control Program
Program Change Proposal
PCR: Page Control Register
Print Command Register
Production Change Request
Program Change Request
Punched Card Requisition
PCS: Personal Computing System
Print Contrast Signal
Production Control System
Programmable Communications Subsystem
Project Control System
Punched Card System
PCSFSK: Phase Comparison Sinusoidal Frequency Shift Keying
pct: percent
percentage
PCT: Peripheral Control Terminal
Processing Control Table
Program Control Table
PCTG: Programmable Channel Termination Group
PCTR: Program Counter
PCU: Peripheral Control Unit
Port Contention Unit
Power Control Unit
Processor Control Unit
Program Control Unit
Programmable Control Unit
Punch Card Unit
Punched Card Utility

PCW: Program Control Word
PCX: Process Control Executive
PD: Panel Display
Physical Distribution
Plasma Display
Potential Difference
Procedure Division
Product Design
PDA: Parallel Data Adapter
Percent Defective Allowable
Physical Device Address
Product Departure Authorization
Pushdown Automation
PDAID: Problem Determination Aid
PDAS: Process Design Analysis System
PDB: Physical Data Base
PDBIN: Processor Data Bus In
PDBM: Pulse Delay Binary Modulation
PDC: Parallel Data Communicator
Parallel Data Controller
Photo-Data Card
Production Decision Criteria
Programmable Data Controller
Programmable Desk Calculator
Project Data Card
PDCS: Parallel Digital Computer System
Performance Data Computer System
Processing Distribution and Control System
PDCU: Plotting Display Control Unit
PDD: Past Due Date
Priority Delivery Date
Processor Description Data Base
Program Description Document
PDDB: Product Definition Data Base

PDDS: Program Definition Data Sheet
PDE: Partial Differential Equations
PDED: Partial Double Error Detecting
PDEL: Partial Differential Equation Language
PDF: Probability Density Function
Program Data File
Program Development Facility
PDG: Program Documentation Generator
PDI: Picture Description Instruction
PDIO: Parallel Digital Input-Output
PDISP: Page Displacement
PDL: Picture Description Language
Process Design Language
Program Design Language
Programmable Data Logger
Programmed Digital Logic
Push Down List
PDM: Physical Distribution Management
Practical Data Manager
Print Down Module
Program Design Manual
Pulse-Duration Modulation
Push Down Memory
PDMM: Push Down Memory Modem
PDMU: Passive Data Memory Unit
pdn: production
PDN: Public Data Network
PD&P: Project Definition and Planning
PDP: Plasma Display Panel
Procedure Definition Processor
Program Development Plan
Programmed Data Processor
Programmed Digital Processor
PDR: Page Data Register
Preliminary Data Report
Preliminary Design Review
Processing Data Rate
PDRL: Procurement Data Requirements List
PDRMA: Portable Drill Rig Manufacturers Association
PDS: Partitioned Data Set
Personnel Data System
Photo-Digital Store
Power Distribution System
Problem Definition/Solution
Procurement Data Sheet
Product Development System
Professional Development Series
Program Data Set
Program Development System
Programmable Data Station
PDSE: Production Sample
PDSMAN: Partitioned Data Set Management System
PDT: Parallel Data Transmission
Programmable Data Terminal
Pushdown Transducer
PDTS: Program Development Tracking System
PDU: Plasma Display Unit
Power Distribution Unit
Programmable Delay Unit
PDX: Program Development Executive
PE: Page-End character
Parity Error
Performance Enhancement
Period Ending
Phase Encoded
Phase Encoding
Probable Error
Processing Element
Pulse Encoding
PEARL: Process, Experiment and Automation Real-Time Language

PEAT: Pricing Evaluation for Audit Technique
PEBS: Pulsed Electron Beam Source
PEC: Program Element Code
PED: Period End Date
PEDS: Packaging Engineering Data System
PEE: Photoferroelectric Effect
PEEP: Production Electronic Equipment Procurement Status Report
PEG: Prime Event Generation
PEIC: Periodic Error Integrating Controller
PEL: Picture Element
PEM: Performance Enhancement Module
Processing Element Memory
Program Element Monitor
PEP: Paperless Electronic Payment
Partitioned Emulation Programming (extension)
Peripheral Event Processor
Program Evaluation Procedure
PEPC: Polynomial Error Protection Code
PEPE: Parallel Element Processing Ensemble
PEPR: Precision Encoding and Pattern Recognition Device
PER: Planning and Engineering for Repairs and Alterations
Post-Execution Reporting
Production Engineering Research Association
Program Error Report
Program Event Recording
Program Execution Request
PER AN: Per Annum
perc: perquisite
PERCOM: Peripheral Communications

PERCOMP: Personal Computing Conference
perf: performance
perif: peripheral
PERM: Permanent Material
Programmed Evaluation for Repetitive Manufacture
PERMACAP: Personnel Management and Accounting Card Processor
PERMACAPS: Personnel Management and Accounting Card Processing System
perp: perpetual
Per Pro: Per Procuration
PERS: Performance Evaluation Reporting System
PERT: Program Evaluation and Review Technique
PERT/COST: Program Evaluation and Review Technique/Cost
PERVAL: Performance/Valuation
PES: Program Execution System
PESD: Program Element Summary Data
PESDS: Program Element Summary Data Sheet
PEST: Parameter Estimation by Sequential Testing
PESY: Peripheral Exchange Synchronization
PET: Process Evaluation Tester
Production Environmental Testing
Program Evaluator and Tester
PEU: Port Expander Unit
pf: picofarad
preferred
PF: Page Format
Permanent File
Program Function
Programmable Format
Punch Off

P&FA: Program and File Analysis
PFA: Production Flow Analysis
PFAM: Programmed Frequency Amplitude Modulation
PFAR: Power Fail Automatic Restart
PFB: Prefetch Buffer
PFDA: Precision Frequency Distribution Amplifier
Pulse Frequency Distortion Analyzer
PFEP: Programmable Front End Processor
PFF: Page Fault Frequency
PFI: Physical Fault Insertion
PFK: Program Function Key
Programmed Function Keyboard
PFM: Performance Monitor
PFN: Permanent File Name
Prime Fanout Node
PFOR: Parallel FORTRAN
PFP: Prefetch Processor
Program File Processor
Programmable Function Panel
PFR: Power Fail Recovery
Power Fail Restart
PFS: Path Fault Secure
Pro-Forma Statement
Programmable Frequency Standard
PFT: Page Frame Table
PFU: Please Follow Up
pg: page
PG: Power Gain
Program Generator
Program Graph
PGA: Programmable Gate Array
PGC: Program Counter
Programmed Gain Control
pgm: program
PGN: Performance Group Number
PGNR: Page Number

PGP: Programmable Graphics Processor
PGS: Program Generation Subsystem
Program Generation System
PGT: Page Table
Program Global Table
PG/ZD: Group Propogate/Zero Detect
ph: phase
PH: Physical Record
PHA: Pulse Height Analysis
PHD: Parallel Head Disk
PHM: Phase Modulation
PHODEC: Photometric Determination of Equilibrium Constants
PHR: Physical Record
phse: phase
P/I: Pressure to Current
PI: Power Input
Processor Interface
Productivity Index
Program Interrupter
Program Interruption
Programmed Information
Programmed Instruction
Proportional-Plus Integral
PIA: Peripheral Interface Adapter
PIB: Programmable Input Buffer
PIC: Position Independent Code
Priority Intercept Controller
Production Inventory Control
Program Interrupt Control
Program Interrupt Controller
PICE: Programmable Integrated Control Equipment
PICRS: Program Information Control and Retrieval System
PICS: Personnel Information Communication System
Plug-In Inventory Control System
Production Information and Control System

PICU: Parallel Instruction Control Unit
Priority Interrupt Control Unit
PID: Personal Identification Device
Pictorial Information Digitizer
Pseudo Interrupt Device
PIDCOM: Process Instruments Digital Communication System
PIDENT: Program Identification
PIDS: Public Investment Data System
PIE: Parallel Interface Element
Program Interrupt Entry
PIG: Passive Income Generator
PIL: Processing Information List
PILP: Parametric Integer Linear Program
PIM: Processor Interface Module
PIML: Polynomial Propagation Time Immediate Language
PIN: Personal Identification Number
PINO: Positive Input-Negative Output
PINT: Processor Interrupt
PINTE: Processor Interrupts Enabled
PIO: Parallel Input-Output
Process Input-Output
Processor Input-Output
PIOCS: Physical Input-Output Control System
PIOSP: Process Input-Output Subroutine Package
PIOU: Parallel Input-Output Unit
PIP: Path Independent Protocol
Peripheral Interchange Program
Personal Identification Project
PIPS: Paperless Item Processing System
Pattern Information Processing System
PIQ: Parallel Instruction Queue

PIR: Program Incident Report
PIRS: Project Information Retrieval System
PIT: Peripheral Input Tape
Physical Inventory Taking
Programmable Interval Timer
Projected Inactive Time
PIU: Path Information Unit
Process Interface Unit
PIVOT: Programmer's Interactive Verification and Organizational Tool
PIXEL: Picture Element
pj: picojoule
pk: peak
PK: Public Key
PKA: Public Key Algorithm
PKC: Position Keeping Computer
PKD: Programmable Keyboard/Display
pkg: package
PK/PK: Peak to Peak
pl: plus
P&L: Profit and Loss
PL: Private Line
Procedure Library
Production Language
Program Library
Program Limit
Programming Language
Pl/1: Programming Language One
PLA: Print Load Analyser
Programmable Line Adapter
Programmed Logic Array
PLAB: Party-Line Adapter Board
PLAN: Program Language Analyzer
PLANCODE: Planning, Control and Decision Evaluation
PLANES: Programmed Language-Based Enquiry System
PLANET: Planning Evaluation Technique
PLANIT: Programming Language for Interactive Teaching

PLANS: Programming Language for Allocation and Network Scheduling
PLAS: Program Logical Address Space
PLATO: Programmed Logic for Automatic Teaching Operations
PLATON: Programming Language for Tree Operation
PLC: Program Level Change
Programmable Logic Controller
PLCB: Pseudoline Control Block
plcy: policy
PLD: Physical Logical Description
PL/E: Programming Language/Edit
PLE: Product Limit Estimator
PLENG: Physical Record Length
PLEX: Programming Language Extension
PLF: Page Length Field
Phone Line Formatter
PLI: Private Line Interface
PL/I: Programming Language One
PLIB: Program Library
PLIC: Procedural Language for Integrity Constraints
PLIMS: Programming Language for Information Management System
PLISN: Provisioning List Item Sequence Number
PLL: Phase Lock Loop
PLLT: Program Load Library Tape
PL/M: Programming Language for Microprocessors
PLM: Passive Line Monitor
Programming Logic Manual
Pulse-Length Manual
PL-MATH: Procedure Library-Mathematics
PLMS: Partitioned Libraries Management System
PLO: Phase-Locked Oscillator
PLOD: Periodic List of Data
PLP: Procedural Language Processor
PLPA: Pageable Link Pack Area
PLRS: Phase Lock Receiving Station
Position Location Reporting System
PLS: Private-Line Service
PLT: Private Line Teletypewriter
PLUS: Program Library Update System
P/M: Put of More
PM: Performance Management
Performance Monitor
Permanent Magnet
Phase Modulation
Planned Maintenance
Prepared Message
Preventive Maintenance
Process Manual
Process Module
Processing Module
Program Memory
PMA: Physical Memory Address
Preamplifier Module Assembly
Priority Memory Access
Protected Memory Address
PMAC: Parallel Memory Address Counter
PMACS: Project Management and Control System
PMAP: Procedure Map
PMAR: Page Map Address Register
PMB: PROM Memory Board
PMBX: Private Manual Branch Exchange
PM&C: Process Monitor and Control
PMC: Performance Management Computer

PMCD: Post Mortem Core Dump
Program Module Connection Diagram
PMD: Post Mortem Dump
Program Management Directive
PME: Processor Memory Enhancement
PMEM: Processor Memory
PMF: Performance Monitor Function
PMG: Phase Modulation Generator
PMH: Productive Man Hour
PMI: Program Management Instruction
PMIC: Parallel Multiple Incremental Computer
PML: Physical Memory Loss
Probable Maximum Loss
PMLC: Previous Microlocation Counter
Programmed Multiline Controller
PMM: Programmable Microcomputer Module
Pulse Mode Multiplex
PMMB: Parallel Memory-to-Memory Bus
PMMI: Packaging Machinery Manufacturers Institute
PMN: Pre-Manufacturing Notice
Program Management Network
Project Management Network
PMON: Performance Management Operations Network
PMOS: P-Channel Metal Oxide Semiconductor
PMP: Parallel Microprogrammed Processor
Parts-Material-Packaging
Performance Management Package
Premodulation Processor
Profit-Maximizing Price
Program Management Plan
PMPM: Phase Margin Performance Measure
PMR: Performance Monitoring Receiver
Power Master Reset
PMRS: Performance Management and Recognition System
PMRT: Program Management Responsibility Transfer
PMS: Performance Management System
Performance Measurement System
Process Management System
Processor Memory Switch
Program Management System
Project Management System
Public Message Service
PMSD: Program Module Sequence Diagram
PMSS: Preventive Maintenance Scheduling System
PMSX: Processor Memory Switch Matrix
PMT: Photo Multiplier Tube
Prepare Master Tape
Program Master Tape
PMTD: Post Mortem Tape Dump
PMU: Portable Memory Unit
PMUX: Programmable Multiplexer
PMX: Packet Multiplexer
Protected Message Exchange
PMY: Productive Man Year
pn: pseudonoise
PN: Packet Number
Page Number
Performance Number
Positive-Negative
Processor Number
Programmable Network
Project Note
PNA: Project Network Analysis

PNAF: Potential Network Access Facility
PNCC: Partial Network Control Center
pnch: punch
pnd: pending
PND: Present Next Digit
PNI: Participate but do Not Initiate
PNM: Path Number Matrix
Pulse Number Modulation
P-N-P: Positive-Negative-Positive
P&O: Planning and Operations
PO: Parity Odd
Planning Objectives
Power on
Pulse Output
Purchase Order
POC: Power On Clear
POD: Program Operation Description
PODA: Priority-Oriented Demand Assignment
PODAF: Post Operation Data Analysis Facility
PODAPS: Portable Data Processing System
PODAS: Portable Data Acquisition System
PODR: Pixel Order
POF: Point Of Failure
Programmed Operator Facility
POGO: Program Oriented Graphics Operation
POI: Plan Of Instruction
Program Of Instruction
pol: policy
POL: Problem Oriented Language
Procedure Oriented Language
POLAR: Production Order Locating And Reports
POLE: Point Of Last Environment
POLGEN: Problem Oriented Language Generator
POM: Program Operation Mode

POMM: Preliminary Operating and Maintenance Manual
POMO: Production Oriented Maintenance Organization
POMS: Professional Office Management System
PON: Power On
POP: Perceived Outcome Potential
Point-Of-Purchase
Power On/Off Protection
Programmed Operators and Primitives
POPO: Push On, Pull Off
POPS: Process Operating System Program for Operator Scheduling
pos: position
positive
POS: Point Of Sale
Primary Operating System
Program Order Sequence
poss: possible
POST: Production Oriented Scheduling Techniques
postp: postprocessor
postpro: postprocessor
POT: Picture Object Table
POWER: Priority Output Writers, Execution Processors, and Input Readers
pp: preprinted
preprocessor
PP: Parallel Processing
Partial Program
Peripheral Processor
Print Position
Production Processes
PPB: Planning-Programming-Budgeting
PROM Programmer Board
PPBAS: Planning, Programming, Budgeting, Accounting System
PPBES: Program Planning-Budgeting-Evaluation System

PPBM: Pulse Polarization Binary Modulation
PPBS: Planning-Programming-Budgeting System
PPC: Personal Programmable Calculator
Platform Position Computer
Print Position Counter
Production Planning and Control
Program Planning and Control
PPDD: Plan Position Data Display
PPDP: Preprogram Definition Phase
PP/E: Parallel Print/Extract
PPE: Premodulation Processing Equipment
Pre-Production Evaluation
Problem Program Evaluator
PPEP: Pen Plotter Emulation Program
PPF: Production Possibility Frontier
P-PH-M: Pulse Phase Modulation
PPI: Program Position Indicator
Programmable Peripheral Interface
PPIB: Programmable Protocol Interface Board
PPICS: Production Planning Inventory Control System
PPIU: Programmable Peripheral Interface Unit
PPL: Polymorphic Programming Language
Print Positions Per Line
Program Production Library
PPLLT: Provisional Program Load Library Tape
PPM: Parts Per Million
Planned Preventive Maintenance

Previous Processor Mode
Pulse Position Modulation
PPP: Parallel Pattern Processor
Programmed Production Planning
PPS: Parallel Processing System
Patchboard Programming System
Programmed Processor System
Project Planning and Control System
Pulses Per Second
PPSAT: Peripheral Processor Saturation
PPT: Periodic Programs Termination
Programmer Productivity Techniques
Punched Paper Tape
PPTC: Purchased Part Tab Card
PPTR: Punched Paper Tape Reader
PPU: Peripheral Processing Unit
PPX: Packet Protocol Extension
Private Packet Exchange
PQA: Protected Queue Area
PQR: Productivity, Quality and Reliability
PQT: Preliminary Qualification Test
pr: prefix
print
printer
program
P&R: Planning and Review
PR: Paper tape Reader
Pattern Recognition
Performance Report
Physical Record
Preliminary Report
Principal Register
Print Restore
Program Register
Progress Report
Project Report

PRA: Page Replacement Alogrithm
Print Alphanumerically
Probabilistic Risk Assessment
Production Reader Assembly
Program Reader Assembly
PRAM: Productivity, Reliability, Availability and Maintainability
Program Requirements Analysis Method
PRAT: Production Reliability Acceptance Test
PRBS: Pseudorandom Binary Sequence
PRC: Printer Control
Procession Register Clock
Programmed Route Control
PRCA: Problem Reporting and Corrective Action
prcessn: processing
pre: prefix
prec: precedent
preceding
PREL: Programmable Rotary Encoded Logic
PREP: Preparation Program
prepak: prepackaging
prepacked
PREST: Party on Scientific and Technical Research Policy (EC)
PREST4: Preprocessor for Structured FORTRAN
PRF: Permanent Requirements File
Potential Risk Factor
Pulse Repetition Frequency
prfm: performance
PRFM: Pseduorandom Frequency Modulated
prgm: program
prgmr: programmer
pri: primary
priority
PRI: Printer Interface
Priority Requirement for Information

Processing Research Institute
Pulse Repetition Interval
PRIDE: Priority Receiving with Inter-Departmental Efficiency
Profitable Information by Design (through Phased Planning and Control)
Programmed Realiability in Design Engineering
PRIME: Planning through Retrieval of Information for Management Extrapolation
Prescribed Right to Income and Maximum Equity
Priority Management Efforts
PRINCE: Programmed International Computer Environment
PRINT: Pre-Edited Interpretive System
prio: priority
PRISM: Personnel Record Information System for Management
Progressive Refinement Integrated Supply Management
Program Integrated System Maintenance
prl: parallel
PRL: Processor Level
prn: printer
PRN: Print Numerically
Pseudorandom Number
PRNET: Packet Radio Network
prntg: printing
prntr: printer
pro: procedure
processor
procurement
PROBFOR: Probability Forecasting
proc: procedure
processing
processor

PROC: Programming Computer Proposed Required Operational Capability
procd: procedure
PROCLIB: Procedure Library
PROCOMP: Process Compiler
PROCOPT: Processing Option
procsd: processed
PROCSEQ: Processing Sequence
PROCTOT: Priority Routine Organizer for Computer Transfers and Operations and Transfers
PRODAC: Programmed Digital Automatic Control
PRODOC: Procedure Documentation
PROF: Prediction and Optimization of Failure Rate
PROFACTS: Production Formulation, Accounting and Cost System
PROFILE: Program Overview and File
PROFIT: Programmed Receiving, Ordering and Forecasting Inventory Technique
PROFITS: Personalized Real-Time-Oriented Financial Institutions Time Saving System
prog: program
　programmer
　programming
PROGDEV: Program Device
PROGOFOP: Program of Operation
progr: programmer
　programming
proj: project
PROJACS: Project Analysis and Control System
PROLAN: Processed Language
PROLOG: Programming in Logic
PROM: Programmable Read-Only Memory

P/ROM: Programmable Read-Only Memory
PROMIS: Project Management Information System
PROMISE: Programming Managers Information System
PROMPT: Production Reviewing, Organizing and Monitoring of Performance Techniques
　Project Management and Production Team Technique
PRONTO: Program for Numeric Tool Operation
　Programmable Network Telecommunications Operating System
PROOF: Projected Return on Open Office Facilities
PROSIM: Production System Simulator
PROSPRO: Process Systems Programs
prot: protect
PRPS: Program Requirement Process Specification
PRR: Pseudoresident Reader
　Pulse Repetition Rate
PRS: Polynomial Remainder Sequence
　Program Requirements Summary
　Pseudorandom Sequence
prt: printer
PRT: Program Reference Table
PRTM: Printing Response Time Monitor
PRTOT: Prototype Real-Time Optical Tracker
prtr: printer
prty: priority
PRU: Packet Radio Unit
　Printer Unit
ps: picosecond
P/S: Parallel to Serial

P&S: Planning and Scheduling
PS: Pace Setter
  Packet Switch
  Packet Switching
  Perfect Shuffle
  Physical Sequential
  Picture System
  Power Supply
  Preliminary Study
  Process Specification
  Processor Status
  Program Start
  Program Summary
  Programming System
  Protect Status
PSA: Polycrystalline Silicon Self-Aligned
PSAD: Prediction, Simulation, Adaptation, Decision
PSAL: Programming System Activity
PSAM: Partitioned Sequential Access Method
PSB: Program Specification Block
PSBNAME: Program Specification Block Name
PSC: Production Scheduling and Control
  Program Schedule Chart
  Program Status Chart
  Project Systems Control
PSCF: Processor Storage Control Function
PSCL: Programmed Sequential Control Logic
PSCS: Program Support Control System
PSD: Packed Switched Data
  Program Status Documents
  Program Status Doubleword
PSDM: Presentation Services for Data Management
PSDR: Program Status Doubleword Register

PS&DS: Program Statistics and Data Systems
PSE: Packet-Switching Exchange
psec: picosecond
PSECT: Program Section
PSF: Point Spread Function
PSG: Planning Systems Generator
PSGEN: Program Specification Block Generation
PSH: Productive Standard Hour
PSI: Personal Security Identifier
  Pounds per Square Inch
  Program Status Information
PSIC: Process Signal Interface Controller
PSK: Phase-Shift Keying
PSKM: Phase-Shift Keying Modem
PSK-PCM: Phase-Shift Keying/Pulse Code Modulation
PSL: Processor Status Longword
  Program Support Library
PSLI: Packet Switch Level Interface
PSM: Packet Switched Signaling Message
  Peak Selector Memory
  Power Supply Module
  Productive Standard Minute
  Program Support Monitor
PSMI: Phase-Shift Modal Interference
PSML: Processor System Modeling Language
psn: position
PSN: Packet Switched Network
  Packet Switched Node
  Program Summary Network
  Public Switched Network
PSOP: Power System Optimization Program
PSOS: Probably Secure Operating System
PSP: Packet Switching Processor
  Planned Standard Programming

Programmable Signal Processor
PSR: Page Send-Receive Performance Summary Report
Processor State Register
Program Status Register
Program Status Report
Program Support Representative
PSRO: Professional Standards Review Organization
PSRR: Product and Support Requirements Request
PSS: Packet Switching Services
Planned Systems Schedule
Printer Storage System
PST: Pair-Selected Ternary
Partition Specification Table
Periodic Self-Test
Program Structure Technology
PSTN: Public Switched Telephone Network
PSU: Packet Switching Unit
Peripheral Switching Unit
Power Supply Unit
Problem Statement Unit
Processor Service Unit
Processor Speed Up
Processor Storage Unit
Program Storage Unit
PSW: Processor Status Word
Program Status Word
PSWR: Program Status Word Register
PSYNC: Processor Synchronous
pt: point
PT: Paper Tape
Performance Test
Printer Terminal
Processing Time
Processor Terminal
Programmable Terminal
Punched Tape

PTA: Paper Tape Accessory
Programmable Translation Array
Pulse Torquing Assembly
Purchase Transaction Analysis
PTB: Page Table Base
PTBR: Punched Tape Block Reader
PTBX: Private Telegraph Branch Exchange
PTCC: Problem Tracking and Change Control
PT CLD: Part Called
PTCPY: Paper Tape Copy
ptd: printed
PTD: Parallel Transfer Disk Drive
Programmable Threshold Detector
PTDOS: Processor Technology Disk Operating System
PTE: Page Table Entry
Potential Toxic Elements
Protect Error
PTF: Program Temporary Fix
PTG: Place To Go
PTH: Project Team Head
PTI: Program Transfer Interface
PTIOS: Paper Tape Input/Output System
PTL: Parameter Table Load
Process and Test Language
PTM: Phase Time Modulation
Programmable Terminal Multiplexer
Programmable Timer Module
Pulse Transmission Mode
PTMS: Pattern Transformation Memory System
PTOP: Program To Program
PTOPC: Program To Program Communications
PTOS: Paper Tape-Oriented Operating System
ptout: printout

PTP: Paper Tape Perforator
Paper Tape Punch
Processor To Processor
ptr: pointer
printer
PTR: Paper Tape Reader
Punched Tape Reader
PTR/P: Paper Tape Reader/Punch
PTS: Paper Tape-to-Magnetic Tape Conversion System
PTS: Paper Tape System
Programmable Terminal System
Public Telephone Service
PTT: Post Telephone and Telegraph Administration
PTTC: Paper Tape and Transmission Code
PTU: Package Transfer Unit
PTV: Punched Tape Verifier
PTX: Plus TWX
PU: Peripheral Unit
Physical Unit
Processing Unit
PUB: Physical Unit Block
PUC: Processing Unit Cabinet
PUD: Physical Unit Directory
Planned Unit Development
PUF: Percent Unaccounted For
PUFI: Pair-Usage-Frequency Indicator
PUL: Program Update Library
pun: punch
punctuation
punc: punch
punctuation
PUNC: Practical, Unpretentious, Nomographic Computer Program Unit Counter
PUP: Performance Units Plan
Peripheral Unit Processor
Peripheral Universal Processor
PUSVC: Physical Unit Services Manager

PUT: Program Update Tape
PV: Path Verification
Process Variable
PVC: Permanent Virtual Circuit
Program and Velocity Computer
PVCS: Portable Voice Communication System
PVD: Plan View Display
PVI: Programmable Video Interface
PVR: Prefix Value Register
Process Variable Record
PVS: Program Validation Services
PVT: Parameter Variable Table
Performance Validation Test
PVTR: Portable Video Tape Recorder
pw: password
PW: Printed Wiring
Private Wire
Processor Write
Pulse Width
PWA: Printed Wire Assembly
Private Write Area
PWAIT: Processor Wait Acknowledge
PWB: Printed Wiring Board
Programmer's Workbench
PWBA: Printing Wiring Board Assembly
PWB/MM: Programmer's Workbench Memorandum Macros
PWCM: Pulse Width with Carrier Modulation
PWEA: Printed Wiring and Electronic Assemblies
PWM: Printed Wiring Master
Pulse-Width Modulation
pwr: power
PWR: Processor Write
PWRNO: Power Failure
PWS: Programmer Work Station
Program Work Statement
PZC: Point of Zero Charge

Q

q: quarterly
query
queue
quotient
Q&A: Questions and Answers
QA: Quality Assessment
Quality Assurance
QAM: Quadrature Amplitude Modulation
QART: Quality Assurance Review Technique
QAS: Question Answering System
QASK: Quadrature Amplitude Shift Keying
QB: Quick Batch
QBD: Quasi-Bidirectional
QBE: Query By Example
QC: Quality Control
Quiesce-Completed
QCB: Queue Control Block
QCD: Query Complexity Degree
QCM: Quantitative Computer Management
QCR: Queue Control Record
QCRT: Quick Change Real-Time
QCS: Quality Control Specification
QDEBUG: Quick Diagnostic Debugging Program
QDM: Quality Assurance, Documentation and Maintenance
QE: Queue Empty
QEC: Quiesce-at-End-of-Chain
QEL: Quality Element
Queue Element
QF: Quality Factor
Queue Full
QIL: Quad-In-Line
QIO: Queue Input/Output
QISAM: Queued Indexed Sequential Access Method
QL: Query Language
QL/1: Query Language/One
QLP: Query Language Processor
QLSA: Queuing Line-Sharing Adapter
QMDO: Quality Material Development Objectives
QMR: Qualitative Material Requirement
QN: Query Normalization
QNS: Quantity Not Sufficient
QPAM: Quadrature Phase and Amplitude Modulation
QPC: Quasi-Public Company
QPL: Qualified Products List
QPS: Query Property Similarity
QPSK: Quaternary Phase Shift Keying
qr: quotient
QR: Quadratic Residues
Quality and Reliability
Q&RA: Quality and Reliability Assurance
QRC: Quick Reaction Communications
QRL: Quick Relocate and Link
QRP: Query and Reporting Processor
QRT: Queue Run-Time
QS: Query Similarity
Query System
Queue Select
QSA: Quad Synchronous Adapter
QSAM: Queued Sequential Access Method
QSL: Queue Search Limit
Q-SYSTEM: Inventory control system with varying reorders

qt: quotient
QTAM: Queued Telecommunications Access Method
Queued Terminal Access Method
QTH: Queued Transaction Handling
QTP: Quality Test Plan
QTR: Quality Technical Requirement
QTS: Quantizer Threshold Spacing
qu: quality
qual: quality
QUALTA: Quad Asynchronous Local Terminal Adapter
QUANSY: Question Answering System
QUEL: Query Language
QUEST: Query Evaluation and Search Technique
QUICO: Quality Improvement through Cost Optimization
QUID PRO QUO: Something for Something
QUIP: Quad In-Line Package
Quota Input Processor
QUO WARRANTO: By what Authority
QXI: Queue Executive Interface

R

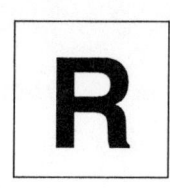

r: radius
range
ratio
read
reader
receive
receiver
record
register
relation
reliability
report
request
research
reset
resistance
resistor
reverse
revolution
right
ring
routine
R&A: Reports and Analysis
Research and Analysis
RA: Random Access
Ratio Actuator
Read Amplifier
Receiver Attenuation
Record Address
Refer to Accepter
Reimbursement Authorization
Relative Address
Reliability Analysis
Reliability Assessment
Relocation Address
Return Address
Rotary Assembly
RAA: Remote Access Audio Device

RAC: Radio Adaptive Communications
Rapid Action Change
Read Address Counter
RACA: Resource Accounting and Cost Allocation
RACE: Random Access Computer Equipment
Research and Development in Advanced Communications for Europe (EC)
Results Analysis, Computation and Evaluation
RACEP: Random Access and Correlation for Extended Performance
RACER: Runner Administration and Computerized Entry Routine
RACF: Resource Access Control Facility
RACS: Random Access Communications System
Remote Access Computing System
Remote Automatic Calibration System
Remote Automatic Control System
RAD: Random Access Device
Random Access Disk
Rapid Access Device
Rapid Access Disk
RADA: Random Access Discrete Address
RADAC: Rapid Digital Automatic Computing
RADACS: Random Access Discrete Address Communications System

147

RADAR: Receivable Accounts Data-entry And Retrieval
RADAS: Random Access Discrete Address System
RADEM: Random Access Delta Modulation
RADIC: Research and Development Information Center
RADIR: Random Access Document Indexing and Retrieval
RADOC: Remote Automatic Detection Contingencies
RADOT: Real-Time Automatic Digital Optical Tracker
RAF: Requirements Analysis Form
RAFT: Recomp Algebraic Formula Translator
RAG: ROM Address Gate
RAI: Random Access and Inquiry
RAIN: Relational Algebraic Interpreter
RAIR: Recordak Automated Information Retrieval
   Remote Access Immediate Response
RAIS: Range Automated Information System
RAK: Read Access Key station
RAL: Rapid Access Loop
RALF: Relocatable Assembly Language Floating point
RALU: Register and Arithmetic Logic Unit
RAM: Random-Access Measurement
   Random-Access Memory
   Reliability, Availability and Maintainability
   Remote Access Monitor
   Remote Area Monitoring
RAMAC: Random-Access Memory Accounting and Control
RAMB: Random Access Memory Buffer
RAMCEASE: Reliability, Availability, Maintainability, Cost Effectiveness and Systems Effectiveness
RAM-D: Reliability And Maintainability-Dependability
   Reliability And Maintainability-Durability
RAMD: Random Access Memory Device
RAMIS: Rapid Access Management Information System
   Receiving, Assembly Maintenance, Inspection, Storage
RAMM: Random Access Memory Module
RAMMIT: Reliability and Maintainability Management Improvement Techniques
RAMS: Random Access Measurement System
   Remote Automatic Multipurpose Station
RAN: Raw Area Normalization
   Request for Authority to Negotiate
RANCID: Real And Not Corrected Input Data
RANCOM: Random Communication Satellite
RAND: Research And Development
RANDAM: Random Access Nondestructive Advanced Memory
RANDID: Rapid Alphanumeric Digital Indicating Device
RAO: Related Application Object
RAP: Random Access Program
   Regulatory Accounting Practices
   Relational Associative Processor
   Remote-Access Point
   Resident Assembler Program

Review and Analysis Program
Revised Accounting Procedures
RAPCOE: Random Access Programming and Checkout Equipment
RAPID: Reactor and Plant Integrated Dynamics
Relative Address Programming Implementation Device
Remote Access Planning for Institutional Development
Retrieval And Processing Information for Display
Retrieval And Production for Integrated Data
Retrieval through Automated Publication and Information Digest
RAPIDS: Rapid Automated Problem Identification System
RAPS: Retrieval Analysis and Presentation System
RAPTAP: Random Access Parallel Tape
RAR: Return Address Register
RARES: Rotating Associative Relational Store
RAS: Regional Automated System
Reliability, Availability, Serviceability
Requirements Audit System
Row Address Strobe
RASER: Random-to-Serial Converter
RASI: Reliability, Availability, Service, Improvement
RASM: Remote Analog Submultiplexer
RASP: Remote Access Switching and Patching
Retrieval And Sort Processor
RAST: Reliability And System Test

RASTAC: Random Access Storage and Control
RASTAD: Random Access Storage and Display
RAT: Remote Area Terminal
RATC: Rate-Aided Tracking Computer
RATE: Remote Automatic Telemetry Equipment
RATFOR: Rational FORTRAN
RAVE: Random Access Video Editing
Random Access Viewing Equipment
RAW: Read After Write
RAX: Random Access
Remote Access
Rural Automatic Exchange
RB: Relay Block
Request Block
Return to Bias
RBA: Relative Byte Address
RBC: Remote Balance Control
Right Bounded Context
RBCS: Retail Batch Communications Subsystem
RBD: Reliability Block Diagram
Reliable Block Design
RBE: Remote Batch Entry
RBF: Remote Batch Facility
RBM: Real-Time Batch Monitor
Relative Batch Monitor
Remote Batch Module
RBOCs: Regional Bell Operating Companies
RBS: Remote Batch System
RBT: Remote Batch Terminal
RBTE: Remote Batch Terminal Emulator
RBTM: Remote Batch Terminal Module
RC: Radix Complement
Reader Code
Real Circuit
Receive Common
Receiver Card
Remote Computer

Remote Concentrator
Remote Control
Resistance-Coupled
Resistor-Capacitor
RCA: Reaction Control Assembly
Remote Control Adapter
RCAC: Remote Computer Access Communications Service
RCB: Resource Control Block
RCC: Read Channel Continue
Real-Time Computer Complex
Remote Center Compliance
Remote Communications Complex
Reset Control Center
RCCAM: Remote Computer Communications Access Method
rcd: record
RCD: Registered Connective Device
RCE: Relay Communications Electronics
Reliability Control Engineering
Remote Control Equipment
RCF: Remote Call Forwarding
Retail Computer Facilities
RCHM: Remote Computer Controlled Hardware Monitor
RCI: Read Channel Initialize
RCI: Remote Control Interface
RCIS: Remote Computer Interface Subsystem
RCIU: Remote Computer Interface Unit
rcl: recall
RCL: Reliability Control Level
RCN: Receipt of Change Notice
Record Control Number
Report Change Notice
Report Control Number
RCP: Receive Clock Pulse
Recognition and Control Processor
Remote Computer Pool
Remote Control Panel

RCR: Required Carrier Return character
RCS: Reloadable Control Storage
Remote Computing Service
Remote Control Switch
Remote Control System
RCSDF: Reconfigurable Computer System Design Facility
RCSS: Random Communication Satellite System
RCT: Regional Control Task
Reversible Counter
RCTL: Resistance Coupled Transistor Logic
Resistor-Capacitor-Transistor Logic
RCU: Remote Control Unit
rcv: receive
RCV: Remote Controlled Vehicle
rcvd: received
RCW: Return Control Word
R&D: Research and Development
rd: read
RD: Read Data
Receive Data
Refer to Drawer
Reference Document
Register Drive
Required Data
Research and Development
Rotational Delay
RDA: Register Display Assembly
Run-Time Debugging Aid
RDAL: Representation Dependent Accessing Language
RDAU: Remote Data Acquisition Unit
RDAV: Reset Data Available
RDB: Relational Data Base
RDBA: Remote Data Base Access
RDC: Remote Data Collection
Remote Data Concentrator
RDCM: Reduced Delta Code Modulation
RD&D: Research, Development, and Demonstration

RDDSEM: Real Data System Element Model
RD&E: Research, Development, and Engineering
Research, Development, and Evaluation
RDE: Receive Data Enable
RDF: Record Definition Field
RD/I: Research, Development, and Innovation
RDI: Remote Data Input
RDIU: Read Interface Unit
Remote Device Interface Unit
rdj: readjustment
RDL: Random Dynamic Load
Report Definition Language
Resistor Diode Logic
RDM: Real-Time Data Base Manager
Remote Digital Multiplexer
RDMS: Relational Data Management System
RDO: Regular Data Organization
RDOS: Real-Time Disk Operating System
RDP: Remote Data Processor
RDPI: Real Personal Disposable Income
rdr: reader
RDR: Receive Data Register
Remote Digital Readout
RDSM: Remote Digital Submultiplexer
RDT: Remote Data Transmitter
Resource Definition Table
RDT&E: Research, Development, Test, and Engineering
Research, Development, Test, and Evaluation
rdy: ready
R&E: Research and Engineering
RE: Request Element
REACT: Register Enforced Automated Control Technique
Resource Allocation Control Tool
READ: Real-Time Electronic Access and Display
REAL: Relocatable Assembler Language
rec: receipt
receive
record
recover
REC: Remote Console
RECAPS: Read Encode/Capture/Proof/Sort
recd: received
RECEP: Relative Capacity Estimating Capacity
RECFM: Record Format
RECFMS: Record Formatted Maintenance Statistics
RECMF: Radio and Electronic Component Manufacturers Federation
RECMS: Record Maintenance Statistics
RECNUM: Record Number
RECON: Remote Console
recov: recovery
RECSYS: Recreation Systems Analysis
red: reduction
REDAC: Real-Time Data Acquisition
REDC: Read Control
REDE: Receiving Decoding
ref: reference
REFS: Remote Entry Flexible Security
reg: register
regular
REG: Range Extender with Gain
REGAD: Regenerate Address
REGIO: European Community regional statistical databank (EC)
regis: register
REGIS: Relational General Information System
regs: regulations
REINIT: Recovery Initialization

REINS: Requirements Electronic Input System
rej: reject
REJEN: Remote Job Entry
rel: relative
    release
    relocatable
RELQ: Release-Quiesce
rem: remark
REM: Recognition Memory
REMAC: Remote Data Acquisition Subsystem
REMAP: Record Extraction, Manipulation and Print
REMAS: Remote Energy Monitor/Alarm System
REMICS: Real-Time Manufacturing Information Control System
REMS: Rohm Electronic Message System
REN: Remote Enable
rep: reply
REP: Re-Entrant Processor
REP-OP: Repetitive Operation
REPORTER: Report Writer
repr: representation
REPROM: Reprogrammable Read-Only Memory
req: request
reqd: required
reqs: requires
reqt: requirement
RER: Residual Error Rate
res: reserve
    reset
    restore
RES: Reader Stop
    Remote Entry Service
RESLOAD: Resident Loader
RESQ: Research Queueing
resrt: restart
ret: return
retd: returned
REU: Ready Extension Unit
rev: reverse
    revolution

REVS: Requirements Engineering and Validation System
REX: Real-Time Executive Routine
    Real-Time Executive System
    Regression Expert
RF: Radio Frequency
    Rating Factor
    Read Forward
    Register File
    Reliability Factor
    Reporting File
    Remote File Access
RFAM: Remote File Access Monitor
RFB: Reliability Functional Block
    Request For Bid
RFCP: Request For Computer Program
RFD: Ready For Data
RFG: Report Format Generator
RFI: Radio Frequency Interference
    Ready For Issue
    Request For Information
RFMS: Remote File Management System
RFNM: Ready For Next Message
RFO: Request for Factory Order
RFP: Request For Programming
    Request For Proposal
RFQ: Request For Quotation
rfrsh: refresh
RFS: Random Filing System
    Report Forwarding System
rfsh: refresh
RFSP: Request For System Proposal
RFT: Request For Test
RGB: Red, Green and Blue
RGCAS: Remote Global Computer Access Service
RGP: Remote Graphics Processor
RH: Request/Response Header
RHA: Records Holding Area
RHR: Receiver Holding Register
RHS: Right Hand Side
RI: Radio Interface
    Register Immediate
    Reliability Index
    Ring Indicator

RIA: Regulatory Impact Analysis
RIC: Radar Interface Control
Read-In Counter
RICS: Reports Index Control System
RID: Rapidate Interactive Debugger
Review Item Disposition
RIDF: Random Input Describing Function
RIF: Relative Importance Factor
Reliability Improvement Factor
RIGFET: Resistive Insulated-Gate Field Effect Transistor
RIH: Read Inhibit
RIL: Representation Independent Language
RIM: Read-In Mode
Read Interrupt Mask
RIMS: Remote Information Management System
Requestor-Oriented Information Management System
RINT: Reverse Interrupt
RIO: Relocatable Input/Output
RIOC: Remote Input/Output Controller
RIOS: Rotating Image Optical Scanner
RIOT: RAM Input/Output Timer
Real-Time Input-Output Transducer
Real-Time Input-Output Translator
Remote Input/Output Terminal
Resolution of Initial Operational Techniques
Retrieval of Information by On-Line Terminal
RIP: Random Input Sampling
RIPFCOMTF: Rapid Item Processor to Facilitate Complex Operations on Magnetic Tape Files
RIPL: Representation-Independent Programming Language

RIQS: Remote Information Query System
RIR: Request Immediate Reply
ROM Instruction Register
RI/RO: Roll-In/Roll-Out
RIS: Record Input Subroutine
Remote Information System
Rotating Image Scanner
RISC: Reduced Instruction Set Computing
Remote Information Systems Center
RISOS: Research in Secured Operating Systems
RISS: Relational Inquiry and Storage System
RITREAD: Rapid Iterative Reanalysis for Automated Design
RJE: Remote Job Entry
RJET: Remote Job Entry Terminal
RJEX: Remote Job Entry Executive
RJF: Remote Job Entry Processor
RJO: Remote Job Output
RJP: Remote Job Processing
Remote Job Processor
RKM: Radar Keyboard Multiplexer
RKR: Rack Register
R-L: Right to Left
R/L: Rotate/Length
RL: Record Length
Remote Loopback
RLA: Remote Loop Adapter
RLC: ROM Location Counter
Run Length Coding
RLD: Relocation Dictionary
RLE: Receiver Latch Enable
Request Loading Entry
RLIN: Research Library Information Network
RLL: Relocating Linking Loader
RLR: Record Length Register
RLSD: Received Line Signal Detector
R&M: Reports and Memoranda
R/M: Reliability/Maintainability

RM: Register Memory
Remote Manipulator
Resource Manager
Revolutions per Minute
Routine Maintenance
RMA: Random Multiple Access
Reliability, Maintainability, Availability
RMAG: Recursive Macroactuated Generator
RMAX: Range Maximum
RMB: Rightmost BIT
RMC: Rack-Mount Control
Rack-Mounted Computer
Rod Memory Computer
rmdr: remainder
RME: Rack-Mount Extender
Request Monitor Entry
RMF: Resource Management Facility
Resource Measurement Facility
RML: Radar Microwave Link
Relational Machine Language
Remote Maintenance Line
RMM: Read Mostly Memory
Read Mostly Mode
Remote Maintenance Monitor
RMMU: Removable Media Memory Unit
RMNAME: Randomizing Module Name
RMON: Resident Monitor
RMOS: Refractory Metal Gate Metal Oxide Semiconductor
R/MOS: Refractory Metal Gate Metal Oxide Semiconductor
RMPI: Remote Memory Port Interface
RMS: Random Mass Storage
Record Management Service
Record Management System
Recovery Management Support
Resource Management System
Root Mean Square
RMSE: Root Mean Square Error
RMSR: Recovery Management Support Recorder
rmt: remote
RMTB: Reconfiguration Maximum Theoretical Bandwidth
RMU: Remote Multiplexer Unit
Resource Management Unit
RMW: Ready-Modify-Write
RMX: Remote Multiplexer
RN: Reception Node
Requisition Number
RNAC: Remote Network Access Controller
RNB: Received - Not Billed
RNC: Request Next Character
RNET: Remote Network
rngt: renegotiate
RNMC: Regional Network Measurement Center
RNP: Remote Network Processor
RNR: Receive Not Ready
RNSC: Reference Number Status Code
RO: Read Only
Receive Only
Regional Office
Register Output
ROADS: Roadway Analysis and Design System
ROAR: Royal Optimizing Assembly Routine
ROBAR: Read Only Back-Up Address Register
ROC: Recovery Operations Center
Reliability Operating Characteristic
Remote Operator's Console
Required Operational Capability
ROCR: Remote Optical Character Recognition
ROD: Reorder On Demand
RODIAC: Rotary Dual Input for Analog Computation

ROF: Remote Operator Facility
ROIN: Reorganization of the Interconnection Network
ROLS: Remote On-Line Subsystem
ROM: Read-Only Memory
ROMAD: Read Only Memory Automatic Design
ROMM: Read-Only Memory Module
ROMON: Receiving-Only Monitor
RONS: Read Only Nano Store
ROP: Receive Only Printer
ROPES: Remote On-Line Print Executive System
ROPP: Receive-Only Page Printer
ROS: Read-Only Storage
Real-Time Operating System
Resident Operating System
ROSAR: Read Only Storage Address Register
ROSCOE: Remote Operating System Conversational Operating Environment
ROSDR: Read Only Storage Data Register
ROSE: Retrieval by On-Line Search
ROSS: Route-Oriented Simulation System
rot: rotate
ROT: Remaining Operating Time
ROTH: Read Only Tape Handler
ROTR: Receive-Only Typing Reperforator
ROTSAL: Rotate and Scale
RQL: Rejectable Quality Level
RP: Reader-Printer
Reader/Punch
Receive Processor
RPB: Remote Programming Box
RPC: Regional Processing Center
Registered Protective Circuit
Remote Position Control
RPCS: Reject Processing and Control System
RPE: Relative Price Effect
Required Page-End character
RPG: Report Program Generator

RPI: Read, Punch and Interpret
Rows Per Inch
RPL: Remote Program Loader
Robot Programming Language
Running Program Language
RPM: Read Program Memory
Repeats Per Minute
Revolutions Per Minute
Rotations Per Minute
RPMC: Remote Performance Monitoring and Control
RPN: Real Page Number
Regular Processor Network
Reverse Polish Notation
RPPE: Research, Program, Planning, Evaluation
RPROM: Reprogrammable Read-Only Memory
RPS: Real-Time Programming System
Records Per Sector
Remote Printing System
Requirements Planning System
Revolutions Per Second
Rotational Position Sensing
rpt: repeat
RPT: Records Per Track
Repeat character
Request Programs Termination
RPTC: Relative Priority Test Circuit
RPU: Regional Processing Unit
Remote Processing Unit
RQ: Repeat Request
R&QA: Reliability and Quality Assurance
R&QC: Reliability and Quality Control
R&R: Reliability and Response
RR: Receive Ready
Register to Register
Research Report
Return Register
RRA: Remote Record Access

RRAR: ROM Return Address Register
RRDS: Relative Record Data Set
RRG: Resource Request Generator
RRIN: Readiness Risk Index Number
RRN: Relative-Record Number
Remote Request Number
RROS: Resistive Read-Only Storage
RRR: Run-Time Reduction Ratio
RRT: Relative Retention Time
RRTS: Remote Radar Tracking System
R&S: Register and Storage
Reliability and Serviceability
RS: Reader Stop
Real Storage
Record Separator (character)
Register Select
Remote Site
Request to Send
R-S: Reset-Set
Rotate-Shift
Run-Stop
RSA: Remote Storage Activities Requirements Statement Analyzer
RSB: Remote System Base
RSC: Remote Store Controller
RSCC: Remote Site Computer Complex
RSCS: Remote Spooling Communications Subsystem
RSDP: Remote Site Data Processor
RSDT: Remote Station Data Terminal
RSE: Record Selection Expression
Request Select Entry
RSET: Register Set
RSEU: Remote Scanner-Encoder Unit
RSEXEC: Resource-Sharing Executive
RSF: Remote Support Facility
RSG: Reference Signal Generator
RS&I: Rules, Standards and Instructions

RSID: Resource Identification Table
RSL: Requirements Statement Language
RSM: Real Storage Management
RSN: Rearrangeable Switching Network
RSP: Reader/Sorter Processor
Record Select Program
Required Space (character)
RSPT: Real Storage Page Table
RSS: Real-Time Switching System
Relational Storage System
Resource Security System
Routing and Switching System
rst: reset
RST: Read Symbol Table
Remote Station
RSTC: Remote Siter Telemetry Computer
RSTCP: Remote Synchronous Terminal Control Program
RSTS: Resource-Sharing Time-Sharing System
RSTS/E: Resource-Sharing Time-Sharing System/Extended
RSU: Register Storage Unit
Relay Storage Unit
Remote Service Unit
RSVP: Rapid Serial Visual Presentation
RSX: Real-Time Resource-Sharing Executive
rt: right
R&T: Research and Technology
RT: Real Time
Receive Timing
Register Transfer
Remote Terminal
Reperforator/Transmitter
Run Time
RTA: Real-Time Accumulator
Real-Time Analyzer
Reliability Test Assembly
Remote Trunk Arrangement
Resident Transient Area

RTAC: Real-Time Adaptive Control
RTAM: Remote Telecommunications Access Method
Remote Terminal Access Method
RTB: Real Time BASIC
Response/Throughput Bias
RTBM: Real Time BIT Mapping
RTC: Real-Time Clock
Real-Time Command
Real-Time Computer
Relative Time Clock
Remote Terminal Controller
RTCAD: Register Transfer Computer Aided Design
RTCC: Real-Time Computer Complex
RTCF: Real-Time Computer Facility
RTCS: Real-Time Communication System
R&TD: Research and Technological Development Policy
RTD: Research and Technology Development
Resistance Temperature Detector
RTDBUG: Real-Time Debug
RTE: Real-Time Executive
Remote Terminal Emulator
Request To Expedite
RTE-B: Real-Time Basic
RTES: Real-Time Executive System
RTF: Real-Time FORTRAN
RTI: Real-Time Interface
Referred To Input
RTIO: Real-Time Input/Output
Remote Terminal Input/Output
RTIP: Remote Terminal Interface Package
RTIRS: Real-Time Information Retrieval System
RTJ: Return Jump
RTL: Real-Time Language
Real-Time Link
Register Transfer Level
Resistor-Transistor Logic
Run Time Library
RTM: Real-Time Management
Real-Time Monitor
Register Transfer Module
Research Technical Memoranda
RTMBEP: Real-Time Minimal Byte Error Probability
RTMS: Real-Time Memory System
Real-Time Multiprogramming System
RTMTR: Remote Transmitter
rtn: return
routine
RTN: Remote Terminal Network
RTO: Real-Time Operation
RTOP: Real-Time Optical Processing
RTOS: Real-Time Operating System
RTP: Remote Terminal Processor
Remote Test Processor
Run Time Package
RTPL: Real-Time Procedural Language
RTPS: Real-Time Programming System
RTR: Response Time Reporting
rts: rights
RTS: Real-Time System
Remote Terminal System
Request To Send
RTSW: Real Time Software
RTT: Request To Talk
RTTY: Radio Teletypewriter
RTU: Remote Terminal Unit
RTVS: Run Time Variable Stack
RTX: Real-Time Executive
RTYPE: Relation Type
RTZ: Return To Zero
RU: Are You....?
Request/Response Unit
RUC: Reporting Unit Code
RUD: Recently Used Directory
RUF: Resource Utilization Factor
Revolving Underwriting Facility

RUG: Regional Unit Group
Resource Utilization Graph
RUM: Resource Utilization Monitor
RUP: Remote Unit Processor
RUT: Resource Utilization Time
RVA: Recorded Voice Announcement
Relative Virtual Address
RVC: Relative Velocity Computer
RVI: Reverse Interrupt
RVN: Requirements Verification Network
RVS: Relative Value Studies
RVT: Reliability Verification Tests
Resource Vector Table
RW: Read-Write
R/W: Read/Write
RWED: Read, Write, Extend and Delete
RWI: Read-Write-Initialize
RWM: Read/Write Memory
R/WM: Read/Write Memory
rwnd: rewind
RWO: Routine Work Order
RWR: Read Writer Register
RWX: Read Write Execute
rx: receive
R&X: Register and Indexed
RXM: Read/Write Expandable Memory
RX(NP): Nonpolarized Return-to-Zero recording
RXVP: A FORTRAN Automated Verification System
RZ: Reset (Return) to Zero
RZ: Return to Zero Level
RZM: Return to Zero Mark
RZ(P): Polarized Return-to-Zero recording

S

s: scalar
second
sender
server
set
sign
single
slave
software
source
stack
state
storage
switch
switching
synchronous
system
sa: semiannual(ly)
semiautomatic
SA: Sample Array
Scaling Amplifier
Security Assistance
Sense Amplifier
Servo Amplifier
Shift Advance
Signal Analyzer
Signal Attenuation
Source Address
Speaker Analysis
Stack Access
Store Address
Structured Analysis
Swing Arm
Synchro Amplifier
System Administrator
Systems Address
Systems Analysis
Systems Analyst
SAA: Satellite Attitude Acquisition
Service Action Analysis
Servo-Actuated Assembly
Slot Array Antenna
Step Adjustable Antenna
SAAC: Schedule Allocation And Control
SAAM: Simulation Analysis And Modeling
SAAOC: System of Analysis and Assignment of Operations according to Capacities
SAB: Solid Assembly Block
Stack Access Block
System Advisory Board
SABE: Society for Automation in Business Education
SABF: Subarray Beam Former
SABIR: Semiautomatic Bibliographic Information Retrieval
SABO: Sense Amplifier Blocking Oscillator
SABOD: Same As Basic Operations Directive
SABR: Symbolic Assembler for Binary Relocatable Programs
SABRE: Semiautomated Business Research Environment
SAC: Secondary Accountability Center
Semiautomatic Coding
Serving Area Concept
Servo Adapter Coupler
Single Address Code
Special Area Code
Storage Access Channel
Storage Access Control
Store And Clear

159

SACA: Service Action Change Analysis
SACCS: Schedule And Cost-Control System
SACE: Semiautomatic Checkout Equipment
SACI: Secondary Address Code Indicator
SACK: Selection Acknowledge
SACMAP: Selective Automatic Computational Matching and Positioning System
SACNET: Secure Automatic Communications Network
SACS: Simulation for the Analysis of Computer Systems
Synchronous Altitude Communications Satellite
SA&D: Structured Analysis and Design
SAD: Sealed And Delivery
Store Address Director
System Analysis Drawing
SADAP: Simplified Automatic Data Plotter
SADC: Sequential Analog-Digital Computer
SADD: Semiautomatic Detection Device
SADIC: Solid-State Analog-to-Digital Computer
SADP: System Architecture Design Package
SADS: Single Application Data Sheet
SADSAC: Sampled Data Simulator And Computer
SADT: Structured Analysis and Design Technique
SAE: Self-Addressed Envelope
Stand Alone Executive
SAF: Segment Address Field
Specification Approval Form
Structural Adjustment Facility

SAFER: Structual Analysis, Frailty Evaluation and Redesign
SAFF: Store And Forward Facsimile
SAFRAS: Self-Adaptive Flexible Format Retrieval and Storage System
SAG: Systems Analysis Group
SAGE: Semiautomatic Ground Environment
SAI: Subarchitectural Interface
SAIC: Switch Action Interrupt Count
SAID: Semiautomatic Integrated Documentation
SAIM: Systems Analysis and Integration Model
SAINT: Symbolic Automatic Integrator
SAL: Service Action Log
Structured Assembly Language
Symbolic Assembly Language
Systems Assembly Language
SALE: Simple Algebraic Language for Engineers
SALINET: Satellite Library Information Network
SALS: Solid-State Acoustoelectric Light Scanner
SALT: Symbolic Algebraic Language Translator
SAM: Selective Automatic Monitoring
Sequential Access Memory
Sequential Access Method
Service Attitude Measurement
Simulation of Analog Methods
System Activity Monitor
System Analysis Machine
Systems Adaptor Module
SAMA: Scientific Apparatus Makers Association

SAMANTHA: System for the Automated Management of Text from a Hierarchical Arrangement
SAMI: Single Action Maintenance Instruction
SAMIS: Structural Analysis and Matrix Interpretation System
SAMM: Systematic Activity Modeling Method
SAMOS: Silicon and Aluminum Metal Oxide Semiconductor
samp: sample
SAMPS: Subdivision And Map Plotting System
SAMS: Sampling Analog Memory System
Satellite Automatic Monitoring System
SAMSON: Strategic Automatic Message Switching Operational Network
SAN: Small Area Network
Subsidiary Account Number
SAND: Sorting and Assembly of New Data
SANDA: Supplies And Accounts
SANDS: Structural Analysis Numerical Design System
SANR: Subject to Approval-No Risks
SANS: Simplified Account - Numbering System
SAO: Select Address and Operate
Systems Analysis Office
SAOS: Select Address Output Signal
SAP: Share Assembly Program
Soon As Possible
Structural Analysis Program
Symbolic Assembly Program
SAPR: Semi-Annual Progress Report

SAR: Segment Address Register
Semiannual Report
Source Address Register
Storage Address Register
SARA: System Availability and Reliability Analysis
Systems Analysis and Resource Accounting
SARG: Self-Adapting Report Generator
SARM: Set Asynchronous Response Mode
SARP: Standards And Recommended Practices
SARTS: Switched Access Remote Test System
SAS: Statistical Analysis System
Switched Access System
SASR: Semi-Annual Status Report
Systems Approach to Training
SAT: System Access Technique
SATF: Shortest Access Time First
SATNET: Satellite Network
SAU: Smallest Addressable Unit
sav: save
SAVE: System for Automatic Value Exchange
SAVT: Secondary Address Vector Table
sb: sideband
standby
SB: Stabilized Breakdown
Stack Base
Statistical Bulletins
Straight Binary
Synchronous Bit
SBA: Shared Batch Area
Shipping and Billing Authorization
Strategic Business Area
SBC: Single Board Computer
Small Business Computer
SBCA: Sensor Based Control Adapter

SBCU: Sensor Based Control Unit
SBD: Structured Block Diagram
SBI: Single Byte Interleaved
SBIR: Storage Bus In Register
SBM: Space Block Map
sbmdl: submodel
SBN: Strontium Barium Niobate
SBP: Semiconductor Bipolar Processor
SBR: Storage Buffer Register
SBS: Satellite Business Systems
 Special Block Sale
 Subscript Character
SBT: Six BIT Transcode
SBU: Station Buffer Unit
sc: semiconductor
SC: Satellite Communication
 Satellite Computer
 Saturable Core
 Selector Channel
 Self Contained
 Send Common
 Sequence Controller
 Sequence Counter
 Session Control
 Set Clear
 Short Circuit
 Signal Comparator
 Sine-Cosine
 Single Column
 Single Counter
 Software Contractor
 Solid-state Circuit
 Source Code
 Special Circuit
 Start Computer
 Statistical Control
 Stop-Continue
 Storage Capacity
 Stored Command
 Subscriber Computer
 Symbolic Code
 System Control
 System Controller
SCA: Synchronous Communications Adapter
 System Control Area
SCAC: Syntax-Controlled Acoustic Classifier
SCAD: Database on documents published by the Community and periodical articles on the Community (EC) Schedule, Capability, Availability, Dependability
 Subprogram Change Affect Diagram
SCADA: Supervisory Control And Data Acquisition
SCALD: Structural Computer Aided Logic Design
SCAM: Synchronous Communications Access Method
SCAN: Schedule Analysis
SCANNET: Scandanavian Network
SCAR: Subcell Address Register
SCARA: Selective Compliance Assembly Robot Arm
SCARS: Status, Control Alerting and Reporting System
SCAT: Schottky Cell Array Technology
SCATS: Sequentially Controlled Automatic Transmitter Start Start
SCB: Stack Control Block
 Station Control Block
 Stream Control Block
 Subscriber Control Block
SCC: Satellite Communications Concentrator
 Satellite Communications Controller
 Security Commodity Code
 Sequential Control Counter
 Single Channel Communications Controller
 Specialized Common Carrier
 Standard Commodity Classification

Standard Commodity Codes
Standards Council of Canada
Synchronous Communications Controller
System Control Center
SCCB: Software Configuration Control Board
SCCC: Shared Contingency Computer Center
SCCFF: Second Check Character Flip-Flop
SCCS: Source Code Control System
Standard Commodity Classification System
SCCU: Single Channel Control Unit
SCD: Serial Cryptographic Device
Service Computation Date
System Contents Directory
SCDC: System Control Distribution Computer
SCDP: Society of Certified Data Processors
SCDR: Subsystem Controller Definition Record
SCDT: Special Committee on Data Transmission
SCE: Standard Card Enclosure
SCERT: Systems and Computer Evaluation and Review Technique
SCEU: Selector Channel Emulation Unit
SCF: Satellite Control Facility
Synchronous Communications Feature
sch: schedule
scheduler
SCI: Science Citation Index
Stacker Control Instruction
System Control Interface
SCIM: Selected Categories in Microfiche
SCIP: System Control Interface Package

SCL: Sequential Control Logic
Supervisory Control Language
System Control Language
SCLA: Section Carry Look Ahead
SCM: Single Channel Monitoring
Small Core Memory
SCMP: Simple Cost-Effective Microprocessor
scn: scanner
SCOM: System Communication
SCOOP: System for Computerization Of Office Processes
SCOPE: Schedule-Cost-Performance
Supervisory Control of Program Execution
SCORE: System Cost and Operational Resource Evaluation
SCORPIO: Subject-Content-Oriented Retriever for Processing Information On-Line
SCP: Supervisory Control Program
System Control Program
SCPC: Single Channel Per Channel
SCPD: Scratch Pad
SCR: Scan Control Register
Silicon-Controlled Rectifier
Single Character Recognition
Software Change Report
System Change Request
SCRIBE: System for Computerized Reporting of Information for Better Education
SCS: Secondary Clear to Send
Small Computer System
Society for Computer Simulation, The
SCSS: SPSS Conversational Statistical System
SCT: Service Counter Terminal
Special Characters Table
Step Control Table
SCTR: Sector Register

SCU: Sequence Control Unit
Station Control Unit
Storage Control Unit
System Control Unit
SCULL: Serial Communication Unit for Long Links
SCX: Selector Channel Executive
S-D: Synchro to Digital
SD: Sample Data
Schematic Diagram
SD: Send Data
Signal Distributor
Single Density
Sort file Description
Space Division
Specification for Design
Standard Deviation
Standardization Data
Switch Driver
System Description
System Development
Systems Design
SDA: Source Data Acquisition
Source Data Automation
SDAL: Switched Data Access Line
SDB: Safe Deposit Box
Segment Descriptor Block
Software Development Board
Storage Data Bus
SDBD: Software Data Base Document
SDBI: Storage Data Bus-In
SDBO: Storage Data Bus-Out
SDC: Signal Data Converter
Software Distribution Center
SDCS: Systems & Data Control Staff
SDCU: Satellite Delay Compensation Unit
SDD: Stored Data Description
System for Distributed Data Bases
SDDL: Stored Data Definition Language
SDE: Source Data Entry
SDEP: Source Data Entry Package

SDF: Software Development Facility
SDFS: Standard Disk Filing System
SDFT: Schottky-Diode Field Effect Transistor Logic
SDI: Selective Dissemination of Information
SDILINE: Selective Dissemination of Information On-Line
SDIO: Serial Digital Input/Output
SDK: System Design Kit
SDL: Software Design Language
System Design Language
System Directory List
SDLC: Synchronous Data Link Control
SDM: Selective Dissemination on Microfiche
Semiconductor Disk Memory
Synchronous Digital Machine
Systems Development Methodology
SDMA: Space-Division Multiple Access
SDMAC: Shared Direct Memory Access Controller
SDMSS: Software Development and Maintenance Support System
SDN: Synchronous Digital Transmission Network
SDOS: Scientific Disk Operating System
S&DP: Systems and Data Processing
SDP: Source Data Processing
SDR: Statistical Data Recorder
Storage Data Register
System Definition Record
System Design Review
SDS: Software Development System
Software Distribution Services
SDSI: Shared Data Set Integrity

SDSU: Switched Data Service Unit
SDT: Syntax-Directed Translation
System Down Time
SDTS: Syntax-Directed Translation Scheme
SDU: Signal Distribution Unit
Source Data Utility
Station Display Unit
SDW: Segment Descriptor Word
SDX: Satellite Data Exchange
SE: Sign Extended
Single End
Single Entry
Software Engineering
Special Equipment
Stack Empty
Standard Error
System Element
System Engineer
System Extension
Systems Engineering
SEA: Static Error Analysis
SEAC: Standards Eastern Automatic Computer
SEACOST: Systematic Equipment Analysis and Cost Optimization Scanning Technique
SEAM: Software Engineering and Management
SEAS: SHARE European Association
sec: second
SEC: Single Error Correcting
SECAM: Sequential Couleur à memoire
SECDED: Single Error Correcting and Double Error Detecting
SECORD: Secure-Voice-Cord Board
SECPDED: Single Error Correcting and Partial Double Error Detecting
SECS: Severe Environment Controller System
SECU: Slave Emulator Control Unit
SEDED: Single Error and Double Erasure Detecting
SEDIT: Source Program Editor
SEE: Standard Error of Estimate
Systems Effectiveness Engineering
SEEA: Software Error Effects Analysis
SEEC: Single Error and Erasure Correcting
SEED: Self-Explaining Extended DBMS
SEER: Systems Engineering, Evaluation, and Research
SEF: Software Engineering Facility
Standard External File
seg: segment
sel: select
selector
SEL: Self-Extensible Programming Language
SELDAM: Selective Data Management system
SELEAC: Standard Elementary Abstract Computer
SEM: Standard Electronic Module
Systems Engineering Management
SEMBEGS: Simply Extended and Modified Batch Environmental Graphical System
SEMCAP: Specification and Electromagnetic Compatibility Analysis Program
SEMCOR: Semantic Correlation
SE/ME: Single Entry/Multiple Exit
SEMI: Semiconductor Equipment and Materials Institute
SEMICON: Semiconductor Conference
SEMP: Standard Electronic Modules Program

SEN: Scanning Encoding
Software Error Notification
SENET: Slotted Envelope Network
SENSEG: Sensitive Segment
SEPOL: Soil-Engineering Problem-Oriented Language
seq: sequence
sequential
SEQ-IC: Sequencer - Iteration Control
SEQUEL: Structured English Query Language
ser: serial
SER: Sequential Events Recorder
SER/DES: Serializer/Deserializer
SEREP: System Error Recording Editing Program
SERF: System for Equipment Requirements Forecasting
SERLINE: Serials On-Line
SES: System External Storage
Systems Engineering Services
SE/SE: Single Entry/Single Exit
SESR: Segment Entry Save Register
SET: Stepped Electrode Transistor
SEU: Source Entry Utility
sev: several
SEW: Software Engineering Workbench
S&F: Store and Forward
SF: Safety Factor
Scale Factor
Select Frequency
Shift Forward
Short Format
Side Frequency
Signal Frequency
Single-Frequency signaling
Skip Flag
Special Facilities
Square Foot
Stack Full
SFA: Segment Frequency Algorithm

SFAR: System Failure Analysis Report
SFBF: Standard Forms Bureau Form
SFC: Sales Finance Companies
Sectored File Controller
Selector File Channel
SFCU: State and Function Control Unit
SFD: Software Functional Description
SFDI: Standard Format of Digital Images
SFE: Smart Front End
SFFT: Semifast Fourier Transform
SFIS: Small Firms Information Service
SFL: Substrate Fed Logic
SFORTRAN: Structured FORTRAN
SFP: Security Filter Processor
SFS: Symbolic File Support
Sft: shift
SFU: Special Front End Unit
Special Function Unit
SG: Scanning Gate
Signal Generator
Single Ground
Specific Gravity
Symbol Generator
System Gain
SG&A: Selling, General, and Administrative expenses
SGA: Shareable Global Area
SGD: Self-Generating Dictionary
SGDF: Supergroup Distribution Frame
SGEN: System Generator
SGG: Samarium Gallium Garnet
SGJP: Satellite Graphic Job Processor
SGML: Standard Generalized Markup Language
SGP: Statistical Gathering Program
SGS: Status Group Select
SGT: Segment Table

S&H: Sample and Hold
SH: Session Handler
  Source Handshake
  Super High Frequency
shf: shift
SHF: Super High Frequency
SHIOER: Statistical Historical Input/Output Error Rate Utility
ship: ship
shipmt: shipment
SHOC: Software/Hardware Operational Control
SHP: Standard Hardware Program
shr: share
SHR: Synchronous Hubbing Regeneration
SHY: Syllable Hyphen (character)
S&I: Storage and Immediate
si: superimpose
SI: International System of Units
  Scientific Instrument
  Selected Item
  Serial Input
  Shift-In (character)
  Short Interest
  Signal Interface
  Signaling Rate Indicator
  Single Instruction
  Special Instruction
  Square Inch
  Systemè International
  System Integration
SIA: Semiconductor Industry Association
  Software Industry Association
  Standard Interface Adapter
SIAM: Society for Industrial and Applied Mathematics
SIB: Screen Image Buffer
  Serial Input-Output Board
  Serial Interface Board
  System Interface Bus
SIC: Semiconductor Integrated Circuit
  Special Interest Committee
  Standard Industrial Classification (system)
SID: Society for Information Display
  SWIFT Interface Device
SIDES: Source Input Data Edit System
SIDF: Standard Interchange Data Form
SIF: Storage Interface Facility
  System's Information File
SIFT: Software Implemented Fault Tolerance
sig: signal
SIG: Special Interest Group
SIGACT: Special Interest Group on Automata and Computability Theory
SIGARCH: Special Interest Group on Computer Architecture
SIGART: Special Interest Group on Artificial Intelligence
SIGBDP: Special Interest Group on Business Data Processing
SIGBIO: Special Interest Group on Biomedical Computing
SIGCAPH: Special Interest Group on Computers and the Physically Handicapped
SIGCAS: Special Interest Group on Computers And Society
SIGCOMM: Special Interest Group on Data Communication
SIGCOSIM: Special Interest Group on Computer System Installation Management
SIGCPR: Special Interest Group on Computer Personnel Research

SIGCSE: Special Interest Group on Computer Science Education
SIGCUE: Special Interest Group on Computers Use in Education
SIGDA: Special Interest Group on Design Automation
SIG/DAT: Signal/Data
SIGDOC: Special Interest Group on Documentation
SIGEFT: Special Interest Group on Electronic Funds Transfer
SIGFIDET: Special Interest Group on File Description and Translation
SIGGRAPH: Special Interest Group in Computer Graphics
SIGI: System of Interactive Guidance and Information
SIGIR: Special Interest Group on Information Retrieval
SIGLASH: Special Interest Group on Language Analysis and Studies in the Humanities
SIGLE: System for Information on Grey Literature in Europe
SIGMAP: Special Interest Group on Mathematical Programming
SIGMETRICS: Special Interest Group on Measurement and Evaluation
SIGMICRO: Special Interest Group on Microprogramming
SIGMINI: Special Interest Group in Minicomputers
SIGMOD: Special Interest Group on Management of Data
SIGNUM: Special Interest Group on Numerical Mathematics
SIGOA: Special Interest Group on Office Automation
SIGOPS: Special Interest Group on Operating Systems
SIGOUT: Signal Output
SIGPC: Special Interest Group on Personal Computing
SIGPLAN: Special Interest Group on Programming Languages
SIGSAM: Special Interest Group on Symbolic and Algebraic Manipulation
SIG/SDI: Special Interest Group for Selective Dissemination of Information
SIGSIM: Special Interest Group on Simulation
SIGSOC: Special Interest Group on Social and Behavioral Science Computing
SIGSOFT: Special Interest Group on Software Engineering
SIGUCC: Special Interest Group on University Computing Centers
SIG/ZBB/ADP: Special Interest Group on Zero-Based Budgeting and Automated Data Processing
SIL: Scanner Input Language
    Store Interface Link
    System Information Library
SILC: System for Interlibrary (Loan) Communication
SILT: Stored Information Loss Tree
sim: simulator
SIM: Set Interrupt Mask
    Synchronous Interface Module
    System Information Management
SIMCOM: Simulation and Computer
SIMCON: Simulation Control

SIMD: Single Instruction/Multiple Data
SIMGEN: Simulation Generating System
SIML: Simulation Language
SIMON: Software Implementation Monitor
SIMOS: Stacked-Gate Injection Metal Oxide Semiconductor
SIMP: Satellite Information Message Protocol
Satellite Interface Message Processor
SIMPA: Simplified Parallel
SIMPAC: Simulation Package
SIMPARAG: Simultaneous Parallel Array Grammers
SIMPLE: System for Integrated Maintenance and Program Language Extension
SIMPS: Simple and Mnemonic File Processing System
SIMSER: Simple Serial
SIMSYS: Simulation System
simul: simultaneous
SIMULA: Simulation Language
SIN: Symbolic Integrator
SINGAN: Singularity Analyzer
SIO: Serial Input-Output
Start Input-Output
SIOC: Serial Input-Output Channel
SIOH: Supervision, Inspection, and Overhead
SIOP: Selector Input-Output Processor
SIOT: Step Input-Output Table
SIP: Self-Interpreting Program Generator
Simulated Input Processor
Single In-Line Package
SIPROS: Simultaneous Processing Operation System
SIPS: Statistical Interactive Programming System

SIR: Segment Identification Register
Selective Information Retrieval
Semantic Information Retriever
Stratified Indexing and Retrieval (Japan)
SIRW: Stuffed Indirect Reference Word
SIS: Scientific Information System
Scientific Instruction Set
Software Integrated Schedule
Special Interest Subgroup
Standard Instruction Set
System Interrupt Supervisor
SISD: Single Instruction, Single Data
SIS-MDS: Single Instruction Stream, Multiple Data Stream
SIS-SDS: Single Instruction Stream, Single Data Stream
SIT: Stand-alone Intelligent Terminal
Static Induction Transistor
SITA: Societe Internationale de Telecommunication Aeronautique
SITAR: System for Interactive Text-Editing Analysis and Retrieval
SITC: Standard International Trade Classification
SITPRO: Simplification of International Trade Procedures
SIU: System Interface Unit
SJ: Single Job
Source Jamming
SJF: Shortest Job First
SJP: Serialized Job Processor
SJV: Standard Journal Voucher
sk: safekeeping
skip
SKB: Skew Buffer

SKIL: Scanner Keyed Input Language
S&L: Supply and Logistics
SL: Sample Laboratory
Section List
Shift Left
Signal Level
Simulation Language
Standard Label
Statement List
Statistical List
Straight Line
Systems Language
SLA: Shared-Line Adapter
Stored Logic Array
Synchronous Line Adapter
SLAM: Symbolic Language Adapted for Microcomputers
SLANG: Systems Language
S&LB: Sale and Lease-Back
SLC: Selector Channel
Shift Left and Count Instructions
Subscriber Line Charge
Systems Life Cycle
SLCC: Store Level Communications Controller
SLCM: Software Life Cycle Management
SLCU: Synchronous Line Control Unit
SLD: Synchronous Line Driver
SLDR: System Loader
SLDTSS: Single Language Dedicated Time-Sharing System
SLI: Suppress Length Indicator
Synchronous Line Interface
System Load and Initialization
SLIB: Source Library
Subroutine Librarian
Subsystem Library
SLIC: Silent Liquid Integral Cooler
SLICE: System Life Cycle Estimation

SLIDE: Source Library Image Delivery Expediter
SLIH: Second Level Interrupt Handler
SLIM: Software Life Cycle Management
SLIMS: Supply Line Inventory Management System
SLIP: Symbolic List Processor
Symmetric List Interpretive Program
Symmetric List Processor
SLIS: Shared Laboratory Information System
SLM: Synchronous Line Module
SLO: Segment Limits Origin
SLO/SRI: Shift Left Out/Shift Right In
SLPQ: Sleep Queue
SLR: Service Level Report
Storage Limits Register
SLRUM: Simple Least Recently Used Stack Model
sls: sales
SLS: Source Library System
SLSI: Super Large-Scale Integration
SLT: Solid Logic Technology
SLTF: Shortest Latency Time First
SLU: Secondary Logic Unit
Serial Line Unit
Source Library Update
SLV: Stipulated Loss Value
S&M: Service and Maintenance
Supply and Maintenance
S/M: Signal to Mean
Sort-Merge
SM: Scientific Memorandum
Semiconductor Memory
Sequence Monitor
Service Manual
Set Mode
Sort Merge
Special Memorandum
Specification Memo
Standard Matched

Structure Memory
Structured Macroassembly
Supply Manual
Synchronous Modem
SMA: Structured Markov Algorithm
SMAC: Store Multiple Access Control
SMACC: Scheduling, Manpower Allocation, and Cost Control
SMAL: Structured Macroassembly Language
SMART: Scheduling Management and Allocating Resources Technique
Standard Memories Add-On and Replacement Technology
Systems Management Analysis, Research and Test
SMB: System Monitor Board
Systems Message Block
SMC: Storage Module Controller
System Monitor Controller
SMD: Storage Module Drive
SMDR: Station Message Detail Recorder/Recording
SME: Society of Manufacturing Engineers
SMF: System Management Facility
Systems Measurement Facility
SMG: System Management Group
SMI: Static Memory Interface
System Memory Interface
SMIMD: Switched Multiple Instruction, Multiple Data Stream
SMIP: Structure Memory Information Processor
SMIS: Society for Management Information Systems
Symbolic Matrix Interpretation System

SMK: System Monitor Kernal
sml: small
SML: Spool Multileaving
Symbolic Machine Language
SMM: Semiconductor Memory Module
SMMP: Standards Methods of Measuring Performance
SMP: Symmetric Multiprocessing
System Modification Program
smpl: sample
SMR: Series Mode Rejection
Shiftout Modular Redundancy
SMRA: Stepwide Multiple Regression Analysis
SMRT: Single Message Rate Timing
SMS: Shared Mass Storage
Standard Modular System
SMSA: Standard Metropolitan Statistical Area
SMT: Systems Management Team
SMU: Store Monitor Unit
System Monitoring Unit
S/N: Signal-to-Noise ratio
SN: Sector Number
Selective Notification
Sequence Number
Serial Number
Shaping Network
Signal Node
Switched Network
Systems Network
SNA: Systems Network Architecture
SNAC: Single Number Account Control
SNBU: Switched Network Backup
sngl: single
SNI: Selective Notification of Information
SNOBOL: String Oriented Symbolic Language
SNP: Statistical Network Processor

Synchronous Network Processor
SNQ: Shared Enqueue
SNR: Signal-to-Noise Ratio
SO: Sales Order
Send Only
Serial Output
Shift-Out (character)
Shuttoff sequence
Slow Operate
Special Operations
Stop Order
Substance Of
Support Operations
System Operation
System Override
Systems Orientation
SOA: Start Of Address
State Of the Art
SOAR: Safe Operating Area
SOB: Start Of Block
SOC: Span Of Control
SOCOCO: Symposium of Software for Computer Control
SOD: Serial Output Data
System Operational Design
SODA: System Optimization and Design Alogorithm
SODAS: Satellite Operation Planning and Data Analysis System
SOF: Start-Of-Format control
Start Of Frame
Structured Oriented FORTRAN
soft: software
SOH: Start-Of-Heading (character)
SOLINET: Southeastern Library Network
SOLOMON: Simultaneous Operation Linked Ordinal Modular Network
SOM: Self-Organizing Machine
Start Of Message
SOMS: Systems Optimization and Monitoring Services

SOP: Standard Operating Procedure
SOPAD: Summary Of Proceedings and Debates
SOR: Specific Operational (Operating) Requirement
SORDID: Summary of Reported Defects, Incidents and Delays
SORM: Set Oriented Retrieval Module
SOS: Silicon On Sapphire
Start Of Significance
Station Operator Support
SOS CMOS: Silicon-On-Sapphire Complementary Metal-Oxide Semiconductor
SOSP: Symposium on Operating Systems Principles
SOST: Special Operator Service Traffic
SOT: Start Of Text
SOTUS: Sequentially Operated Teletypewriter Universal Selector
SOUP: Software Updating Package
SOUT: Swap Out
SOW: Statement Of Work
sp: space
S&P: Systems and Procedures
S-P: Serial to Parallel
SP: Satellite Processor
Science Plot
Scratch Pad
Send Processor
Sequence Processor
Sequential Phase
Sequential Processing
Set Point
Signal Processor
Single-Phase
Single Programmer
Single Purpose
Special Purpose
Stack Pointer

Standing Procedure
Start Permission
Structured Programming
Subscriber Processes
Summary Plotter
Switch Panel
Symbol Programmer
System Parameter
Systems Procedures
Systems Programmed
SPA: Scratch Pad Area
Shared Peripheral Area
Single Parameter Analysis
Systems Programmed Application
SPACE: Sales Profitability And Contribution Evaluator
SPAD: Scratch Pad Memory
SPADE: Single-Channel Per Carrier, Pulse-Code Modulation, Multiple Access, Demand Assignment Equipment
SPAU: Signal Processing Arithmetic Unit
SPB: Stored Program Buffer
SPC: Small Peripheral Controller
Stored Program Control
Switching and Processing Center
SPCL: Single Product Cost Leadership
SPCS: Storage and Processing Control System
SPD: Software Product Description
System Program Director
SPDM: Subprocessor with Dynamic Microprogramming
SPDT: Single Pole, Double Throw
SPE: Single Processing Element
Special Purpose Equipment
System Performance Effectiveness
SPEAC: Special Purpose Electronic Area Correlator
spec: specification

SPECLE: Specification Language
SPECOL: Special Customer Oriented Language
SPECTA: Structure-Preserved Error-Correcting Tree Automata
SPEED: Systematic Plotting and Evaluation of Enumerated Data
SPF: Structured Programming Facility
SPH: Strokes Per Hour
SPI: Shared Peripheral Interface
Single Processor Interface
Single Program Initiator
Specific Productivity Index
SPIC: Spare Parts Inventory Control
SPIE: Society of Photo-Optical Instrumentation Engineers
SPIN: Searchable Physics Information Notices
spkt: sprocket
SPL: Signal Processing Language
Simulation Programming Language
Source Program Library
System Program Loader
System Programming Language
SPLC: Standard Point Location Code
SPLICE: Shorthand Programming Language in COBOL Environment
SPLIT: Space Programming Language Implementation Tool
SPM: Scratch Pad Memory
Source Program Maintenance
System Planning Manual
SPMAR: Scratch Pad Memory Address Register
SPMOL: Source Program Maintenance On-Line
SPMTS: Simplified Predetermined Motion Time System

SPNS: Switched Private Network Service
SPO: Separate Partition Option
Synchronized Power On
SPOOF: Structure and Parity-Observing Output Function
SPOOL: Simultaneous Peripheral Operations On-Line
SPP: Signal Processing Peripheral
Simultaneous Print/Plot
Special Purpose Processor
SPPS: Subsystem Program Preparation Support
SPQE: Subpool Queue Element
SPR: Software Problem Report
Storage Protection Register
System Parameter Record
SPRB: Senior Performance Review Board
SPRINT: Strategic Program for Innovation and Technology Transfer
SPROM: Switched Programmable Read-Only Memory
S-P/ROM: Slave Programmable Read-Only Memory
SPRT: Sequential Ratio Probability Test
SPS: Serial-Parallel-Serial
String Process System
Symbolic Program System
SPSS: Statistical Package for the Social Sciences
SPST: Single Pole, Single Throw
SPT: Sectors Per Track
Structured Programming Techniques
SPTF: Shortest Processing Time First
SPU: Slave Processing Unit
System Processing Unit
SPUR: Source Program Utility Routine
SPUTNIC: Synchronously Programmed user Terminal and Network Interface Control
spx: simplex (circuit)
sq: square
squeezed
SQA: Software Quality Assurance
System Queue Area
SQAP: Software Quality Assurance Procedure
SQD: Signal Quality Detector
sql: sequel
SQPSK: Staggered Quadriphase Shift Keying
SQR: Square Root
SQUARE: Specifying Queries as Relational Expressions
Statistical Quality Analysis Report
sr: senior
subroutine
S/R: Send/Receive
Set/Reset
SR: Sample Rate
Scientific Report
Self-Rectifying
Service Record
Shift Register
Special Register
Special Report
Specification Requirement
Speech Recognition
Standard Requirement
Starting Relay
Status Register
Storage Register
Summary Report
Supporting Research
Switch Register
System Reader
System Residence
SRA: Systems Requirements Analysis
SRAM: Semirandom Access Memory
Sort Re-Entrant Access Method

SRB: Service Request Block
src: source
SRC: Stored Response Chain
 Synchronous Remote Control
SRCCOM: Source Compare Program
SRCR: System Run Control Record
SRD: Software Requirements Document
SRE: Single Region Execution
 Society of Reliable Engineers
SREJ: Selective Reject
SREM: Software Requirements Engineering Methodology
SREP: Software Requirements Engineering Program
 Source Representation
SRF: Software Recording Facility
 Software Recovery Facility
SRIM: Selected Research in Microfiche
SRL: Scheme Representation Language
 Shift Register Latch
SRM: Short Range Modem
 System Resources Manager
SRN: System Reference Number
SRP: Shared Resources Processing
SRQ: Service Request
SRR: Serially Reusable Resource
 System Requirements Review
SRS: Slave Register Set
SRTM: Simplified Real-Time Monitor
SRWG: Software Review Working Group
ss: substructure
 syncsort
S-S: Satellite-Switched Storage to Storage
S/S: Source/Sink
 Spooler/Scheduler
 Start/Stop
SS: Samples per Second
 Satellite Switched
 Satellite System

Select Standby
Selective Signaling
Signal Selector
Single Scan
Single Sideband
Solid State
Start-Stop (character)
Start-Stop (transmission)
Support System
Synchro Standard
System Segment
System Specifications
System Supervisor
SSB: Single-Sideband (transmission)
 Social Security Board
 Social Security Bulletin
SSB AM: Single-Sideband Amplitude Modulation
SSC: Signaling and Supervisory Control
 Station Selection Code
SSCI: Social Science Citation Index
SSCP: System Services Control Point
SSD: Solid State Disk
SSDA: Synchronous Serial Data Adapter
SSDD: Single-Sided Double-Density
SSDM: Systematic Software Development and Maintenance
SSE: Special Support Equipment
SSEC: Selective Sequence Electronic Calculator
SSES: Software Specification and Evaluation System
SSF: Symmetrical Switching Function
SSFT: Self-Service Financial Terminal
SSG: Symbolic Stream Generator
SSI: Small Scale Integration
 Synchronous Systems Interface
SSIA: Subschema Information Area
SSL: Scientific Subroutine Library
 Software Specification Lan-

guage
Source Statement Library
Storage Structure Language
System Specification Language
SSLC: Synchronous Single Line Controller
SSM: Semiconductor Storage Module
Small Semiconductor Memory
SSMA: Spread Spectrum Multiple Access
SSN: Segment Stack Number
Social Security Number
SSP: Scientific Subroutine Package
System Status Panel
SSP-ICF: System Support Program-Interactive Communication Feature
SSPLIB: Scientific Subroutine Package Library
SSR: Software Specification Review
Solid State Relay
System Status Report
SSRS: Source Storage and Retrieval System
SSSD: Single-Sided Single-Density
SST: Scanned Storage Tube
Synchronous System Trap
System Segment Table
SSTDMA: Satellite Switched Time-Division Multiple Access
SSTF: Shortest Seek Time First
SSTV: Slow Scan Television
SSU: Subsequent Signal Unit
System Services Unit
SSW: Satellite-Switched
SSYN: Slave Synchronization
st: status
S&T: Scientific and Technical
ST: Self-Test
Sequence Timer
Set Trigger
Special Text
Special Tools
Start Signal
Station Manager
Storage Tube
Stored Time
Straight Time
System Test
sta: station
status
STAC: Software Timing and Control
STACK: Start Acknowledge
STAD: Subprogram/Table Affect Diagram
STAE: Specify Task Asynchronous Exit
STAI: Subtask ABEND Intercept
STAIRS: Storage And Information Retrieval System
STAM: Shared Tape Allocation Manager
stan: standard
standardization
STAR: Scientific and Technical Aerospace Reports
Self-Testing And Repairing
Special Telecommunications Action for Regional Development (EC)
STARS: Standard Time And Rate Setting
Status And Revision System
stat: status
STATDSB: Status Disable
STATPAC: Statistical Package
STAT-PACK: Statistical Package
STATPAK: Statistical Package
STC: Serving Test Center
Start Conversion
STCB: Subtask Control Block
STCK: Store Clock
std: standard
STD: Science and Technology for Development (EC)
Subscriber Trunk Dialing

STDM: Statistical Time-Division Multiplexor
Synchronous Time-Division Multiplexor
STE: Segment Table Entry
Special Test Equipment
Standard Test Equipment
Subscriber Terminal Equipment
STEP: Specification Technology Evaluation Program
STEPPS: Some Tools For Evaluating Parallel Programs
STESD: Software Tool for Evaluating System Designs
STF: Supervisory Time Frame
STG: Subtree Transformational Grammar
STH: Satellite To Host
STI: Scientific and Technical Information
STIDC: Scientific and Technical Information and Documentation Committee (EC)
STIG: Storage Tag In Register
stk: stack
STL: Schottky Transistor Logic
STLB: Segment Table Look-Aside Buffer
STM: Short Term Memory
stmt: statement
STN: Switched Telecommunication Network
stnd: standard
STO: Segment Table Origin
Standing Order
STOIC: Stack-Oriented Interactive Compiler
STOL: Systems Test and Operation Language
STOQ: Storage Queue
STOQUE: storage Queue
stor: storage
store
STOR: Storage Tag Out Register
STORET: Storage and Retrieval
STP: Signal Transfer Point
Stop character
STR: Segment Table Register
Status Register
Synchronous Transmit Receive
Synchronous Transmitter Receive
STRADIS: Structured Analysis, Design and Implementation of Information Systems
STRAIN: Structural Analytical Interpreter
strd: stored
STRESS: Structural Engineering System Solver
STRIDE: Science and Technology for Regional Innovation and Development in Europe (EC)
strt: start
STRUBAL: Structured Basic Language
struc: structure
STRUDL: Structural Design Language
STRUM: Structured Microprogramming
sts: status
S/TS: Simulator/Test Set
STSN: Set and Test Sequence Number
Space Time Space Network
STSTB: Status Strobe
STT: Seek Time per Track
Single Transition Time
STTL: Schottky Transistor-Transistor Logic
STU: Segment Time Unit
STUFF: System To Uncover Facts Fast
STV: Subscription Television
STX: Start-of-Text (character)
su: supply

SU: Selectable Unit
   Signaling Unit
   Speed Up
   Standard Upkeep
   Statute of Uses
   Storage Unit
   Switching Unit
sub: subroutine
   subscriber
   substitute
   subtractor
Substn: substitution
SUDM: Single User Drive Module
SUE: System User Engineered
SUI: Standard Universal Identifying Number
SUM: System Utilization Monitor
sup: supervisory
SUPER: System Used for Prediction and Evaluation of Reliability
supvr: supervisor
sur: surplus
SURP: Service and Unit Record Processor
SUT: System Under Test
SUTY: System Utility
SV: Single Value
   Status Valid
SVA: Shared Virtual Area
svc: service
SVC: Supervisor Call (instruction)
   Switched Virtual Circuit
SVD: Simultaneous Voice/Data
   System Validation Diagram
SVDF: Segmented Virtual Display File
SVP: Service Processor
SVR: Super Video Recorder
SVRB: Supervisor Request Block
SVS: Single Virtual Storage
   Single Virtual System
SVSPT: Single Virtual Storage Performance Tool
SVT: System Validation Testing
sw: software
   switch

SW: Single Weight
   Specific Weight
   Status Word
   Structured Walkthrough
SWA: Scheduler Work Area
   System Work Area
SWADS: Scheduler Work Area Data Set
SWAMI: Software Aided Multifont Input
SWAP: Standard Wafer Array Programming
swch: switch
SWE: Status Word Enable
SWI: Software Interrupt
SWIFT: Society for Worldwide Interbank Financial Telecommunications
SWL: Software Writer's Language
SWM: Software Monitor
SWORD: Software Optimization for the Retrieval of Data
SWORDS: Standard Work Order Recording and Data System
swp: swapper
SWS: Software Services
SWU: Switching Unit
SX: Secondary Instruction
SXS: Step-by-Step (system)
SXTN: Sixteen Acknowledge
SXTRQ: Sixteen Request
sy: system
SYCOM: System Communication Module
SYD: Sum of the Years Digits depreciation
SYFA: System For Access
SYLCU: Synchronous Line Control Unit
sym: symbol
   system
SYMBUG: Symbolic Debugger
symp: symposium
syn: synchronous
SYN: Synchronous idle (character)

sync: synchronization
synchronous
synch: synchronous
SYNGLISH: Synthetic English
SYRIUS: Symbolic Representations for Image Understanding System
sys: system
SYSADMIN: System Administrator
SYSCAP: System of Circuit Analysis Programs
SYSCOM: System Communication
SYSEX: System Executive
SYSGEN: System Generation
SYSIN: System Input Stream
SYSIPT: System Input Stream
SYSL: System Description Language
SYSLIB: System Subroutine Library
SYSLOG: System Log
SYSMON: System Monitor
SYSOPO: System Programmed Operator
SYSOUT: System Output Stream
SYSPCH: System Punch
SYSRDR: System Reader
SYSRES: System Residence
syst: system
systematic
SYU: Synchronization Signal Unit

T

t: temperature
tera
terminal
test
testator
time
timer
track
transaction
transformation
transmit
transmitter
tree
true
T&A: Taken and Accepted
TA: Tape Adapter
Technical Analysis
Technology Assessment
Telegraphic Address
Telex Network Adapter
Terminal Access
Transfer Address
TAA: Tactical Asset Allocation
TAC: Terminal Access Controller
Transformer Analog Computer
Transistorized Automatic Computer
TACADS: Tactical Automated Data Processing System
TACINTEL: Tactical Intelligence
TACOS: Tool for Automatic Conversion of Operational Software
TACT: Terminal Activated Channel Test
TAD: Terminal Address Designator
Time Available for Delivery
Transaction Applications Driver
TAEB: Technology Assessment and Evaluation
TAF: Time And Frequency
Transaction Facility
TAG: Time Automated Grid
TAG: Transfer Agent
TAL: Terminal Application Language
Transaction Application Language
TAM: Task Analysis Method
Telecommunications Access Method
Telephone Answering Machine
Terminal Access Method
TAMALAN: Table Manipulation Language
TAMOS: Terminal Automatic Monitoring System
TAMPR: Transformation Aided Multiple Program Realization
TAP: Terminal Access Processor
Time Sharing Assembly Program
TAPGEN: Terminal Applications Program Generator
TAPS: Terminal Application Processing System
TAR: Terminal Address Register
Total Assets Reporting
Track Address Register
Transfer Address Register
Turnaround Ratio
TARAN: Test And Repair As Necessary
Test And Replace As Necessary
TARP: Test And Repair Processor

TAS: Telephone Answering Machine
Terminal Automation System
Test And Set
TAT: Time and Attendance Terminal
Transatlantic Telephone Cable
TAU: Trunk Access Unit
TAXIR: Taxonomic Information Retrieval
TB: Terminal Block
Time Base
Tone Burst
Transmitter-Blocker
Trial Balance
TBA: To Be Announced
TBEM: Terminal Based Electronic Mail
TBI: Time Between Inspections
TBM: Tone Burst Modulation
TBMT: Transmitter Buffer Empty
TBP: Telephone Bill Payment
TBR: Table Base Register
TBS: Tokyo Broadcasting System
tc: telecommunications
T&C: Terms and Conditions
T/C: Trust or Complement
TC: Tabulating Card
Tape Core
Technical Committee
Technical Cooperation
Technological Change
Terminal Computer
Terminal Concentrator
Terminal Control
Terminal Controller
Test Conductor
Test Coordinator
Time Clock
Time to Computation
Transfer Count
Transmission Control
Trunk Control
TCA: Telecommunications Association
Terminal Communication Adapter
TCAM: Telecommunication Access Method
TCB: Task Control Block
Transaction Control Block
Transfer Control Block
TCC: Technical Control Center
Transmission Control Characters
TCE: Top Computer Executive
Transaction Cost Estimator
TCF: Terminal Configuration Facility
TCIS: TELEX Computer Inquiry Service
TCL: Terminal Command Language
Terminal Control Language
Transaction Control Language
TCM: Telecommunications Manager
Telecommunications Monitor
Terminal, Computer and Multiplexer
TCMS: Telecommunications Management System
TCO: TELENET Central Office
Termination Contracting Office
TCP: Tape Conversion Program
Task Control Program
Terminal Control Program
Time, Cost and Performance
Tool Center Point
Transmission Control Program
Transmission Control Protocol
Transmitter Clock Pulse
TCPC: Telephone Cable Process Controller
TCR: Tape Cassette Recorder
TCS: Telecommunications Control System
Terminal Control System
Tool Coordinate System
Transaction Control System

Transmission-Controlled Speed
TCS-AF: Telecommunications Control System-Advanced Function
TCT: Terminal Control Table
Transaction Control Table
TCTS: Trans-Canada Telephone System
TCU: Tape Control Unit
Telecommunications Control Unit
Teletypewriter Control Unit
Terminal Control Unit
Timing Control Unit
Transmission Control Unit
TCV: Terminal Configures Vehicle
T-D: Transmitter-Distributor
TD: Tape Drive
Technical Data
Telemetry Data
Test Data
Time Delay
Time Division
Top Down
Track Data
Transmit Data
Tunnel Diode
TDA: Tunnel Diode Amplifier
TDB: Temporary Disability Benefits
TDC: Total Distributed Control
TDCS: Time Division Circuit Switching
TDD: Tod Down Development
TDE: Total Data Entry
TDEM: Test Data Effectiveness Measurement
TDF: Transnational Data Flows.
TDG: Test Data Generator
TDGL: Test Data Generating Language
TDI: Telecommunications Data Interface
Two-Wire Direct Interface
TDL: Transaction Definition Language

Transformation Definition Language
TDM: Template Descriptor Memory
Time-Division Multiplexing
Time Driven Monitor
TDMA: Tape Direct Memory Access
Time Division Multiple Access
TDMC: Time Division Multiplexed Channel
TDMS: Time-Shared Data Management System
TDOA: Time Deposit Open Account
TDOS: Tape Disk Operating System
TDP: Test Data Package
TDPL: Top Down Parsing Language
TDR: Tape Data Register
Time Delay Relay
Time Domain Reflectometry
Tone Dial Receiver
Transmit Data Register.
Treasury Deposit Receipt
TDRS: Tracking and Data Relay Satellite
TDRSS: Tracking and Data Relay Satellite System
TDS: Transaction Distribution System
TDSP: Top Down Structured Programming
TDX: Time Division Exchange
T&E: Test and Evaluation
TE: Task Element
Technical Engineer
Terminal Equipment
Text Editor
Trailing Edge
TEAM: Teleterminals Expandable Added Memory
Terminology, Evaluation and Acquisition Method
TEAMS: Test Evaluation And Monitoring System
TEAS: Time Elapsed After Study

TEBOL: Terminal Business Oriented Language
TEC: Triple Erasure Correction
tech: technical
TECHEVAL: Technical Evaluation
TECH EX: Technical Exchange
TECH MEMO: Technical Memorandum
TECH REPT: Technical Report
TECO: Text Editor and Corrector
TED: Text Editor
TEGAS: Test Generation And Simulation System
TEL: Task Execution Language
TELCO: Telephone Industry
telec: telecommunication
telecc: telecommunication
telecom: telecommunication
telecomm: telecommunication
teleg: telegram
TELEMUX: Telegraph Multiplexer
TELEX: Teletype Exchange
TELNET: Telecommunications Network
TELOPS: Telemetry On Line Processing System
TELSAM: Telephone Service Attitude Measurement
TEM: Test Equipment Manufacturing
TEMA: Telecommunication Engineering and Manufacturing Association
TEMOD: Terminal Environment Module
temp: temporary
TEMPOS: Timed Environment Multipartitioned Operating System
TEP: Terminal Error Program
TEPE: Time-Sharing Event Performance Evaluator
TEPOS: Test Program Operating System
term: terminal
termination
TES: Text Editing System
tex: telex
TF: Tabulating Form
Tape Feed
Technological Forecasting
Terminal Frame
Time Frame
Transfer Function
Transmit Filter
Transmitter Frequency
TFA: Test Form Analyzer
Transaction Flow Auditing
TFC: Total Fixed Cost
TFM: Tape File Management
TFMS: Text and File Management System
TFP: Total Factor Productivity
TFPIA: Textile Fabric Products Identification Act
TFR: Transaction Formatting Routines
TFS: Task Form Specification
Tape File Supervisor
TFSF: Time To First System Failure
tg: telegraph
TG: Task Group
Technology Gap
Terminal Guidance
Terminator Group
Test Group
TGC: Terminator Group Controller
TGID: Transmission Group Identifier
TH: Temporary Hold
Transmission Header
THD: Total Harmonic Distortion
THP: Terminal Handling Processor
THP: Terminal Holding Power
Transmitter Holding Register
THREAD: Three-Dimensional Reconstruction and Display
T&I: Test and Integration
TI: Tape Inverter
Technical Information

Technical Integration
Temporary Instructions
Terminal Instruction
Terminal Interface
Test Instrumentation
Transformational Implementation
Transmission Identification
TIA: Task Item Authorization
Telecommunications Information Administration
TIAS: Team Integrated Avionic System
TIC: Terminal's Identification Code
TICCIT: Time-Shared Interactive Computer-Controlled Information Television
TICS: Telecommunication Information Control System
TID: Tuple Identifier
TIDMA: Tape Interface Direct Memory Access
TIE: Terminal Interface Equipment
TIES: Total Information Educational Systems
TIF: Tape Inventory File
Terminal Independent Format
TIGS: Terminal Independent Graphics System
TIH: Trunk Interface Handler
TIM: Table Input to Memory
TIMS: The Institute of Management Science
Transmission Impairment Measuring Set
TI-NET: Transparent Intelligent Network
TIO: Test Input/Output
Time Interval Optimization
TIOC: Terminal Input/Output Coordinator
TIOT: Task Input/Output Table
TIOWQ: Terminal Input/Output Wait Queue
TIP: Technical Information Program

Terminal Interface Processor
Transaction Interface Processor
TIPS: Text Information Processing System
TIP TOP: Tape Input-Tape Output
TIQ: Task Input Queue
TIR: Target Instruction Register
TIRKS: Trunks Integrated Records Keeping System
TIT: Test Item Taker
TIU: Terminal Interface Unit
TJB: Time-Sharing Job Control Block
TJID: Terminal Job Identification
tk: track
TK: Teletype Keyboard
Ten Keyboard
TKB: Task Builder
TKTN: Task Termination Notice
TL: Target Language
Technical Library
Total Load
Transaction Language
Transaction Listing
Transmission Level
Transmission Line
Tuple Length
TLA: Time Line Analysis
Transmission Line Adapter
Transmission Line Assembly
TLB: Table Lookaside Buffer
Translation Lookaside Buffer
TLC: Task Level Controller
True Liquid Cooling
TLCT: Total Life Cycle Time
TLI: Transferable Loan Instrument
TLMS: Tape Library Management System
TLN: Trunk Line Network
TLO: Total Loss Only
TLP: Telephone Line Patch
Transmission Level Point
TLS: Tape Librarian System
Typed Letter Signed
TLSA: Transparent Line-Sharing Adapter

TLU: Table Look-Up
T&M: Time and Materials
TM: Tabulating Machine
    Tape Mark
    Tape Module
    Technical Manual
    Terminal Monitor
    Test Mode
    Test Model
    Time Monitor
    Training Manual
    Transaction Manager
    Turing Machine
TMC: Tape Management Catalog
TMIS: Technician Maintenance Information System
tml: terminal
TMO: Time Out
TMP: Terminal Monitor Program
TMR: Triple Modular Redundancy
TMS: Table Management System
    Tape Management System
    Text Management System
    Time and Motion Study
TMU: Test Maintenance Unit
    Transmission Message Unit
TMX: Transaction Management Executive
TN: Technical Note
    Terminal Node
    Test Number
    Transferable Notice
    Transport Network
TNC: Total Numerical Control
    Transport Network Controller
TNET: Terminal and Computer Network
TNF: Third Normal Form
tngwe: tonnage
TNS: Transaction Network Service
TNV: Total Net Value
TNZ: Transfer on NonZero
to: turnover
TO: Table of Organization
    Technical Order
    Test Operation
    Time Out
    Transfer Order
    Transmitter Order
    Travel Order
TOA: Total Obligational Authority
TOADS: Terminal Oriented Administrative Data System
TOC: Time Out Circuit
TOCS: Terminal Oriented Computer System
TOCTTOU: Time Of Check To Time Of Use
TOD: Time Of Day
TODS: Test-Oriented Disk System
TOF: Top Of File
    Top Of Form
TOL: Test Oriented Language
TOLAR: Terminal On-Line Availability Reporting
TOLT: Total On-Line Testing
TOLTEP: Teleprocessing On Line Test Executive Program
TOLTS: Total On-Line Testing System
TOOL: Test-Oriented Operator Language
TOPP: Task Oriented Plant Practice
TOPS: Time-Sharing Operating System
    Total Operations Processing System
TOS: Tape Operating System
    Team Operating System
    Top Of Stack
TOSCW: Top Of Stack Control Word
TOSL: Terminal-Oriented Service Language
TOSP: Top Of Stack Pointer
TOSS: Terminal-Oriented Support System
tot: total
TOT: Transfer Overhead Time
TOTE: Teleprocessing On-Line Test Executive
TOX: Time Of Expiration

TOXBACK: Toxicology Information Back-Up
TOXLINE: Toxicology Information On-Line
tp: teleprinter
teleprocessing
TP: Technical Paper
TELENET Processor
Teletype Printer
Terminal Point
Terminal Printer
Terminal Processor
Terminal Protocol
Test Procedure
Total Parts
Transaction Processing
Transaction Processor
Transition Period
TPA: Transient Program Area
TPAM: Teleprocessing Access Method
TPAP: Transaction Processing Applications Program
TPB: Teletype Printer Buffer
TPD: Thermoplastic-Photoconductor Device
Transaction Processing Description
TPDT: Tree-walking Pushdown Transducer
TPE: Transaction Processing Executive
TPFI: Terminal Pin Fault Insertion
TPFP: Transaction Processing Function Processor
TPFS: Teleprocessing Performance Forecasting System
TPG: Telecommunication Program Generator
tph: telephone
TPI: Tracks Per Inch
TPIS: Telecommunications Products Information Retrieval and Simulation
TPL: Table Producing Language
Terminal Processing Language
Terminal Programming Language
Test Procedure Language
Traditional Products Line
Transaction Processing Language
TPLAB: Tape Label
TPL/F: FORTRAN Test Procedure Language
TPM: Technical Performance Measures
Teleprocessing Monitor
TPMM: Teleprocessing Multiplexor Module
TPMS: Teleprocessing Monitor System
TPNS: Teleprocessing Network Simulator
TPR: Transaction Processing Routine
TPS: Tape to Print System
Terminal Polling System
Terminal Programming System
Transaction Processing System
TPTC: Teleprocessing Test Center
TPU: Telecommunications Processing Unit
Terminal Processing Unit
TPVM: Teleprocessing Virtual Machine
TQC: Total Quality Control
TQE: Timer Queue Element
TQS: Transaction Query Subroutine
TQTBL: Task Queue Table
tr: track
T&R: Transmit and Receive
TR: Tape Reader
Tape Resident
Technical Report
Technical Requirement
Test Request
Test Run
Throughput Ratio
Transfer Reset

Transformer-Rectifier
Translation Register
Trouble Report
tra: transfer
TRAC: Text Reckoning and Compiling
TRACE: Total Remote Access Center
Total Risk Assessing Cost Estimate
TRAD: Transportation, Allocation or Distribution
TRAFFIC: Transaction Routing And Form Formatting in COBOL
TRAM: Test Reliability And Maintainability
Trademark Reporting And Monitoring System
tran: transaction
transmit
TRAN-PRO: Transaction Processing
trans: translator
TRANSFOR: Translator for Structured FORTRAN
TRC: Transmit/Receive Control Unit
Tuple Relational Calculus
TRC-AS: Transmit/Receive Control Unit–Asynchronous Start/Stop
TRC-SC: Transmit/Receive Control Unit–Synchronous Character
TRC-SF: Transmit/Receive Control Unit–Synchronous Framing
TREM: Tape Reader Emulator Module
TRENDS: Transmission Line Environmental Digital Studies
trf: transfer
TRIAL: Technique for Retrieving Information from Abstracts of Literature
TRIB: Transfer Rate of Information BITs
TRI-BITS: Three-BITs
TRIM: Tailored Retrieval and Information Management
TRIS-On-LINE: Transportation Research Information Services On-Line
trk: track
TRL: Transistor-Resistor Logic
TRM: Terminal Response Monitor
TRMS: Technical Requirements Management System
TROLL: Time-Shared Reactive On-Line Laboratory
TROS: Transformer Read-Only Storage
trp: trap
TRQ: Task Ready Queue
TRR: Tape Read Register
Transaction Routing Routines
TRS: Terminal Receive Side
trx: transaction
TS: Technical Specification
Telecommunication System
Test Specification
Time Sharing
Time Switch
Transit Storage
Transmission Service
Transport Station
Type Specification
TSA: Time Series Analysis
Time Slot Access
TSAM: Time Series Analysis and Modeling
TSAS: Time-Sharing Accounting System
TSAU: Time Slot Access Unit
TSB: Terminal Status Block
TSC: Three State Control
Time Share Control
Totally Self-Checking
Transmitter Start Code

TS/DMS: Time-Shared Data Management System
TSE: Terminal Source Editor
Time Sharing Executive
TSF: Time to System Failure
TSFP: Time to System Failure Period
TSGAS: Time-Shared General Accounting System
TSI: Test Structure Input
TSID: Track Sector Identification
TSIU: Telephone System Interface Unit
tsk: task
TSL: Test Source Library
Time Series Language
Time Sharing Library
TSM: Terminal Support Module
Time Sharing Monitor
TSMS: Time Series Modeling System
TSO: Technical Standards Orders
Time-Sharing Option
TSODB: Time Series Oriented Data Base
TSOS: Time Sharing Operating System
TSO/VTAM: Time Sharing Option for the Virtual Telecommunications Access Method
TSP: Time Series Processor
TSPL: Telephone Systems Programming Language
TSPS: Traffic Service Position System
TSR: Technical Summary Report
Temporary Storage Register
Translation State Register
TSS: Terminal Send Side
Time Sharing Service
Time Sharing Subsystem
Time Sharing System
tst: test
TST: Transaction Step Task
TSV: Turnkey Systems Vendor
TSX: Time Sharing Executive
tt: teletype
T/T: Telegraphic Transfer
TT: Technical Test
Teller Terminal
Transaction Telephone
Transaction Terminal
TTBL: Task Table
TT&C: Telemetry, Tracking and Command
TTD: Temporary Text Delay
TTDL: Terminal Transparent Display Language
TTF: Time to Time Failure
TTF&T: Technology Transfer, Fabrication and Test
TTK: Tie Trunk
TTL: Transistor-Transistor Logic
TTL/LS: Transistor-Transistor Logic–Low Power Schottky
TTLS: Transistor-Transistor Logic Schottky
tts: teletypesetting
TTS: Transmission Test Set
TTSPN: Two Terminal Series Parallel Networks
ttw: teletypewriter
tty: teletype
teletypewriter
TTY: Telephone-Teletypewriter
TU: Tape Unit
Technology Utilization
Time Unit
Timing Unit
Transfer Unit
Transmission Unit
Transport Unit
TUF: Time of Useful Function
Transmitter Underflow
T&UG: Telephone and Utilities Group
TUR: Traffic Usage Recorder
TUT: Transistor Under Test
tv: television
TV: Transfer Vector

TVC: Television Camera
TVRO: Television Receive Only Earth Station
TVS: Transient Voltage Suppressor
TVT: Television Typewriter
tw: typewriter
TW: Time Word
  Wait State
TWA: Transaction Work Area
  Typewriter Adapter
TWI: Trade-Weighted Index
TWIMC: To Whom It May Concern
TWODEPEP: Two Dimensional Elliptic, Parabolic and Eigenvalue Problems
TWP: Twisted Wire Pair
TWR: Tape Writer Register
TWS: Translator Writing System
TWT: Traveling Wave Tube
TWX: Teletypewriter Exchange
tx: telex
  transmit
  transmitter
TX: Terminal Executive
TXA: Terminal Exchange Area
TXD: Transmit Data
txt: text
TXTM: Text Maintenance
typ: type
  typewriter
  typical
  typically
typwrtr: typewriter

U

u: unified
unit
universal
universe
update
user
UA: Unnumbered Acknowledge
User Area
UAC: Uninterrupted Automatic Control
UACN: Unified Automated Communication Network
UACTE: Universal Automatic Control and Test Equipment
UADP: Uniform Automatic Data Processing
UADPS: Uniform Automatic Data Processing System
UADS: User Attribute Data Set
UAF: Unit Authorization File
UAL: Unit Authorization List
UAP: User Area Profile
UAR: Unit Address Register
UART: Universal Asynchronous Receiver Transmitter
UAS: Uniform Accounting System
UAT: User Accounting Table
UB: Upper Bound
User Board
UBC: Universal Block Channel
Universal Buffer Controller
UBD: Utility Binary Dump
UBHR: User Block Handling Routine
UBITA: Upper Bound of Information Translation Amount
UBS: Unit Backspace character
uc: unichannel
UC: Up Converter
Upper Case

Usable Control
Utilization Control
UCA: Upper Control Area
UCB: Unit Control Block
Universal Character Buffer
UCBTAB: User Control Block Table
UCC: Uniform Commercial Code
Universal Copyright Convention
UCCC: Uniform Consumer Credit Code
UCD: Unemployment Compensation Deduction
Unemployment Compensation Disability
UCDP: Uncorrected Data Processor
UCF: Utility Control Facility
UCI: Utility Card Input
UCIS: Uprange Computer Input System
UCLAN: User Cluster Language
UCM: Universal Communications Monitor
UCN: Uniform Control Number
UCP: Uninterruptible Computer Power
UCS: Universal Call Sequence
Universal Character Set
Universal Classification System
User Control Store
UCSB: Universal Character Set Buffer
UCT: Universal Coordinated Time
UCV: Unimproved Capital Value
UCW: Unit Control Word
UD: Undetected Defect
Usage Data
UDAC: User Digital Analog Controller

UDAS: Unified Direct Access Standards
UDC: Universal Decimal Classification
Universal Digital Control
UDE: Universal Data Entry
UDF: Unit Development Folder
U-DID: Unique Data Item Description
UDL: Uniform Data Language
UDP: Uniform Delivered Price
UDTS: Universal Data Transfer Service
UE: Unit Equipment
User Equipment
Utility Expenditures
UET: Universal Emulating Terminal
UETS: Universal Emulating Terminal System
UF: Used For
Utility File
UFA: Until Further Advised
UFAM: Universal File Access Method
UFAS: Universal File Access System
UFC: Universal Frequency Counter
UFD: User File Directory
UFF: Universal Flip-Flop
UFI: Usage Frequency Indicator
User Friendly Interface
UFM: User-to-File Manager
UFO: User Files On-Line
UFP: Utility Facilities Program
UFS: Universal Financial System
UG: User Group
UGA: Unity Gain Amplifier
UGLI: Universal Gate for Logic Implementation
UGT: User Group Table
UH: Unit Head
Upper Half
UHF: Ultra High Frequency
UHL: User Header Label
UHM: Universal Host Machine

UIC: User Identification Code
UICP: Uniform Inventory Control Program
UIG: User Instruction Group
UIM: Ultraintelligent Machine
UIO: Units In Operation
Universal Input/Output
UIOD: User Input Output Devices
UIR: User Instruction Register
UIS: Unit Identification System
UIT: Union Internationale des Telecommunications (International Telecommunications Union)
UJCL: Universal Job Control Language
UKB: Universal Keyboard
UKITO: United Kingdom Information Technology Organization
U/L: Upper/Lower
UL: Underwriters' Laboratories
Upper Limit
User Language
ULA: Uncommitted Logic Array
ULC: Uniform Loop Clock
Universal Logic Circuit
Upper-Lower Case
ULCC: Ultra-Large Crude Carrier
ULE: Unit Location Equipment
ULM: Universal Line Multiplexer
Universal Logic Module
ULS: Unit Level Switchboard
ULSI: Ultra Large-Scale Integration
ult: last
UM: Unit of Measure
Universal Measuring Amplifier
Universal Monitor
Unscheduled Maintenance
UMC: Unibus Microchannel
UMCS: Unattended Multipoint Communications Station
UMF: Ultra Microfiche
UMI: Ultra Microfiche

UMLC: Universal Multiline Controller
UMOD: User Module
UMS: Universal Multiprogramming System
UNA: Unattended Answering Accessory
UNADS: UNIVAC Automated Documentation System
UNALC: User-Network Access Link Control
UNCM: User Network Control Machine
UNCOL: Universal Computer-Oriented Language
undef: undefined
UNIBUS: Universal Bus
UNICOMP: Universal Compiler Fortran Compatible
UNIMOD: Universal Module
UNIPOL: Universal Procedure Oriented Language
UNIPRO: Universal Processor
UNIQUE: Uniform Inquiry Update and Edit
Uniform Inquiry Update Element
UNISTAR: UNIVAC Storage and Retrieval System
User Network for Information Storage Transfer, Acquisition and Retrieval
UNISWEP: Unified Switching Equipment Practice
UNIVAC: Universal Automatic Computer
unprot: unprotect
U&O: Use and Occupancy
UOA: Used On Assembly
UODDL: User-Oriented Data Display Language
UOF: Unusual Order Form
up: uniprocessing
uniprocessor
UP: Uncovered Position

UPA: Unique Product Advantage
Units Per Assembly
UPACS: Universal Performance Assessment and Control System
UPB: Upper Bound
UPC: Uniform Practice Code
Unit of Processing Capacity
Universal Peripheral Control
Universal Product Code
UPI: Universal Peripheral Interface
UPIC: Universal Personal Identification Code
UPL: Universal Programming Language
User Programming Language
UPP: Universal PROM Programmer
UPS: Uninterrupted Power Supply
Uninterruptible Power Supply
Uninterruptible Power System
Universal Processing System
UPSI: User Program Sense Indicator
UPT: User Process Table
UPU: Universal Postal Union
UQT: User Queue Table
UR: Unit Record
Unit Register
Utility Register
URA: User Requirements Analysis
Utilization Review Agency
URC: Unit Record Control
URDS: User Requirements Data Base
URL: User Requirements Language
URP: Unit Record Processor
US: Unit Separator (character)
USA: United States of America
USACII: United States of America Standard Code for Information Interchange
USACSC: United States Army Computer Systems Command

USAM: Unique Sequential Access Method
USART: Universal Synchronous-Asynchronous Receiver/Transmitter
USAS: United States of America Standard
USASCII: United States of American Standard Code for Information Interchange
USASCSOCR: United States of America Standard Character Set for Optical Character Recognition
USASI: United States of America. Standards Institute
USBA: United States Bureau of Standards
USC: User Service Center
USDA/CRIS: United States Department of Agriculture/ Current Research Information System
USE: Univac Scientific Exchange
usec: microsecond
USER: User System Evaluator
USERID: User Identification
USG: United States Government
USI: User System Interface
USIO: Unlimited Sequential Input/Output
USIS: United States Information Service
USITA: United States Independent Telephone Association
USNC: United States National Committee of the International Electrotechnical Commission
USOA: Uniform Systems Of Accounts
USOC: Universal Service Order Code
USPO: United States Post Office
USPS: United States Postal Service
USQ: Squeezed files
USR: User Service Routine
USRT: Universal Synchronous Receiver/Transmitter
UST: User Symbol Table
USU: Unbundled Stock Unit
UT: Unit Tester
Universal Time
User's Terminal
UTA: User Transfer Address
UTC: Utilities Telecommunications Council
UTD: Universal Transfer Device
util: utilization
UTL: User Trailer Label
UTOL: Universal Translator Oriented Language
UTR: Unprogrammed Transfer Register
UTS: Universal Timing-Sharing System
UTT: Unit Under Test
UU: Ultimate User
UUT: Unit Under Test
uv: ultraviolet
UVPROM: Ultraviolet Programmable Read Only Memory
UV-PROM: Ultraviolet Programmable Read Only Memory
UW: Used With
UWA: User Working Area

V

v: overflow
variable
vector
verification
verify
vertical
virtual
volt
voltage
V-A: Volt-Ampere
VA: Value Analysis
Video Amplifier
Virtual Address
VAA: Voice Access Arrangement
VAB: Voice Answer-Back
vac: vacancy
VAC: Value Added Carrier
Vector Analog Computer
VACC: Value Added Common Carrier
VAD: Voltmeter Analog-to-Digital Converter
VADAC: Voice Analyzer Data Converter
VADC: Video Analog to Digital Converter
VADE: Versatile Automatic Data Exchange
VAG: Vertex Adjacency Graph
val: valuation
value
VALDEFD: Value Defined
VAMP: Vector Arithmetic Multiprocessor
VAN: Value Added Network
VANS: Value Added Network Service
VAPS: Volume, Article, Paragraph, Sentence
var: variable
variation
VAR: Value-Added Remarketer
Vector Autoregressive Model
VARBLK: Variable Blocked
VARUNB: Variable Unblocked
VAS: Value Added Service
Value Added Statement
Vector Addition System
VAT: Virtual Address Translator
VATE: Versatile Automatic Test Equipment
VAU: Vertical Arithmetic Unit
VAX: Virtual Address Extended
VB: Voice-Band
VBOMP: Virtual Base Organization and Maintenance Processor
VBP: Valid BIT Register
Virtual Block Processor
VC: Vector Control
Verification Condition
Virtual Circuit
Virtual Computer
Volume Control
VCA: Voice Connecting Arrangement
VCBA: Variable Control Block Area
VCC: Video Compact Cassette
VCD: Variable Capacitance Diode
VCF: Verified Circulation Figure
Voltage Controlled Filter
VCG: Verification Condition Generator
Voltage Controlled Generator
VCGEN: Verification Condition Generator
VCO: Voltage Controlled Oscillator
VCR: Valuation by Components Rule
Video Cassette Recorder

195

VCS: Validation Control System
Video Communications System
VCTCA: Virtual Channel to Channel Adapter
VCTD: Vendor Contract Technical Data
VCV: Variable Compression Vector
vd: void
VD: Virtual Data
Volume Deleted
VDAM: Virtual Data Access Method
VDB: Vector Data Buffer
Video Display Board
VDC: Vendor Data Control
Video Display Controller
Voltage Doubler Circuit
VDD: Version Description Document
Visual Display Data
VDDL: Virtual Data Description Language
VDDP: Video Digital Data Processing
VDE: Variable Display Equipment
VDETS: Voice Data Entry Terminal System
VDG: Video Display Generator
VDI: Video Display Input
Video Display Interface
Visual Display Input
VDL: Virtual Data Base Level
VDLIB: Virtual Disk Library
VDM: Video Display Module
VDP: Vertical Data Processing
Video Data Processor
Video Display Processor
Voice Digitization Rate
VDPS: Voice Data Processing System
VDR: Vendor Data Request
VDS: Vendor Direct Shipment
Voice/Data Switch
VDT: Video Data Terminal
Video Display Terminal
Visual Display Terminal

VDU: Video Display Unit
Visual Display Unit
VE: Value Engineering
VEA: Value Engineering Audit
VEC: Value Engineering Change
Vector Analog Computer
VECP: Value Engineering Change Proposal
VEFCA: Value Engineering Functional Cost Analysis
VEM: Value Engineering Model
Vendor Engineering Memorandum
VENUS: Valuable and Efficient Network Utility Service
ver: verify
vert: vertical
VERT: Venture Evaluation and Review Technique
VES: Variable Elasticity of Substitution
V-F: Voltage to Frequency
VF: Variable Factor
Variable Frequency
Video Frequency
Visual Field
Voice Frequency
VFB: Vertical Format Buffer
VFC: Variable File Channel
Vector Function Chainer
Vertical Format Control
Vertical Forms Control
Voltage Frequency Channel
VFD: Value For Duty
VFFT: Voice-Frequency Facility Terminal
VFL: Variable Field Length
VFMED: Variable Format Message Entry Device
VFO: Variable Frequency Oscillator
VFT: Voice Frequency Telegraph
VFU: Vertical Format Unit
Vocabulary File Utility
V-F-V: Voltage to Frequency to Voltage
VG: Vector Generator

VGAM: Vector Graphics Access Method
VGCA: Voice Gate Circuit Adaptors
V-H: Vertical-Horizontal
V&H: Vertical and Horizontal
VHD: Video High Density
VHF: Very High Frequencies (Frequency)
VHFO: Very High Frequency Oscillator
VHFR: Very High Frequency Receiver
VHM: Virtual Hardware Monitor
VHOL: Very High Order Language
VHS: Video Home System
VHSI: Very High Speed Integration
VHSIC: Very High Speed Integrated Circuits
VI: Variable Interval Volume Indicator
VIA: Vertatile Interface Adapter
VIBROT: Vibrational-Rotational
VIC: Variable Instruction Computer
Virtual Interaction Controller
Visibility of Intransit Cargo
VICAM: Virtual Integrated Communications Access Method
VICAR: Video Image Communication and Retrieval
VICC: Visual Information Control Console
vid: video
VIDEO: Visual Data Entry On-Line
VIEW: Visible, Informative, Emotionally Appealing, Workable
VIL: Vendor Item List
VIM: Vendor Initial Measurement
VIMTPG: Virtual Interactive Machine Test Program Generator
VIN: Vehicle Identification Number
Vendor Identification Number
VIO: Very Important Object
Video Input/Output
Virtual Input/Output

VIP: Valuable-Items Policy
Value Improving Products
Value in Performance
Variable Individual Protection
Variable Information Processing
Variable Interest Plus
Vector Instruction Processor
Verifying Interpreting Punch
Versatile Information Processor
Video Programming
VIPS: Variable Item Processing System
VIR: Vendor Information Request
Vendor Item Release
VIS: Vector Instruction Set
Verification Information System
VISAM: Variable-Length Indexed Sequential Access Method
VISDA: Visual Information System Development Association
VISPA: Virtual Storage Productivity Aid
VITA: Volunteers for International Technical Assistance
VITAL: Virtual Image Take-off And Landing
VIURAM: Video Interface Unit Random Access Memory
VL: Vector Length
VLAM: Variable Level Access Method
VLCBX: Very Large Computerized Branch Exchange
VLDB: Very Large Data Base
VLF: Variable Length Field
Very Low Frequency
VLP: Video Long Player
VLS: Virtual Linkage Subsystem
VLSI: Very Large Scale Integration
VLSW: Virtual Line Switch
VLT: Video Layout Terminal

VLTP: Variable Length Text Processor
VM: Vertical Merger
Virtual Machine
Virtual Memory
VMA: Valid Memory Address
Virtual Machine Assist
VMAPS: Virtual Memory Array Processing System
VMBLOK: Virtual Machine Control Block
VMC: Virtual Memory Computer
VMCF: Virtual Machine Communication Facility
VMD: Vector Memory Display
VME: Virtual Machine Environment
VMF: Virtual Machine Facility
VML: Virtual Memory Level
VMM: Virtual Machine Monitor
VMOS: Verticle Metal Oxide Semiconductor
V-Groove Metal Oxide Silicon
Virtual Memory Operating System
VMPE: Virtual Memory Performance Enhancement
VMR: Violation Monitor and Remover
VMS: Virtual Memory System
Voice Message System
VMT: Variable Microcycle Timing
Virtual Memory Technique
VNC: Voice Numerical Control
VNL: Via Net Loss
VNLF: Via Net Loss Factor
VOB: Vacuum Optical Bench
VOBANC: Voice Band Compression
VOC: Variable Output Circuit
voc: vocational
vocab: vocabulary
VOCAL: Vocabulary Language
VOCOM: Voice Communications
VODACOM: Voice Data Communications

VODAS: Voice-Operated Device Anti-Sing
VODAT: Voice-Operated Device for Automatic Transmission
VODER: Voice Coder
VOF: Variable Operating Frequency
VOGAD: Voice-Operated Gain-Adjustment Device
Voice-Operated Gaining-Adjusting Device
vol: volume
VOLCAL: Volume Calculator
VOLID: Volume Identifier
VOLSER: Volume/Serial
vom: voltohmmeter
voltohmmilliammeter
VOM: Volt-Ohm Meter
Volt-Ohm Milliammeter
VOS: Virtual Operating System
Voice-Operated Switch
VOX: Voice Operated Device
Voice Operated Keying
Voice Operated Transmission
VP: Vector Processor
Verifying Punch
Vertical Parity
Virtual Processor
VPB: Vendors Per Block
VPE: Vector Processing Element
VPF: Vector Parameter File
VPI: Vendor Parts Index
VPM: Vendor Part Modification
Versatile Packaging Machine
Vibrations Per Minute
Virtual Processor Monitor
VPN: Vendor Parts Number
Virtual Page Number
VPP: Value Payable by Post
VPS: Vector Processing System
Vibrations Per Second
VPSS: Vector Processing Subsystem Support
VPTR: Value Pointer
VPU: Virtual Processing Unit
VPZ: Virtual Processing Zero

VQA: Vendor Quality Assurance
VQC: Vendor Quality Certification
VQD: Vendor Quality Defect
VQZD: Vendor Quality Zero Defects
V&R: Validation and Recovery
VR: Virtual Route
　Visible Record
V = R: Virtual Equal Real
VRA: Value Received Analysis
VRAM: Variable Random Access Memory
　Variable Rate Adaptive Multiplexing
　Video Random Access Memory
VRC: Vertical Redundancy Check
VREF: Voltage Reference
VRM: Voice Recognition Modules
VRP: Visual Record Printer
VRS: Voice Recognition System
　Voice Recording System
VRT: Visual Reaction Time
VRU: Voice Response Unit
VRX: Virtual Resource Executive
VS: Vendor Supplier
　Virtual Storage
　Virtual System
　Vocal Synthesis
VSA: Value Systems Analysis
　Visual Scene Analysis
　Voltage Sensitive Amplifier
VSAM: Virtual Sequential Access Method
　Virtual Storage Access Method
　Virtual System Access Method
VSB: Vestigial Sideband
VSBS: Very Small Business System
VSC: Virtual Subscriber Computer
VSD: Variable Slope Delta
VSDM: Variable Slope Delta Modulation
VSE: Virtual Storage Extended
VSF: Voice Store and Forward system

VSI: Visual Simulator Interface
VSL: Variable Specification List
VSM: Video Switching Matrix
　Virtual Storage Management
　Virtual Storage Memory
VSMF: Visual Search on Microfilm
VSP: Vehicle Scheduling Program
VSPC: Virtual Storage Personal Computing
VSPX: Vehicle Scheduling Program Extended
VSQ: Very Special Quality
VSR: Validation Summary Report
VSS: Video Storage System
　Virtual Storage System
　Voice Signaling System
VSTOL: Vertical and (very) Short Takeoff and Landing
VSWR: Voltage Standing Wave Ratio
VSYNC: Vertical Synchronous
VT: Variable Time
　Vertical Tabulation
　Video Terminal
　Virtual Terminal
VTA: Variable Transfer Address
　Virtual Terminal Agent
VTAB: Vertical Tabulation (character)
VTAC: Video Timing and Controller
VTAM: Virtual Telecommunications Access Method
　Virtual Terminal Access Method
　Vortex Telecommunications Access Method
VTB: Video Terminal Board
VTC: Virtual Terminal Control
VTD: Variable Time Delay
　Vertical Tape Display
VTDI: Variable Threshold Digital Input
VTE: Visual Task Evaluation
　Visual Task Evaluator

VTI: Video Terminal Interface
Voluntary Termination Incentive
VTLC: Virtual Terminal Line Controller
VTM: Vocal Tract Models
VTOC: Volume Table Of Contents
VTOHL: Vertical Takeoff and Horizontal Landing
VTOL: Vertical Takeoff and Landing
VTP: Verification Test Plan
Virtual Terminal Protocol
VTR: Video Tape Recorder
Video Tape Recording
VTRS: Videotape Recording System
VTRU: Variable Threshold Recently Used
VTS: Vessel Traffic System
Virtual Terminal System
VTVM: Vacuum Tube Voltmeter
VU: Vertical Arithmetic Unit
Voice Unit
Volume Unit
V&V: Verification and Validation
VV: Volume in Volume
V = V: Virtual Equal Virtual
VV & C: Verification, Validation and Certification
VWS: Variable Word Size
vx: videotex
VZ: Virtual Zero

W

w: wait
watt
weight
wide
width
word
write
wrong
W: Wait Time
WA: Weighted Average
Will Advise
With Answers
With Average
Word Added
WAA: World Aluminum Abstracts
WAB: When Authorized By
WAC: Wage Analysis and Control
Weapon Arming Computer
Working Address Counter
WACK: Wait Acknowledge
Wait before Transmit Positive Acknowledgement
WACS: Wire Automated Check System
WAD: Work Authorization and Delegation
Work Authorization Document
WADS: Wide Area Data Service
WAF: With All Faults
Word Address Format
WAI: Wait for Interrupt
WAK: Wait Acknowledge
Write Access Key
WAKPAT: Walking Pattern
WAM: Words A Minute
Work Analysis and Measurement
Worth Analysis Model

WAN: Wide Area Network
Work Authorization Number
WAP: Work Assignment Procedure
WAR: With All Risks
Work Authorization Routine
WARC: World Administrative Radio Conference
WARES: Workload And Resources Evaluation System
WARF: Weekly Audit Report File
WARP: Worldwide Automatic Digital Information Network Restoral Plan
WASAR: Wide Application System Adapter
WASP: Work Activity Sampling Plan
Workshop Analysis and Scheduling Programming
WATS: Wide Area Telecommunications Service
Wide Area Telephone Service
WATTC: World Administrative Telegraph and Telephone Conference
WAVES: Weight And Value Engineering System
wb: weber
WB: Write Buffer
WBA: Wire Bundle Assembly
WBAT: Wideband Adapter Transformer
WBC: Wideband Coupler
WBCT: Wideband Current Transformer
WBD: Wideband Data
WBDX: Wideband Data Switch
WBS: Work Breakdown Structure

WBTS: Wideband Transmission System
W&C: Write and Compute
WC: Wage Class
Word Count
Work Card
Work Control
Write Control
WCB: Way Control Block
Will Call Back
WCC: Work Center Code
Work Control Center
WCDB: Work Control Data Base
WCF: Workload Control File
WCGM: Writable Character Generation Memory
WCL: Word Control Logic
WCM: Wired-Core Matrix
Wired-Core Memory
Word Combine and Multiplexer
Writable Control Memory
WCP: Work Control Plan
WCR: Word Control Register
Word Count Register
WCS: Work Control System
Writable Control Storage
Writable Control Store
wd: width
word
WD: Work Description
Work Directive
Write Data
WDB: Word Driver BIT
Working Data Base
WDC: Wideband Directional Coupler
World Data Center
WDCS: Writable Diagnostic Control Store
WDIR: Working Directory
WDL: Wireless Data Link
WDM: Wavelength Division Multiplex
WDP: Work Distribution Policy
wdt: width

WDT: Watch Dog Timer
Wear Durability Trial
WDV: Written Down Value
WE: With Equipment
Write Enable
WEFAX: Weather Facsimile
WEI: Work Experience Instructor
WEN: Waive Exchange if Necessary
WESTAR: Western Union Satellite
WETARFAC: Work Element Timer and Recorder for Automatic Coupling
WF: Write Fault
Write Forward
Wrong Font
WFL: Work Flow Language
WG: Weight Guaranteed
Working Group
Write Gate
WGS: Working Group Standards
wgt: weight
WI: Word Intelligibility
WIB: When Interrupt Block
WIBFD: Will Be Forwarded
WIBIS: Will Be Issued
wid: width
WILCO: Will Comply
WIMC: Whom It May Concern
WIP: Work In Process
Work In Progress
WISE: World Information Systems Exchange
wk: week
work
wkg: working
wl: workload
WL: Word Line
Work Level
WLM: Wire Line MODEMS
WLR: Wrong Length Record
WM: Words per Minute
WMMW: Work Measurement and Methods Engineering
Work Measurement System
WNL: Within Normal Limits

WNP: Will Not Process
   Wire Non-Payment
wo: without
W/O: Write-Off
WO: Wait Order
   Wipe Out
   Wiped Out
   Write-Off
   Write Only
   Write Out
WOA: Work Order Authorization
WOCS: Work Order Control System
WOE: Without Equipment
WOLAP: Workplace Optimization and Layout Planning
WOM: Write Only Memory
WON: Waiver Of Notice
WOPAST: Work Plan Analysis and Scheduling Technique
WOPE: Without Personnel and Equipment
WOR: Work Order Release
WORAM: Word-Oriented Random Access Memory
WORLDCOM: World Communications
WORP: Word Processing
WOUDE: Wait-On-User-Defined Event
WP: Word Processing
   Word Processor
   Workspace Pointer
   Write Protection
WPA: With Particular Average
WP/AS: Word Processing/Administrative Support
WPB: Write Printer Binary
WPC: Wired Program Computer
   Word Processing Center
WPD: Write Printer Decimal
WPDA: Writing Pushdown Acceptor
WPI: World Patent Index
WPM: Words Per Minute
   Work Package Management
   Write Program Memory
   Write Protect Memory
WPOE: Word Processing and Office Equipment
WPR: Work Planning and Review
WPS: Word Processing System
   Words Per Second
WPSI: Word Processing System Incorporated
WPU: Write Punch
wr: write
WR: Wire Recorder
   Word Request
   Work Request
   Working Register
W/R: Write/Read
WRAIS: Wide Range Analog Input Subsystem
WRAP: Weighter Record Analysis Program
WRAPS: World Bank Retrieval Array Processing System
WRBND: Wire Bound
WRE: Write Enable
WRIU: Write Interface Unit
WRO: Work Release Order
WRPT: Write Protect
   Write Protection
WRS: Word Recognition System
wrt: write
WRTC: Write Control
WRU: Who Are You?
ws: worksheet
WS: Word Station
   Word Sync
   Work Simplification
   Work Space
   Work Station
   Working Space
   Working Storage
WSDCU: Wideband Satellite Delay Compensation Unit
WSF: Work Station Facility
WSS: Work Summarization System
WST: Word Study
   Word Synchronizing Track

WSU: Work Station Utility
wt: weight
WT: Waiting Time
Wait Time
Walk Through
Waveguide Transmission
Word Terminal
Word Type
WTBD: Work To Be Done
WTD: World Telecommunications Directory
WTO: Write-To-Operator
WTOR: Write-To-Operator with Reply
WTR: Work Transfer Record
Work Transfer Request
WTS: Word Terminal, Synchronous
WTT: Working Timetable
WU: Work Unit
WUDB: Work Unit Data Bank
WUI: Western Union International
WUS: Word Underscore character
WV: Weight in Volume
Working Voltage
WW: Wire Wrap
W/W: Wire Wrap
WXTRN: Weak External Reference

X

x: experiment
express
index
indexed
transmission
X: Recommendation Designation of the Consultative Committee on International Telegraph & Telephone International Telecommunication Union Index Register
XA: Auxiliary Amplifier
Cross-Assembler
Transmission Adapter
XALC: Extended Assembler Language Coding
XAM: External Address Modifier
XASM: Cross Assembler
xb: crossbar (Bell System)
XBASE: Data Base Management Software Package
XBC: External Block Controller
XBM: Extended Basic Mode
XCONN: Cross Connection
XCT: X-Band Communications Transponder
xcvr: transceiver
XDFLD: Secondary Index Field
XDMS: Experimental Data Management System
xdr: transducer
xducer: transducer
XDUP: Extended Disk Utilities Program
xec: execute
XEC: Extended Emulator Control
xeq: execute
XFC: Extended Function Code
xfer: transfer
XFM: X-Band Ferrite Modulator
xfmr: transformer
xge: exchange
XIC: Transmission Interface Converter
XIM: Extended IO Monitor
XI/O: Execute Input/Output
XIT: Extra Input Terminal
XL: Cross Reference List
Execution Language
XLP: Extra Large Scale Packaging
XM: Expanded Memory
xmit: transmit
transmitter
XMP: Experimental Mathematical Programming System
xmsn: transmission
xmt: transmit
transmitter
XMT-REC: Transmit-Receive
XMTR-REC: Transmitter-Receiver
XN: Execution Node
XNOS: Experimental Network Operating System
X-OFF: Transmitter Off
X-ON: Transmitter On
XOP: Extended Operation
XOR: Exclusive OR
XOT: Extra Output Terminal
xpd: expedite
XPSW: External Processor Status Word
xpt: crosspoint
X-PUNCH: Eleven Punch
XQ: (Cross) Question
XR: External Reset
Index Register
XREF: Cross-Reference Listing
XREP: Extended Reporting
XRM: Extended Relational Memory

XS: Cross Section
  Transform Services
XSECT: Cross Section
XSP: Extended Set Processor
xstr: transistor
XTA: X-Band Tracking Antenna
XTC: External Transmit Clock
XU: X Unit
XUV: Extreme Ultraviolet
xvers: transverse
xvtr: transverter
XX: Double Excellent
XY: Cartesian Coordinate System
X-Y: Cartesian Coordinate System
XYAT: X-Y Axis Table
XYP: X-Y Plotter

Y

y: yield
YACC: Yet Another Compiler-Compiler
YAP: Yield Analysis Pattern
YDC: Yaw Damper Computer
YEC: Youngest Empty Cell
YG: Yield Grade
YMS: Yield Measurement System
YN: Yes-No
YOE: Year Of Entry
YP: Yield Point
YPS: Yards Per Second
yr: year
YS: Yield Strength
YSF: Yield Safety Factor
YTC: Yield To Call
YTD: Year To Date

Z

z: impedance
zero
Z243: Canadian Standards Association Data Processing Standard Designation
Z&A: Zero and Add
ZA: Zero Adder
ZAI: Zero Address Instruction
ZB: Zero Bit
ZBA: Zero-Bracket Amount
ZBB: Zero-Base Budgeting
ZBOP: Zero-Base Operational Planning and budgeting
ZCO: Zero Crossover
ZCR: Zero Crossing Rate
ZDC: Philip Crosby Associates Inc. (ASE)
ZE: Zero Balance Entry
ZFC: Zero Failure Criteria
Z-FOLD: Fan-Fold paper
ZI: Zero Input
ZIP: Zone Improvement Plan
ZLL: Zero Lot Line
ZO: Zero Output
ZOD: Zero Order Detector
ZOH: Zero Order Hold
ZRE: Zero Rate Error
ZS: Zero Shift
ZSG: Zero Speed Generator
ZWC: Zero Word Count
ZWC: Zero Wind Computer
ZZC: Zero-Zero Condition